Tax Ti~~~
Canadian~~~

MW00965081

Answers to the Five Most Commonly Asked Tax Questions

✔ Where do I file?

If you choose to paper-file your return, the address where you send your tax return depends on where you live. The Canada Revenue Agency (CRA) sends you mailing labels in your tax package each year, but if you've misplaced them you can visit the CRA Web site at www.cra-arc.gc.ca/contact/t1addr-e.html to obtain the address of the tax office where you should send your return. You can also call 1-800-959-8281 to request this information.

✔ When is my return due?

Your 2006 income tax return is due on Monday, April 30, 2007 (or June 15, 2007, if you or your spouse ran a business in 2006, although if you owe tax your payment is due on or before April 30). If you owe taxes, make sure that your return is transmitted or postmarked before midnight on the due date to avoid late-filing penalties and interest.

✔ What happens if I file late?

If you file your return late and you owe taxes, you'll automatically be charged a penalty of 5 percent of your balance owing. On top of that, you'll face a penalty of 1 percent of the balance owing for each month your return remains outstanding, to a maximum of 12 months. And don't forget the interest: the CRA charges interest, compounded daily, on outstanding balances and penalties. At the time of writing, the interest rate on overdue taxes was 8 percent, but this could change quarterly!

✔ Can I change my return if I find a mistake?

Yes, you can file a T1 Adjustment using form T1-ADJ, "T1 Adjustment Request," to amend your return for any mistakes you may find after the fact. You can also request changes online under the "My Account" option on the CRA Web site (www.cra-arc.gc.ca).

✔ Where can I get missing forms?

The majority of the CRA forms are available for download from the CRA Web site (www.cra-arc.gc.ca). To order forms by phone, call 1-800-959-2221. If you're missing the package and guide sent to you by the CRA, you can pick up a copy at your local post office.

For Dummies: Bestselling Book Series for Beginners

Tax Tips 2007 For Canadians For Dummies®

Cheat Sheet

Where Do I Turn for Help?

- ✔ CRA Web site: www.cra-arc.gc.ca
- ✔ Have an income tax question? Call 1-800-959-8281
- ✔ Wondering where your refund is? Call 1-800-959-1956
- ✔ Waiting for your GST credit? Call 1-800-959-1953
- ✔ Waiting for your Child Tax or Universal Child Care Benefit? Call 1-800-387-1193

2006 Top Marginal Tax Rates

	Regular/ Interest	Canadian Dividends[1]	Capital Gains
British Columbia	43.70	31.58	21.85
Alberta	39.00	24.08	19.50
Saskatchewan	44.00	28.33	22.00
Manitoba	46.40	35.24	23.20
Ontario	46.41	31.34	23.20
Quebec	48.22	36.35	24.11
New Brunswick	46.84	37.25	23.42
Nova Scotia	48.25	33.06	24.13
Prince Edward Island	47.37	31.96	23.69
Newfoundland and Labrador	48.64	37.33	24.32
Yukon	42.40	28.62	21.20
N.W.T.	43.05	29.64	21.53
Nunavut	40.50	28.96	20.25

(1) These rates are for Canadian non-eligible dividends (generally those paid from private companies). The dividend tax rates for publicly listed Canadian stocks are less than those reflected above, however, at printing time, all the provinces/territories had not yet announced their rates so the rates on these dividends have been excluded. See Chapter 6 for details.

For Dummies: Bestselling Book Series for Beginners

Tax Tips 2007
For Canadians
FOR
DUMMIES®

by Christie Henderson, CA, CFP, TEP
Brian Quinlan, CA, CFP, TEP
Suzanne Schultz, CA, CFP
Leigh Vyn, CA, CFP

BICENTENNIAL
1807
WILEY
2007
BICENTENNIAL

John Wiley & Sons Canada, Ltd.

Tax Tips 2007 For Canadians For Dummies®

Published by
John Wiley & Sons Canada, Ltd
6045 Freemont Boulevard
Mississauga, Ontario, L5R 4J3
www.wiley.com

Library and Archives Canada Cataloguing in Publication

Tax tips 2007 for Canadians for dummies / Christie Henderson ... [et al.]. – 2007 ed.

Includes index.

2001-2003 eds. published under title: Taxes for Canadians for dummies.

ISBN-13: 978-0-470-84054-2

ISBN-10: 0-470-84054-4

    1. Income tax–Law and legislation–Canada–Popular works. 2. Tax returns–
Canada–Popular works. 3. Tax planning–Canada–Popular works. I. Henderson, Christie

KE5682.T39 2006a   343.7105'2   C2006-905799-0

KF6290.ZA2T39 2006a

Printed in Canada

1 2 3 4 5 TRI 10 09 08 07 06

Distributed in Canada by John Wiley & Sons Canada, Ltd.

For general information on John Wiley & Sons Canada, Ltd., including all books published by Wiley Publishing, Inc., please call our warehouse, Tel 1-800-567-4797. For reseller information, including discounts and premium sales, please call our sales department, Tel 416-646-7992. For press review copies, author interviews, or other publicity information, please contact our marketing department, Tel 416-646-4584, Fax 416-236-4448.

For authorization to photocopy items for corporate, personal, or educational use, please contact in writing The Canadian Copyright Licensing Agency (Access Copyright). For an Access Copyright license, visit www.accesscopyright.ca or call toll free, 1-800-893-5777.

WILEY

About the Authors

Christie Henderson, CA, CFP, TEP, is a partner with Henderson Partners LLP, specializing in tax and financial planning. Christie qualified for the Chartered Accountant designation with Ernst & Young, Toronto. Christie is a Certified Financial Planner, a Trust and Estate Practitioner, and has completed the CICA's in-depth Tax Course, the Canadian Securities Course, and the Canadian Investment Funds Course. Christie's clientele consists largely of entrepreneurial owner-managers, executives, and their families. She provides comprehensive financial planning, including retirement planning, investment planning, insurance needs, estate planning, stock option planning, and business succession planning. Christie makes appearances on various Canadian radio and television programs and contributes articles to business publications. Christie would like to thank her husband, Kirk, and their two young sons, Charlie and Finlay, for being just plain wonderful!

Brian Quinlan, CA, CFP, TEP, is a partner with Campbell Lawless Professional Corporation in Toronto. He works with individuals and owner-managed businesses to maximize cash by minimizing tax. Brian serves as a contributing editor at *Canadian MoneySaver Magazine*; he has been a guest on a number of TV and radio call-in shows and is a frequent speaker at tax and financial planning seminars. He has instructed tax courses for Ryerson University and the Institute of Chartered Accountants of Ontario. Brian has two income-splitting vehicles: Andrew, 16, and Tara, 13.

Suzanne Schultz, CA, CFP, is a Financial Planning Specialist with RBC Investments, where she works with investment advisors to provide tax, estate, and financial planning services to their clients. Previously, Suzanne worked as a tax manager at a national accounting firm and as Associate Vice President of a wealth management firm where she provided tax education and consulting services to financial advisors and their clients across Canada. In her career she's helped a wide range of clients with their tax concerns, including high net worth individuals, owner-managers, and those with cross-border tax issues. She has appeared as a tax commentator in the media and has been a featured speaker at financial services events across the country. Suzanne is a graduate of Dalhousie University, has completed the CICA's in-depth tax course, and is a member of the Canadian Tax Foundation. Aside from her career, Suzanne enjoys a busy family life with her husband, Kevin, sons Carter, 6, and Ben, 3, and daughter Claire, 1.

Leigh Vyn, CA, CFP, is Vice President, Taxation, at The WaterStreet Group Inc., one of Canada's first and largest multiple-office firms. There she provides financial, tax, and estate planning to a select group of families. Previously, she was an Associate Vice President at an investment counsel firm where she played an essential role in providing financial advisers across Canada with a broad range of tax and estate planning services. She has written for a number of tax publications, has made frequent media appearances, and has become a frequently requested speaker. Leigh received her Honours Bachelor of Commerce at McMaster University, in Hamilton, Ontario. She began her accounting career at KPMG and then went on to obtain her CA designation. Leigh has also completed the CICA's in-depth tax course and is a member of the Canadian Tax Foundation. Leigh enjoys spending time with her husband, Dave, her daughter, Abby, 3, and son, Joshua, 1.

Authors' Acknowledgments

We're proud to say that *Tax Tips For Canadians For Dummies* has become one of the top-selling tax books in Canada. But by no means have we done this alone. With four authors contributing to this book, we'd like to recognize the following people for their assistance: First, a special thank you to our families for their patience and support while we wrote this book. It's no small feat keeping up with family and work obligations while writing a book on the side, and the encouragement of our families was essential to getting this project done. Another thanks to our co-workers, too numerous to mention, for being there to throw tax ideas around with, making us all better tax professionals.

A sincere thanks to our editor, Robert Hickey, and the staff at John Wiley & Sons Canada for helping to make *Tax Tips For Canadians For Dummies* such a success. We'd also like to thank them for helping us transform what is normally a very dry subject into one that is fun to read and easy to understand.

Publisher's Acknowledgments

We're proud of this book; please send us your comments at canadapt@wiley.com. Some of the people who helped bring this book to market include the following:

Acquisitions, Editorial, and Media Development

Editor: Robert Hickey

Copy Editor: Lisa Berland

Cartoons: Rich Tennant
(www.the5thwave.com)

Composition

Publishing Services Director: Karen Bryan

Publishing Services Manager: Ian Koo

Project Manager: Elizabeth McCurdy

Project Coordinator: Pam Vokey

Layout and Graphics: Wiley Indianapolis Composition Services

Proofreader: Evelyn Still

Indexer: Colborne Communications Inc.

John Wiley & Sons Canada, Ltd

Bill Zerter, Chief Operating Officer

Jennifer Smith, Publisher, Professional and Trade Division

Publishing and Editorial for Consumer Dummies

Diane Graves Steele, Vice President and Publisher, Consumer Dummies

Joyce Pepple, Acquisitions Director, Consumer Dummies

Kristin A. Cocks, Product Development Director, Consumer Dummies

Michael Spring, Vice President and Publisher, Travel

Suzanne Jannetta, Editorial Director, Travel

Publishing for Technology Dummies

Andy Cummings, Vice President and Publisher, Dummies Technology/General User

Composition Services

Gerry Fahey, Vice President of Production Services

Debbie Stailey, Director of Composition Services

Contents at a Glance

Table of Contents

Part III: Tax Preparation Tips: Claiming Deductions and Credits.....................211

Chapter 11: Tips for Deductions in Calculating Taxable Income 213

Introduction

● ●

*O*kay, we know what you're thinking. This is a tax book. How fun a read can it be? How can it possibly keep my attention? How will I ever get through enough of this tome to learn what I need to prepare my tax return accurately and on time? We're pretty good mind readers, aren't we? But you're right on only one account: this is a tax book. You'll be pleasantly surprised, though (amazed and astounded, really), to find that this book does hold your attention, and you don't have to pore over it from start to finish to get out of it what you need to do your taxes. As for the fun part, well . . . we promise this will be more fun than a root canal!

Why Buy This Tax Book?

Like most *For Dummies* books, this one is easy to read. And reading from cover to cover isn't necessary. In fact, a good way to use this book is to simply dive in to the particular topic you need help with — that's what the table of contents and the index are for, Dummy. Just kidding — we won't make that assumption about you. The truth is, all across Canada very intelligent people like you are reading this very same book, as you read this. We understand. Taxes are a tough topic, and you should feel no shame about needing help in preparing your return!

This is the 2007 version of *Tax Tips For Canadians For Dummies,* where you will find help for preparing your 2006 personal tax return, plus tips to reduce your tax bill in future years. We're sure you'll find that the book lives up to the *For Dummies* reputation. It's full of expert advice topped off with a little humour. Very little humour, actually. But hey, some is better than none.

Excuse us while we give ourselves a collective pat on the back, but we really couldn't have assembled a better team of authors to put this book together. Each author is a chartered accountant and certified financial planner with considerable expertise in tax matters. Our combined years of experience span more decades than even an accountant can count. Each author contributed hours of work to this project to ensure the 2007 edition is up-to-date and reflects all the new tax rules and rates. Trust us, at the hourly rates we charge, this book is a deal. The bottom line? You can't beat the advice you get in this book, and the value is outstanding.

Your Tax Road Map

By now you've probably had a glance at the table of contents. If so, you'll notice that the book is divided into five parts:

Part I: Getting Ready to File

This part helps you understand Canada's tax system, including our tax rates and our provincial tax systems, too. We also talk about how to organize your receipts and other tax information, and the various ways to file your return (no, it's not good enough to simply dump your receipts in an envelope and mail them to the tax collector!).

Part II: Tax Preparation Tips: Reporting Income

What type of income do you earn? Believe it or not, it can make a huge difference in how much tax you pay each year. Perhaps you're an employee receiving salary or wages, or maybe you're retired and receive pension income or income from your Registered Retirement Savings Plan (RRSP). And let's not forget about investment income. Your investments can generate interest, dividends, rents, royalties, and capital gains — or losses. In this part, we look at how the various types of income are taxed, and how to report them on your tax return.

Part III: Tax Preparation Tips: Claiming Deductions and Credits

Here's the real reason why you bought this book, right? You'd like to know about all the tax deductions and credits you're entitled to. Part III covers in detail the many types of available deductions and credits. Chances are that a number of the tax deductions and credits don't apply to your situation — but you'll want to make sure that you claim those that do, and take advantage of the tax relief you're rightfully entitled to.

Part IV: After You've Filed Your Tax Return

After you've filed your tax return, what's next? You sit and wait to hear from the tax collector to see whether you've bypassed the long arm of the tax auditors one more time, right? Not quite. In Part IV we talk about your Notice of Assessment, filing objections to your assessment, and fixing any mistakes after you've filed. We also discuss dealing with the CRA.

Part V: The Part of Tens

Every book should have a place for a top-ten list. Enter the Part of Tens — Part V. You will find invaluable tidbits of useful information in this perennial *For Dummies* favourite. Specifically, we cover the ten major tax changes that have taken place for 2006, the top ten ways to reduce your risk of an audit, and more. We also wanted to include the top ten chocolate chip cookie recipes we've stumbled across, and the top ten verbal insults for 2006, but the publisher thought these lists would best belong in other books. So we focused solely on tax issues.

Icons Used in This Book

This nerdy guy appears beside discussions that aren't critical if you just want to know the basic concepts and get answers to your tax questions — that is, if you're using the book as a quick reference days before your return is due (you wouldn't do that, now, would you?). However, actually reading these little information gems can deepen and enhance your tax knowledge. You'll be the tax-savviest person around the office water cooler.

The bull's-eye marks the spot for smart tax tips and timesavers to help you get your tax return done quickly and with a minimum amount of pain. This is definitely the icon to look for if you're pulling an all-nighter on April 29th.

When you see this icon, you'll find a friendly reminder of stuff we discuss elsewhere in the book or of points we really, really want you to remember.

Don't make these common but costly mistakes with your taxes! Aren't we nice folks to point them out?

This icon highlights tax provisions that went into effect in the 2006 tax year. Quite a few changes were made this year, so pay close attention to this icon so you are aware of the many new deductions and credits you may be entitled to!

Part I
Getting Ready to File

"I got excellent advice on my tax return from a very knowledgeable guy. All the while he cleaned my windshield and checked the air pressure in my tires."

In this part . . .

This is the beginning, so sit down and get comfortable! You'll be glad to know that in these first few chapters you'll find very few numbers and complicated calculations. Instead, we're going to ease you in gently: Have you ever wanted to know how Canada's tax system works? And how, in the midst of all the paper, do you figure out what forms to fill out? If so, you've come to the right place. We'll also give you some handy pointers on how to stay organized, or — for all you procrastinators out there — how to get organized in the first place. And for those who are not do-it-yourselfers, we'll let you know when it's okay to throw in the towel and call for help!

> *"Isn't it appropriate that the month of the tax begins with April Fool's Day and ends with the cries of 'May Day!'"*
>
> —Robert Knauerhase

Chapter 1

Canada's Tax System and Rates

*T*hough it can be confusing at times, Canada's income tax system has two very straightforward purposes. One, of which we are all quite aware, is to finance government expenditures. A second purpose, which is not as obvious as the first, is to encourage certain expenditures by Canadians. That's right — our government cuts you a tax break when you spend money in ways that it approves of. In other words, income tax legislation acts as a tool for the government's desired fiscal policies.

Let's look at a few examples. The government wants to encourage you to:

✔ **Save for retirement.** Tax rules are favourable for registered retirement savings plans (RRSPs). To ensure you are up to date on these tax-friendly plans, don't miss Chapter 10, line 208.

✔ **Pursue post-secondary education.** Tuition fees are eligible for a tax credit (Chapter 12, line 323), as is interest incurred on student loans (Chapter 12, line 319). Don't forget that an education credit (Chapter 12, line 323) is allowed to both full-time and part-time students. In fact, starting this year, there is also a textbook tax credit available (Chapter 12, line 323) and you'll find that scholarships, fellowships, or bursaries received (Chapter 8, line 130) are completely tax free!

✔ **Work.** If you have kids who need to be taken care of, a deduction is available for childcare expenses (Chapter 10, line 214). And new for 2006, a Canada employment credit (see Chapter 12) is available to all employees in recognition that we all incur some expenses out of our own pockets in order to work.

✔ **Invest in shares.** Dividends from Canadian corporations are taxed at a favourable rate (see Chapter 13), and only one-half of the capital gain (see Chapter 7) on a sale of investments is subject to tax. Moreover, if you borrow to invest, the interest you incur is generally tax deductible (Chapter 10, line 221).

The government also recognizes that some of us incur additional costs to earn income due to disabilities, illness, and living in remote locations. Therefore, the income tax rules include tax savings provided by the following:

✔ The disability tax credit (Chapter 12, lines 316 and 318)

✔ The medical expense tax credit (Chapter 12, line 330)

✔ The northern residents tax deduction (Chapter 11, line 255)

The government wants you to give to charities — hence, the charitable tax credit (Chapter 12, line 349).

And finally, you can get a federal tax break by contributing to your favourite federal politician or party (Chapter 13, lines 409 and 410). Tax breaks are also available for contributions to provincial and territorial politicians and parties (Chapter 14). (Yes, we agree — the political tax credit seems to be a little self-serving for the politicians.)

Make use of the various tax incentives in your spending, investing, and lifestyle decisions — *and save tax!*

You Have the Right to Pay Less Tax!

You have the right to arrange your affairs to minimize the tax you pay. A U.S. federal judge, Learned Hand (1872–1961), is often quoted:

There is nothing sinister in so arranging one's affairs as to keep taxes as low as possible. Everybody does so, rich or poor, and all do right. Nobody owes any public duty to pay more than the law demands.

Canada's tax system is based on self-assessment. Each of us has the responsibility to ensure our tax return includes all necessary information for reporting income, claiming tax deductions and tax credits, and, finally, calculating our tax liability. In complying with the tax laws, we all have the right to pay as little tax as is *legally* possible. We stress *legally*. Planning to minimize your tax is legal. Tax evasion is not!

Throughout this book we offer many tips on how to minimize the tax you will pay. All these tips are legal, of course — all work within the tax law, not against it. We stand behind the tips we offer, based on the tax law and the currently proposed changes. Remember, however, that as tax laws change some tips will no longer be valid — and new tips will apply. (Okay, we're done with the disclaimer now.)

Tax evasion occurs when you purposely understate the amount of income tax you should pay. This can occur when you don't report all your income, or when you overstate tax deductions and credits to which you are entitled. At worst, tax evasion can result in a charge being laid under the *Criminal Code* (which often means jail time). This is scary!

Tax planning is a continuous process. With the ever-changing economy and tax legislation, and the investment vehicles available in the market, you should always be planning ways to minimize your taxes. Many opportunities for tax planning arise when you experience significant change in your life — a new job, a new child or grandchild, a new marriage or the end of one, a relocation, a business start-up, a business sale, retirement, death of a family member, and so on.

The Provincial and Territorial Tax Systems

To make taxes just a little more confusing, we all have more than one tax collector to deal with. Canada's constitution gives income-taxing powers to both the federal and provincial governments. (Somehow the territories get covered in there, too.) In Canada, taxpayers are liable for both federal and provincial/territorial taxes. With the exception of taxpayers in Quebec, individuals need to deal with one tax collector — the Canada Revenue Agency (referred to throughout the book as the CRA).

The CRA administers the tax system for our federal government and all the provinces/territories except Quebec. Taxpayers in Quebec need to deal with both the CRA (for federal taxes) and the Ministère du Revenu du Québec (for Quebec taxes).

Taxes in Quebec

Unlike the other provinces and territories, Quebec has its own tax return — form TP.1-D-V. Residents of Quebec on December 31, 2006 must separately file a 2006 federal tax return *and* a 2006 Quebec tax return. The Ministère du Revenu du Québec administers the Quebec tax system. Its Web site is www.revenu.gouv.qc.ca; service is offered in English and French.

Many of the federal tax rules discussed in this book also apply to the Quebec return. However, Quebec does have some of its own unique rules and calculations. So, if you need to complete a Quebec return this year, you have a little more work ahead of you than those of us who can get by with simply completing the federal return. See Chapter 14 for more information on Quebec's income tax.

My Taxes Are How High?

There's no doubt about it, Canada is a high-tax nation — which means all the more reason to ensure the taxes paid by you and your family are minimized. Take advantage of the tax-saving tips in this book, plus ensure you take advantage of all the tax deductions and credits available to you. Canada's income tax system is a progressive tax rate system. The percentage of your income that goes to fund your tax liability increases as your income increases. This is easily illustrated. Take a look at the four federal tax brackets in Table 1-1.

Table 1-1   2006 Federal Income Tax Brackets and Rates
             (Provincial and Territorial Taxes Not Included)

Tax Bracket	Tax Rate
$0 to $36,377	15.25%
$36,378 to $72,755	22%
$72,756 to $118,284	26%
$118,285 and over	29%

As you can see, the greater your taxable income through the four federal tax brackets, the greater the percentage of tax that is applied to that additional income.

The tax rates in Table 1-1 are only the federal tax rates, and do not include provincial/territorial income taxes (see Chapter 14). When your taxable income falls into the top federal tax bracket (that is, greater than $118,285), your combined federal and provincial/territorial tax rate on the portion of your taxable income in the top tax bracket can be as high as the tax rates summarized in Table 1-2. However, the tax rates in the charts shown are before any tax credits (except the basic personal amount) that may be available to individuals. Your tax liability is based on your taxable income. Once the liability is calculated, it is reduced by tax credits available to you. These tax credits are discussed in Chapter 12.

Table 1-2   2006 Top Tax Rates (Federal and Provincial/ Territorial Taxes Combined)

Province	Salary & Interest	Capital Gains	Non-eligible Dividends
Alberta	39.00	19.50	24.08
British Columbia	43.70	21.85	31.58
Manitoba	46.40	23.20	35.24
New Brunswick	46.84	23.42	37.26
Newfoundland and Labrador	48.64	24.32	37.32
Northwest Territories	43.05	21.53	29.65
Nova Scotia	48.25	24.13	33.06
Nunavut	40.50	20.25	28.96
Ontario	46.41	23.20	31.34
Prince Edward Island	47.37	23.69	31.96
Quebec	48.22	24.11	36.35
Saskatchewan	44.00	22.00	28.33
Yukon	42.40	21.20	28.63

Note: Figures are current to August 2006

Starting in 2006, two different tax rates apply to dividends. The actual rate that will apply to your dividends will depend on their source. *Noneligible* dividends are generally dividends paid after December 31, 2005, from small businesses in Canada. If you own your own company and receive dividends from it, these rates likely apply to you. Alternatively, *eligible* dividends are those paid by public corporations resident in Canada. It is these eligible dividends that most investors in Canada receive when they invest in a non-registered account. Due to changes announced in the 2006 federal budget, eligible dividends will be taxed at a lower rate than non-eligible dividends. See Chapter 6 for more details.

As Table 1-2 indicates, *capital gains* (the excess of sale proceeds over the cost of an asset) are the most tax-efficient sources of income because they are taxed at the lowest rate. Dividends come in second. (If you are not taxed at the highest rate you might find that dividends are taxed at a lower rate than capital gains in your province.) Remember when we talked about how our government cuts you a tax break when you spend money in ways that it approves of? That's why dividends and capital gains are given preferential treatment.

Tallying up your effective tax rate

Your effective tax rate is the percentage your tax is of your total taxable income. It is easy to calculate. It is simply your tax liability (after you have taken all the tax credits you are entitled to) over your taxable income.

$$\frac{\text{Tax liability}}{\text{Taxable income}} = \text{Effective tax rate}$$

Take a look at Micha's 2006 tax return. Micha lives in Thompson, Manitoba. Her taxable income is $53,000. She calculates the tax on the $53,000 and then reduces the amounts for any tax credits she is entitled to. After these credits are deducted, her federal/Manitoba tax liability is $13,353. Her effective tax rate is then 25.2 percent ($13,353/$53,000).

The calculation of your effective tax rate takes into account that portions of your income are taxed in different tax brackets. The effective tax rate calculation "averages" the rates of tax paid in these brackets. The more income you have taxed in the highest tax bracket (taxable income in excess of $118,285), the higher your effective tax rate.

Calculating your marginal tax rate

When tax geeks talk about marginal tax rates, they are referring to the tax rate that applies to your next dollar of taxable income.

Assume your taxable income is $120,000. You are clearly in the top tax bracket. Further assume you live in Alberta. If you were to earn $1 of additional interest income, you would pay 39¢ in tax on this dollar. In other words, your marginal tax rate is 39 percent (see Table 1-2). On an after-tax basis, that extra dollar of income leaves you with only 61¢, or 61 percent. This is referred to as your *after-tax rate of return*. It can be calculated as:

1 – Your marginal tax rate = Your after-tax rate of return

The calculation of your marginal tax rate ignores that portions of your income are taxed in different tax brackets and subject to different tax rates. The marginal tax rate is focused on your *next* dollar of taxable income — not your overall taxable income.

The marginal tax rate is an easy way to assess the impact of a raise. With a marginal tax rate of 39 percent, you know that if you receive a $10,000 raise you will be taking home only an additional $6,100. When looking at investment returns from alternative investment opportunities, ensure you compare after-tax rates of return.

A marginal tax rate can also be used to calculate the tax savings that a deduction will provide. Assume your taxable income is $130,000 and you live in Alberta. You are wondering what the impact would have been if you had contributed $5,000 to your RRSP and taken a deduction on your 2006 return. Your taxable income would have been reduced to $125,000 by the $5,000 RRSP deduction. You know your marginal tax rate on that $5,000 would have been 39 percent. The tax saving you would enjoy if you were able to deduct the $5,000 RRSP contribution is $1,950 ($5,000 multiplied by 39 percent)! You can clearly see why there is so much talk about the tax-saving qualities of RRSP contributions!

Chapter 2

Getting and Staying Organized

● ●

In This Chapter

▶ Understanding the necessity of keeping good books and records

▶ Knowing how long to keep your records

▶ Dealing with the loss of information slips and receipts

▶ Taking a look at the Merchant Rule

● ●

*D*o you want to know the secret to making sure you claim every deduction you're entitled to? To saving money when you have a tax preparer do your tax return? To surviving a CRA audit unscathed? We'll tell you: Keep good records!

That's all there is to it, really! In this chapter we give you our tried, tested, and true methods of keeping things organized — methods that will save you time and money, not to mention headaches!

Did you know that when dealing with the CRA, the burden of proof is on you to provide support for the deductions you have claimed? The CRA is considered by law to be correct unless you can prove otherwise. This is one case where you are guilty until proven innocent.

Keeping Good Books and Records

You may think that by filing a tax return for the year you've absolved yourself of any further CRA requirements. Unfortunately, that's not true. You see, the CRA requires every person who pays or collects taxes, or who is carrying on a business in Canada, to keep books and records. This requirement means you have to keep

Information pertaining to your taxes in case the CRA asks to review
it in the future. Your books and records must enable the CRA to
determine your taxes payable for the year and must be supported
by source documents to verify the amounts reported.

Make sure you keep all source documents pertaining to your tax
return. These include such documents as the following:

- ✔ Sales invoices
- ✔ Purchase invoices
- ✔ Cash-register receipts
- ✔ Written contracts
- ✔ Credit card receipts
- ✔ Delivery slips
- ✔ Deposit slips
- ✔ Cheques
- ✔ Bank statements
- ✔ General correspondence

When deciding what type of document to keep, consider this: What
document will best verify your tax records? The stronger the evidence, the less likely it is that your tax records will be rejected by
the CRA.

The original bill is best — the CRA will not always accept cancelled
cheques and credit card statements as authentication of an expense.

Setting up your record-keeping system

In our experience, the number-one reason why people end up
paying more tax than they have to is that they keep lousy records.
We know that taming the paper tiger is no mean feat. What follows
are our best suggestions to make your tax organization and preparation tasks much easier.

Save all receipts and records that you think you might be able to
use, especially those in the list above. It's much more difficult to
recover receipts that have been thrown away than to ceremoni-
ously toss out whatever unnecessary paper you have left after
your tax return is complete.

Our favourite method of organizing tax information is in an accordion file — pick one up at any office supply store. (You could also use file folders or envelopes.) Label each section by expense category. Use the categories listed on the tax form you will be completing; for example, charitable donations, medical expenses, office supplies, parking, advertising, and so on. As you collect receipts throughout the year, periodically sort them into the proper category. When it comes time to file your tax return, all you have to do is take out the receipts, add them up, and enter the total on the tax form. Voila!

You may also want to consider organizing your tax information by the tax schedules you have to file, such as Statement of Real Estate Rentals, Capital Gains and Losses, and Statement of Business Activities. If your tax return is uncomplicated, it might be sufficient to have one file for each year. As you receive your tax information throughout the year, just put it into the file.

Any of these storage methods will save you from tearing your house apart looking for that investment statement or charitable receipt you were using as a bookmark last June. Keep a copy of the tax return you filed for that year and your Notice of Assessment, once received, in the same file folder.

Even if you end up hiring a tax accountant to prepare your tax return for you, you will save money if you sort and organize your information before you hand it over. (*Hint:* Accountants prefer organized clients! Just ask us.)

Your friend the computer

Your computer can be a huge help in tracking your tax information each year. There are many software packages out there, each with its own merits. Speak with a knowledgeable software salesperson before purchasing to make sure you get only what you need. There's no sense in buying an expensive, state-of-the-art accounting package if you are going to use only one or two components.

We recommend the software packages Quicken and Microsoft Money for tracking personal and small business expenses, and QuickBooks for tracking the expenses of larger businesses. These packages will help you do everything from tracking your investment portfolio to balancing your chequebook to monitoring payroll.

Using a software package to enter your data means more of a time commitment up front, but when you need the records for tax time your figures will be added up and ready to go.

If you do use a computer for all your record keeping, or if you have other valuable documents, it makes sense to store a recent backup of your computer files and those valuable documents, or copies of them, off-site. That way, if you suffer a fire or other disaster all will not be lost.

Record-keeping time bombs

Look out for these special situations:

- **Automobile expenses:** If you are claiming automobile expenses for a vehicle used for both business and personal purposes, you must keep a log to support the vehicle's business use, detailing dates, number of kilometres driven, and destinations. (For more on claiming automobile expenses, see Chapter 10.)

- **Charitable receipts:** A receipt from a registered charity is the only document accepted by the CRA for a charitable donation. Cancelled cheques and ticket stubs will not be accepted. And if you want to claim a tax credit, ensure you are donating to a *registered* charity — ask to see a registration number if you're not sure. The registration number must appear on the receipt.

How Long Should I Keep My Tax Records?

One of the questions we are most frequently asked is, "How long do I have to keep my records and receipts?" The answer, according to the CRA, is six years. The books and records must be kept in Canada at your residence or place of business. Remember, these books and records must be made available to the CRA should it ask to see them.

Even though the CRA can't go back and audit your tax return after six years — unless it suspects fraud, in which case all tax years are fair game — you need to keep purchase receipts and investment statements for assets you still own. You may need those records as proof of ownership if you ever have to make an insurance claim or if you sell the asset. And you may need proof of an asset's cost in the future if the gain or loss must be reported on your tax return.

If a particular tax year is under objection or appeal, you should keep your books and records on hand until the objection or appeal has been resolved and the time for filing a further appeal has expired. It would be a shame to throw out your books and records only to have legitimate tax deductions denied down the road.

Missing Information Slips and Receipts

Employers and other issuers of information slips are generally required to send you your slips by the end of February in the year following the year in which you received the payment. This includes slips such as T4s (reporting employment income), T5s (reporting investment income), and slips from the government. However, T3 slips (reporting trust income) are often not available until after March 31. If you are missing any slips, call the issuer for a new one.

Giving the CRA your best estimate

If you've made a reasonable attempt to obtain your slip but you are still "slipless," you should estimate your income and related deductions (that is, CPP, EI, income tax, union dues) and report them on your tax return. (See Chapter 11 for information on these deductions.) Your pay stubs are a good way to make this estimate if it is your T4 that is missing. Attach a note to your return stating you were unable to obtain your slip and summarize the estimated amounts. You should also give the name and address of the person or organization that should have issued the slip.

You must still file your tax return before the April 30 filing deadline (or June 15, if you or your spouse are self-employed) even if you know information is missing. Attach a note to your return explaining what is missing, detail any estimated amounts, and get it in on time! This is especially important if you owe money, since you will be charged a late filing penalty if the return is late — and interest if your balance owing is not paid by April 30.

Missing receipts

Receipts for some deductions, such as RRSP contributions, charitable donations, and medical expenses, must be attached to your tax return when it is filed (assuming you are paper-filing your return). If these receipts are not included with your return, processing will probably be delayed and your deductions may be disallowed. Remember, the onus is on you to prove all your income and deductions!

If a receipt is missing, call the person or organization responsible for issuing it to obtain another copy. If you cannot get another copy before the April 30 tax return filing deadline, you should still file your return on time. You can forward the slip to the CRA when it does finally arrive. Alternatively, you can simply leave the deduction off your tax return and file an adjustment once you receive the receipt. Check out Chapter 15 for tips on filing adjustments to a return you have already filed.

You don't have to attach some types of receipts to your tax return. For example, if you have claims for union dues, tuition fees, or childcare expenses, you don't need to attach the receipts to your return when you file it. However, be aware that the CRA does regular "reviews" of these types of credits and deductions, so you should still ensure you have the proper documentation on hand should the CRA ask to see it in the future.

Don't think you can get away from keeping receipts and other supporting documentation because you are NETFILING, TELEFILING, or EFILING your return. The CRA can and does often ask to see the documentation!

What to Do If the Dog Really Did Eat Your Tax Records

Your worst nightmare has come to life — you're being audited! And to top it off, Sparky has eaten some of your tax receipts. Does this mean you'll lose out on all your legitimate tax deductions? Not necessarily. The CRA does understand that these situations can occur, and will give you the benefit of the doubt (sometimes) if you can show reasonable proof of your income and deductions.

Reconstructing missing or damaged tax records

If the CRA does come calling and you simply don't have the tax records you need to support your tax deductions, all is not lost. You can prove your claims were legitimate in other ways. It may take you some time to reconstruct records, but when you consider the alternatives (additional tax, interest, and penalties on disallowed deductions from an audit) the time you spend will be well worth it.

The simplest way to reconstruct missing tax records is to ask for new ones. For example, if you know you bought a number of prescriptions in 2006 but can't find your receipts, go back to your local pharmacy and ask for a printout of your expenditures for the year. You will be surprised at how many deductions you will be able to reconstruct simply by asking for duplicate receipts.

If you've sold or given an asset in 2006 but you do not have a record of its original cost, either because you lost the relevant documents or because it was a gift, you can establish a cost in one of several ways:

✔ Look in newspapers from the year you purchased or were given an asset to determine what similar assets were selling for. Your local library should have old newspapers on file or on microfiche.

✔ If you're trying to find information on a property, consult with the local real estate board. They usually keep historical data on property in the area. You could also go to the property tax collector's office in your municipality. Their assessed values for the property might be of use.

✔ If you inherited an asset, the easiest way to establish its tax cost to you is to check the deceased's final tax return to see at what price they were deemed to have disposed of the property to you. This disposal price is the same as your tax cost.

✔ Call your financial adviser for help. Your adviser should have historical records of your financial affairs and may be able to help you to calculate the cost of your shares, mutual funds, or other assets he or she manages.

Why is the cost value important? You need to know the original cost of the asset to properly calculate the capital gain or loss when the asset is eventually sold or otherwise disposed of — see Chapter 7 for more details.

If it is your business records that have been lost or destroyed, you can re-create many of your expenses using the following tactics:

✔ Get copies of your phone, utility, credit card, rent, and other bills from the companies that issued the bills. Getting an annual statement from a major vendor shouldn't be too difficult.

✔ Ask for duplicate bank statements from your bank (all for a small fee, of course!) that will help you to establish income and some of your expenses for the year.

✔ Reconstruct automobile expenses based on a reasonable estimation of what it costs to run your type of vehicle. The dealer from whom you bought your car might be helpful in estimating these costs.

✔ Look at your previous years' tax returns to establish your expenses in prior years and also your profit margins. If you have lost those, too, you can obtain copies of previous years' returns on request from the CRA.

The Merchant Rule

Our discussion of record keeping would not be complete if we didn't highlight the "Merchant Rule." This rule is the result of a Canadian tax court case in which a lawyer, named Merchant, attempted to deduct certain expenses for which he had no receipts. The CRA disallowed all of the expenses on the grounds that the taxpayer had no support for his claims and that it was therefore impossible to determine how much had actually been spent. The case was appealed and the taxpayer won. The courts established the rule of *reasonable approximation*.

In other words, for an expense to be deductible taxpayers need only establish that it is *reasonable* to conclude that they had incurred the expenses and that the amounts claimed are *reasonable* in the circumstances.

A similar case in the U.S. courts involved George Cohan, who deducted $55,000 in business-related entertainment expenses in 1921 and 1922. The judges in the Cohan case arrived at the same conclusion. In response to the Cohan decision, U.S. Congress changed the law to make sure taxpayers could no longer deduct expenses without receipts or support. Currently, Canada's Parliament shows no interest in following this U.S. lead.

Are we saying that you no longer have to keep receipts to support your tax deductions? Of course not! However, keep Mr. Merchant and Mr. Cohan in mind if ever you are under the watchful eye of the CRA and have no receipts to prove your expenses. As they've shown us, if you can otherwise corroborate your deductions you may be entitled to tax deductions even if you have no traditional receipts. But be prepared for a fight.

Chapter 3

Going Over Your Preparation Options

· ·

In This Chapter

▶ Using preparation software

▶ Making use of tax help on the Web

▶ Getting help from the tax collector

▶ Assessing tax pros

▶ Evaluating EFILING versus paper filing

▶ Taking a look at TELEFILE

▶ Considering the NETFILE option

▶ Locating forms and other information

· ·

*C*hances are, if you're reading this chapter you've already determined that yes, you need to file a tax return, and yes, you need to do it now. So, now what? Do you prepare your return yourself, or do you throw in the towel and hire someone to do it for you? This chapter gives you some handy advice on when to file your own return and when you should seek help. We will also discuss various options for filing your return.

 Whether you decide to prepare your return yourself or hire someone to help you out, check out the sections of this book that affect your tax return. Not only will you find some handy hints so that you don't make any mistakes, but also you may find some ideas about deductions and credits you did not know are available.

Using Your Computer to Tally Up Your Taxes

Have you ever thought of preparing your tax return using your computer? Think about it. No more adding machines or the dreaded smell of correction fluid. No more tearing through the paper when you've erased the amount on line 150 one too many times. Tax preparation software makes sense for those of you who have already dived into the world of preparing your own return. And even for those of you still sitting on the fence, tax preparation software may be the answer to your phobia.

The perks and perils of going the techno route

Using software to prepare your tax return has a number of advantages. The favourite, of course, is automatic recalculation: When one number on your return changes, the program updates all relevant forms and recalculates your final tax bill.

Another advantage is that most software packages are dummy-proof. Most programs are set up so all you need to do is find the window that corresponds to the particular slip you have — be it a T4, T3, T5, or so on — and fill it in based on what appears in your boxes.

Computers aren't people. They can't look at numbers to determine if they're reasonable, or if they're correct. No computer will tell you to think again before deducting your all-inclusive trip for two to Jamaica as a business expense.

Shopping for tax software

Many tax software programs are available to help taxpayers deal with the headaches that April so often brings.

- **QuickTax Standard** (Windows, download or CD ROM)) or online via **QuickTaxWeb** from Intuit Canada. QuickTax is Canada's best-selling tax software. Gather up your receipts and answer the simple questions posed by EasyStep Interview in English or French. The program takes your information and puts it where it belongs on the federal and Quebec forms. QuickTax reviews your return when you're finished, and even alerts you to any missed deductions or credits. You can NET-FILE your return with both the desktop and online versions. Check out www.quicktax.ca.

✔ **TaxTron:** The software is available in Windows and Macintosh versions, comes in English and French, can handle Quebec returns, and is NETFILE-capable. Support is available online or by phone in English, French, Chinese, Hindi, and Punjabi. For more details, visit www.taxtron.ca.

✔ **UFile by Dr. Tax:** UFile is another program with Quebec and NETFILE capabilities. You can either use the UFile.ca online version or buy UFile for Windows to install on your PC. Check it out at www.ufile.ca.

✔ **H&R Block:** You can have H&R Block complete your return for you, or use their Online Tax Program to do your own taxes and NETFILE your return. Go to www.hrblock.ca for more information.

✔ **myTaxExpress:** For Windows users only, this program boasts a free trial before purchase, can handle Quebec returns, and is NETFILE certified. See www.mytaxexpress.com for details.

✔ **TAXWIZ Deluxe:** This Windows-only product from Intuit Canada is marketed to the beginner. It can handle Quebec and is NETFILE-compatible. Find out more at www.taxwiz.ca.

✔ **GenuTax:** Downloadable multiyear software — you don't pay for annual updates! The software is Windows-only and doesn't support Quebec returns. It's NETFILE-compatible. Visit www.genutax.ca.

✔ **CuteTax Online:** Online software, NETFILE-compatible, but no Quebec returns. Get more info at www.cutetax.ca.

✔ **Taxman:** Free software! Get the details at http://pacificcoast.net/~gthompson, and then download the software at www.winsite.com. Although you can't use a Mac, do Quebec returns, or NETFILE, you can print out the federal forms and mail them to the CRA.

✔ **Others:** T1Filer (www.t1filer.ca), TaxFreeway (www.taxfreeway.ca), CresTax (www.crestax.com), EachTax (www.eachtax.com), EtaxCanada (www.etaxcanada.com), FileTaxOnline (www.filetaxonline.ca), SimTax (www.simtax.com), StudioTax (www.studiotax.com), and WebTax4U (www.webtax4U.ca).

Surfing Your Way to Tax Help

So it's 11 p.m. on April 30, and you need help. What do you do? Well, if you're lucky, you may find the answers to some of your questions via the Internet. Several Web sites provide handy, up-to-the-minute tax tips. Let's take a look at our top picks.

- ✔ **Ernst & Young:** www.ey.com/global/content.nsf/Canada/ Home. This Web site provides you with the latest tax changes, as well as tax calculators. Watch for E&Y tax publications "TaxMatters@EY" and "Tax Alert." You can download the booklet *Managing Your Personal Taxes.*

- ✔ **Deloitte (a.k.a. Deloitte & Touche):** www.deloitte.ca. The daily tax highlights on this Web site will ensure you don't miss any tax changes. Keep your eye open for "TaxBreaks," Deloitte's tax newsletter, and their helpful guides on a variety of tax topics.

- ✔ **KPMG:** www.kpmg.ca. You'll find out all the latest tax changes by visiting KPMG's site and reading its tax publications, "TaxNewsFlash Canada" and the "Canadian Tax Letter."

- ✔ **PricewaterhouseCoopers:** www.pwcglobal.com. Visit the publications area of the site for PWC's tax newsletter "Tax Memo" and tax guides on specific tax subjects.

- ✔ **BDO Dunwoody:** www.bdo.ca. This site is chock-full of tax information ranging from tax facts and figures for each province to weekly tax tips to in-depth bulletins on many tax topics.

When (and How) to Get Help from the Tax Collector

Believe it or not, the CRA Web site (www.cra-arc.gc.ca) is an excellent source for information. Here, you can download a copy of the income tax package and request additional forms, and the site also contains detailed information on all of the most frequently requested topics.

TIPS

If your question relates to your tax situation, try the CRA's automated TIPS line (Tax Information Phone Service). Call 1-800-267-6999.

Personal info

To obtain specific information on your tax account, you need to provide your social insurance number, your month and year of birth, and the total income reported on line 150 of your last assessed return.

Here is what you can find out on TIPS:

- ✔ **Tax refund**: Find out the status of your refund.

- ✔ **Goods and Services Tax/Harmonized Sales Tax (GST/HST) credit:** See if you're eligible to receive the credit and when you can expect to receive a payment.

- ✔ **Child Tax Benefit:** You can find out if you're eligible to receive the benefit and when you can expect to receive a payment.

- ✔ **Universal Child Care Benefit:** Do you have a child under 6? Find out when your payment is coming.

- ✔ **RRSP deduction limit:** Want to know your RRSP deduction contribution limit for the year? TIPS has your answer.

General info

TIPS also provides general recorded information:

- ✔ **Info-Tax:** General tax information on a number of tax topics.

- ✔ **Bulletin Board:** Recent tax and benefit information.

- ✔ **Business Information:** Tax and GST information for those who operate a business or are thinking of starting one up (for example, how to handle payroll tax, CPP, and EI deductions).

My Account

The CRA has an online service, called My Account, where you can access information about your personal tax and benefits. Access is provided 7 days a week, 21 hours a day (in case you're wondering, they shut down for 3 hours each day for maintenance).You can access it through the CRA Web site.

This is quite an innovative service for the CRA. (We're impressed, at least!) The types of personal information you can access online include the following information about your tax account:

- ✔ Tax refund or balance owing
- ✔ Direct deposit
- ✔ RRSP, Home Buyers' Plan, and Lifelong Learning Plan

✔ Account balance and payments made on filing your tax return

✔ Instalments

✔ Child Tax Benefit

✔ Universal Child Care Benefit

✔ GST/HST credit

Sure beats trying to phone in the middle of tax season, when all you get is a busy signal! You can also use My Account to change your filed return, to change your address and/or phone number, and to dispute your notice of assessment.

To access My Account you need to register for a Government of Canada epass. You can do this by going into My Account on the CRA Web site. Once you have completed the registration process (you get to choose your password!) CRA will mail the Activation Code to you. Just key in the CRA Activation Code and your password to get full access to My Account for the first time. After that, you'll just need to enter your password.

As you likely guessed, the idea behind the epass and the CRA Activation Code is to protect your personal data.

Enquiring by phone

Agents are also available to answer your questions by phone, Monday to Friday (except holidays), 8:15 a.m. to 4:30 p.m. To accommodate the flood of calls during tax season, these hours are extended until 10:00 p.m. weekdays, and include weekends from 9:00 a.m. to 1:00 p.m. from mid-February to April 30. Contact the CRA by phone at 1-800-959-8281.

If your query is in regard to electronic services (NETFILE, TELE-FILE, or My Account) call the e-service Helpdesk at 1-800-714-7257, TTY 1-888-768-0951.

If you would like someone else to call the CRA on your behalf, be sure that you've completed and mailed consent form T1013, "Authorizing or Cancelling a Representative," to the CRA. This form gives the CRA permission to discuss your tax affairs with someone other than you.

Visiting your local Tax Services Office

If you can't find the information you need on the Web site, through TIPS, or through Individual Income Tax Enquiries at 1-800-959-8281, try contacting your local Tax Services Office in person or by phone. (Note, though, that they really prefer you to call the 1-800 number — we just want to give you some options!) The TSOs are open Monday to Friday (except holidays, of course), 8:15 a.m. to 4:30 p.m. (sometimes 5:00 p.m.). To find the location of your nearest TSO, visit the CRA's Web site and click "Contact us" at the main menu.

Getting the Most from Tax Pros

If your plumbing is broken, do you immediately call the plumber, or do you try to fix it yourself? For some, calling for help is the last resort — and preparing their own tax return is no exception. Sometimes, however, it's a good idea to admit defeat and hire someone before you get yourself into trouble.

Dealing with a tax professional

 Be sure you have accumulated all the information necessary before sending it to your preparer. If you have a business, your best bet is to summarize all your revenue and expenses ahead of time. This is one way to cut down your fee and ensure no relevant information is omitted.

 Hiring someone may be a good idea if you need some tax planning advice. Sometimes the additional fees you pay may actually be recovered in saved taxes! However, be careful whom you hire for tax planning, since some individuals are more competent than others. We tell you how to find that special person next.

Questions to ask a tax professional

The Yellow Pages has dozens of pages of accounting firms and businesses that specialize in tax. Finding a reputable tax professional is kind of like finding a mechanic — you've got to be careful. In your initial meeting, the tax professional should ask a lot of questions about your situation, and you should ask some questions too, to make sure you've found the right person.

Here's a list of questions to ask your tax professional to ensure he or she can handle your situation.

> ✔ **What services do you offer?** Some tax professionals only prepare tax returns, while others will help you with other matters such as retirement planning or estate planning.

✔ **Have you worked in this area before?** If you have your own business, or are an avid investor, make sure your professional has worked with similar situations before. Many firms have specialists in particular areas, while some may be used to working with employees whose tax documentation consists of a T4 and RRSP slips.

✔ **Who will prepare my return?** Unless you're dealing with a sole practitioner, the person you're speaking to will not necessarily prepare your return. Don't be alarmed if a junior staff member prepares your return — this is common practice and can actually save you preparation fees. However, ensure that a senior tax professional reviews it for errors.

✔ **What is your fee structure?** Most tax professionals charge by the hour, so make sure you ask up front for the hourly fee, as well as for an estimate of the time your project will take to complete.

✔ **What qualifications do you have?** Many tax professionals are chartered accountants, and many are also certified financial planners. Those who specialize in tax should also have completed a two-year in-depth tax course offered by the Canadian Institute of Chartered Accountants.

EFILING versus Paper Filing Your Return

You're now at the point where your tax return is complete. Now what? If you've hired someone to prepare it for you, you have the option of EFILING your return. EFILE is an automated system that allows approved electronic filers to electronically deliver individual income tax return information to the CRA.

You can't EFILE your tax return yourself. You must first have your return prepared by an approved electronic filer. Most businesses that offer tax preparation services are registered to EFILE returns.

Who can EFILE?

The majority of Canadian taxpayers can have their return electronically filed. Individuals who *can't* EFILE include non-residents, individuals who came to or left Canada during the tax year, individuals who have declared bankruptcy, and people who have to pay income tax to more than one province or territory. Tax returns of deceased individuals cannot be EFILED either.

What are the benefits of EFILING?

Most people like EFILING their return because they get their assessment and refunds faster. In fact, the wait is cut to two weeks from the usual four to six if you're a procrastinator and file toward the end of April. If you're one of those who file in the middle of March, you may actually see your refund in just over a week! As well, since electronically transmitting your return saves the CRA from having to manually input your data, it reduces the likelihood of data entry errors. Last but not least, EFILING saves you a stamp.

Are my chances of an audit lower if I EFILE?

No. EFILED returns are selected for review using the same criteria as paper-filed returns. So if you're worried about an audit, don't think you can reduce your odds by EFILING your return.

If you don't like having any contact with the CRA after you file your return other than the report card called the Notice of Assessment, then we don't suggest you EFILE. You see, since no supporting documentation is sent to the CRA when you EFILE, they may contact you asking for backup information for some of your claims. The most common requests are for childcare, medical, and donation receipts. The CRA tries to select only returns for which they think there is a higher probability of non-compliance, but this is not always the case. Don't panic, however, if you receive a request to send more information. It doesn't mean you're being audited.

TELEFILE Your Return

With TELEFILE, you don't need to have someone else prepare and file your return. You can electronically file your own return. All you need is a touch-tone phone, your social insurance number, an invitation from the CRA to TELEFILE if you wish, and a personal access code. The system accepts income tax information such as employment income, pension income, interest income, RRSP contributions, and charitable donations. The more complex returns would take more telephone time, and often the CRA needs to see supporting documentation in order to process them.

Only those individuals who would ordinarily file the T1 Special return instead of the longer T1 "general" return are eligible for TELEFILE.

The T1 Special or T1S is sent to individuals who are wage and salary earners only, students, seniors, and filers who file only to obtain tax credits. When individuals eligible to use TELEFILE receive their tax package from the CRA, they will also receive the TELEFILE invitation along with an access code and instructions on how to use the system.

NETFILE

Now more than ever, Canadians are doing everything from banking to buying cars to planning their family vacations over the Internet. So why not file your income tax return over the Internet, too? NETFILE allows most individuals to file their returns using the Internet.

The CRA has set up a Web site containing a ton of information on NETFILE. Go to www.netfile.gc.ca.

NETFILE cannot be used by individuals that are bankrupt, are a non-resident of Canada or have earned self-employed income in more than one province or territory.

Before you can NETFILE your return to the CRA, you must first prepare it using certified tax preparation software. Basically, all this means is that the software will save your return in a format that the CRA can read. A listing of approved software is available on the CRA's Web site at www.netfile.gc.ca/software-e.html. You can also take a look above where we discuss tax software and the programs that are NETFILE-compatible.

Where to Get Forms and Other Information

The package that's sent by the CRA in mid-February contains only the most commonly used forms. If you didn't receive a package, or need an additional one, you can pick one up at the post office or the Tax Services Office (TSO) nearest you.

If you find that you need a form not contained in your package, getting your hands on one has never been easier! You have three options: visit your local TSO and pick up the form there, download the form from the CRA's Web site, or call and request to have the printed form mailed to you.

Chapter 4

Tips for Employment-Related Income

· ·

In This Chapter

▶ Defining employment income

▶ Establishing the difference between employee and self-employed

▶ Using taxable and non-taxable benefits to your best advantage

▶ Dealing with commission income

▶ Dealing with other employment income

· ·

*I*f you're like many Canadians, much of your time is spent at work. Among us are farmers and bankers and teachers and bus drivers, plus occupations that many of us have yet to imagine. But the one thing that we all have in common is that we work to get paid so that we have income to enjoy the rest of our lives. And, much to the chagrin of many Canadians, employment income is where we pay the bulk of our taxes. But don't despair — with some planning and a better understanding of how the CRA views employment income, we just might be able to help you end up with a few more dollars in your pocket after all is said and done.

What Is Employment Income?

Employment income includes all amounts received in a year as salary, wages, commissions, vacation pay, director fees, bonuses, tips, gratuities, and honoraria. You should report all these items — which, in most cases, have been reported by your employer on your T4 slip in box 14 — on line 101 of your personal tax return. This amount includes commission income, which is reported again on line 102. Record any income from the list above that you received but that is not reported on your T4 on line 104, "Other employment income."

Employee versus Self-Employed

Are you your own boss? For obvious reasons many of us like to think so, and this is yet another question that the CRA wants answered. Plainly stated, the CRA wants to know whether you are an employee or self-employed. For many people the answer may be simple, but for others it's not so obvious. In fact, you may consider yourself to be self-employed, but the taxman may think differently. You see, the CRA makes the distinction between self-employed and employed based on several factors or tests. And make no mistake about it: this distinction can make a huge difference in your taxable income. If you are an employee, the *Income Tax Act* restricts the expenses that you can deduct from your employment income. If a deduction is not specifically mentioned in the Act, the answer's simple — it's not deductible. Self-employed individuals do not have these same restrictions.

If possible, in most situations it's advantageous to arrange your business relationship so that you are an independent contractor (self-employed) rather than an employee. This is because independent contractors are entitled to claim deductions for many expenses not deductible by an employee. See Chapter 9 for a detailed discussion on self-employment and income tax!

Wondering how to set yourself up as an independent contractor? The CRA has a guide entitled *Employee or Self-Employed?* (RC4110) that identifies the factors it looks at to determine your status. You can find the guide under "Forms and publications" on the CRA Web site www.cra-arc.gc.ca).

Self-employment is not for everyone, since it comes with its own pitfalls. As a self-employed person you'll be responsible for paying the employer's share of Canada Pension Plan (CPP) contributions, which doubles your overall contribution. As well, before leaping at the opportunity to become your own boss, remember this: if the company turns sour, there will be no Employment Insurance (EI) or severance waiting for you. And, of course, you won't be entitled to any employment benefits such as medical or dental coverage if you are not considered an employee. (For the complete story on self-employment, see Chapter 9.)

Taxable and Non-Taxable Benefits

An employer will sometimes provide other benefits for your work in addition to your paycheque. These are often referred to as *perks*. The majority of the benefits you receive from your employer are considered taxable income, whether they are received in cash (for example, certain automobile allowances) or in kind (like an all-expense-paid holiday).

Taxable benefits

Even though you may not be pleased that some perks offered by your employer are taxable, a taxable benefit will usually be more financially advantageous than if you had to pay for the benefit yourself. For example, if your employer pays group term life insurance premiums of $4,000 for you annually, and you are taxed on the amount at 40 percent, you will pay tax of only $1,600 — that's much less expensive than having to pay this amount out of your after-tax income.

The following items are some of the more common taxable benefits that may show up on your T4 slip, along with some tips for using these benefits to your best advantage:

- ✔ **Stock options.** The difference between the price you pay (the "exercise price") and the market value of the shares on the exercise date is taxable to you. However, this benefit can be reduced by one-half if certain conditions are met. See Chapter 11, line 249 for details.

- ✔ **Interest-free or low-interest loans.** You are taxable on the difference between the actual interest rate, if any, you pay to your employer and the CRA's "prescribed" interest rate. The CRA's rates are adjusted quarterly and can be found at www.cra-arc.gc.ca.

If the loan from your employer was to help you relocate and purchase a home that's at least 40 kilometres closer to a new work location, you will not need to pay any taxes on the "free interest" on the first $25,000 of the loan during the first five years that the loan is outstanding.

- ✔ **Club dues.** If your employer is willing to pay for your dues to a recreational, sporting, or dining club, ensure that you can show that the membership is primarily to your employer's advantage (think networking and sales prospecting!). If this is the case, the benefit will not be taxable to you.

- ✔ **Car allowances.** If your employer gives you an allowance to help defray the cost of your vehicle, ensure you receive a per-kilometre reimbursement. If you receive a lump-sum allowance that is not based on a per-kilometre rate, you will find yourself with a taxable benefit. The good news is that even if the allowance is taxable, you may be entitled to deduct some of your auto expenses if you use your car for employment purposes. See Chapter 10, line 229 for details.

✔ **Company cars.** If you are provided with a company-owned or leased car, you will pay tax on the benefit for having the car (called a standby charge) for having the car available for personal use — regardless of whether you use the car personally. In addition, if your employer pays for operating costs (such as gas, insurance, or maintenance), you will pay tax on this benefit (referred to as an operating benefit), to the extent the car was used for personal purposes.

Think twice about accepting a company car as part of your compensation. You'll be required to pay tax on two separate benefits: the standby charge (which can be 24 percent of the cost of your car each year or two-thirds the annual lease costs!) and an operating benefit (22¢ per personal kilometre driven). Even though the value of your car is reduced as soon as you drive it off the lot, your standby charge stays the same each year. The car's depreciating value is ignored in calculating the standby charge. Thanks but no thanks!

You can reduce the standby charge if you drive at least 50 percent for employment use and your personal kilometres driven are less than 20,004 in a year. Also, if you are employed principally in selling or leasing automobiles, you are entitled to a lower operating benefit and standby charge.

✔ **Employee profit-sharing plans.** Your employer should provide you with form T4PS, "Statement of Employee Profit-Sharing Plan Allocations and Payments," which details the amounts to include in your income. Amounts received by the plan from your employer and income earned in the plan during the year are included. However, a distribution actually made by the plan to you will generally be tax-free since you've already paid tax on the amount received.

✔ **Employment-related insurance payments you receive.** Payments made to you for loss of income because of disability, sickness or accident, or income maintenance plan are taxable if your employer paid your premiums.

Make sure your plan at work is set up so that you pay the premium. That way any disability payments will be tax-free if you ever have to collect.

✔ **Group term life insurance premiums.** These premiums, paid by your employer, are considered to be a taxable benefit received by you.

✔ **Reimbursements and awards.** Such items received because of your employment — for example, paid holidays or incentive awards from employer-related contests — are taxable to you.

✓ **Rent-free or low-rent housing.** If your employer provides you with rent-free or low-rent accommodations, the difference between the actual market value of that housing and the amount you are required to pay will be included in your employment income. There is an exception if your duties are performed at a remote location or special work site. See Chapter 11, line 255 for further details.

✓ **Spouse's travelling expenses.** If your spouse joins you on a business trip, you'll probably have a taxable benefit equal to your spouse's travelling expenses paid for by your employer, unless your spouse was primarily engaged in business activities on behalf of your employer.

There's no harm in extending your business trip to include a personal vacation. Since the initial trip was for business purposes, the costs paid by your employer will be tax-free benefits. Of course, this is provided you pick up all the additional costs for your extended trip (other than the trip home).

✓ **Gifts from your employer.** You can receive two non-cash gifts per year, and if the combined cost to your employer is $500 or less, the entire amount is non-taxable. But watch out: if the total amount of the gifts you receive cost your employer more than $500, the entire amount becomes taxable — not just the portion above $500.

Gifts that have been personalized with your name or corporate logo will have a reduced market value. When the award is a plaque, trophy, or other memento for which there is no market, there likely will be no taxable benefit.

A prize recognized by the public for certain achievements or services can be non-taxable!

✓ **Frequent-flyer programs.** If you use points earned while travelling for work on personal travel, you'll have to report a taxable benefit for the market value of the points used. The good news (if you can call this "good") is that the value of the benefit is not the normal fare you'd have to pay if you bought the ticket yourself. Due to restrictions on the use of points at the airlines (and boy, there are a lot!), the CRA allows you to use the value of the most heavily discounted economy-class ticket sold for the flight.

✓ **Forgiveness of employee debt.** Do you have a nice employer who has lent you money? Do you have an even nicer employer who forgave some or all of this debt? In this case, your debt may be gone but the value of the forgiven amount is taxable.

Non-taxable benefits

And now for the fun stuff — non-taxable benefits! The following are benefits you can enjoy tax-free from your employer. Keep these benefits in mind if you're negotiating your way into a new job, or simply at your next compensation review:

- **Transportation to the job.** Some employers provide their employees with transportation to and from work, for security or some other reason (think private limo with a driver, not city bus with an employer-provided bus pass). Whatever the reason, there will be no inclusion for the value of the benefit in the employee's income. So now you can sit back and enjoy the ride, without worrying about any tax hit.

- **Moving costs.** If your employer pays for or reimburses you for moving costs where the move is for employment there is no taxable benefit.

Ensure you negotiate this tax-free benefit when considering a new job where a move is necessary.

If your employer compensates you for the diminished value or loss on the sale of your home due to relocation, you are considered to have received a taxable benefit. However, the taxable amount is only half of the amount reimbursed over $15,000. Better than nothing, we say!

- **Food and lodging.** Food and lodging are not taxable benefits if you were required to work at a temporary site for more than 36 hours consecutively. To qualify, the temporary site must be in a remote place or be farther away than a reasonable daily commute from your residence, and you must keep your usual residence.

- **Personal counselling.** Not many people know this, but your employer can pay for counselling related to your or a relative's mental or physical health, and you won't have to report a taxable benefit. The counselling may be related to tobacco, drug, or alcohol abuse; stress management; job placement; or retirement. Be sure to negotiate these payments with your employer if you find yourself or someone related to you in need of these services.

- **Computer and Internet services.** The CRA says that the provision of home computers and Internet services to an employee where the primary use is for work or for the employee to become more computer literate is not a taxable benefit. The CRA suggests the employee pay a nominal fee for personal use.

✔ **Death benefits.** If you pass away and your employer pays a death benefit to your family, the first $10,000 of that benefit is received tax-free.

✔ **Education costs.** If your employer picks up the tab for education, you will not have to pay any additional taxes for taking a course provided that you are benefiting your employer. If the course is of "personal interest," it would result in a taxable benefit since it has nothing to do with your work. So, if your employer kindly agrees to pay for your birdhouse-carpentry course, be prepared to pay taxes for it.

✔ **Scholarship.** If your employer has a scholarship plan to assist children of employees, the scholarship money can now be fully received tax-free by the child. Previously, the child was taxed on amounts received in excess of $3,000.

✔ **Parking space.** The fair market value of an employer-provided parking space, minus any amount you pay for the spot, must usually be included in your income. If your employer provides a parking space to you and you use your vehicle regularly during business hours to carry out your employment duties, it is not a taxable benefit. Of course, when the spot is in a location where free parking is readily accessible, then there will be no taxable benefit.

Other non-taxable benefits you may receive include

✔ Employer contributions to pension plans

✔ Employer contributions to private health services plans

✔ Merchandise discounts, if extended to all employees

✔ Subsidized meals, as long as you pay a reasonable charge for those meals

✔ The cost of uniforms, and the cleaning of them

✔ In-house recreational and fitness facilities

✔ In-house daycare services (but not daycare provided by a third party and paid for by your employer)

Commission Income

If you sell goods or negotiate contracts for a living, you may be compensated partially or wholly by commissions. From a tax point of view, you may be considered either a commissioned employee or self-employed (see our discussion of employee versus self-employed earlier in this chapter).

If you are considered an employee, your commission income will be reported on your T4 slip.

 Although your commissions are separately listed on your T4 slip, don't add this amount to your employment income on line 101. Box 14 of your T4 includes all taxable employment income you earned, including salary and wages, taxable benefits, and commission income.

 As a commissioned employee, you are entitled to deduct many expenses incurred to earn your commissions. See Chapter 10, line 224 for details.

If you are self-employed, you'll have to file a special tax form (T2124, "Statement of Business Income") detailing your commission income and expenses. See Chapter 9 for more information.

Other Employment Income

The CRA asks for certain items that are not technically employment income to be reported on line 104, "Other employment income."

These items include

- Royalties from a work or invention
- Employee GST rebate from the prior year
- Research grants net of expenses
- Amounts received from a supplementary unemployment benefit plan
- The taxable portion of an income maintenance insurance plan
- Director fees
- Signing bonuses
- Termination payments and damages for loss of employment
- Executor fees received for administering an estate

Part II
Tax Preparation Tips: Reporting Income

The 5th Wave   By Rich Tennant

"And just how long did you think you could keep that pot o'gold at the end of the rainbow a secret from us, Mr. O'Shea?"

In this part . . .

*H*ere's where we get into the good stuff. Contrary to popular opinion, every type of income you earn belongs somewhere on your tax return. Unfortunately, it doesn't all belong on the same line. Here's where all the various schedules and forms come into play, and where the confusion may begin. That's why we always say: Start with the identification section, ease into the rest of the return, and be thankful you only have to complete your T1 return once a year.

This part walks you through the various types of income that typical taxpayers may have. In the traditional *For Dummies* format, we've managed to make this as simple and painless as possible. So whether you're an employee, a business owner, an investor, or retired, this part's for you!

"The hardest thing in the world to understand is income tax!"

—Albert Einstein

Chapter 5

Tax Tips for Pension Income

* *

In This Chapter

▶ Making the most of the Old Age Security (OAS) program

▶ Preparing for the OAS "clawback"

▶ Sorting out the Canada Pension Plan (CPP) and the Quebec Pension Plan (QPP)

▶ Understanding other pensions

▶ Handling foreign pension income

▶ Separating non-taxable pension income

▶ Understanding and transferring the pension income credit

* *

*I*f you're a Canadian under age 65, you're probably asking yourself whether you need to bother with this chapter. We suggest you take the time to read it — you might be surprised by all the ways pension income can be part of your tax picture, even if you are a spring chicken.

True, only three lines of the tax return relate to pension income, and reporting OAS, CPP, and other pension income is usually straightforward. In most cases you will be issued an information slip detailing the amounts to be included in line 113 (Old Age Security pension), line 114 (Canada Pension Plan benefits), and line 115 (Other pensions and superannuation). So why is this chapter so long? Well, we decided to give you the lowdown on OAS and CPP to help you determine whether you qualify for these payments, how to go about receiving them, and how to pay the least tax on the amounts received. We also delve into the "OAS clawback" and offer you some pension and tax-planning ideas.

Old Age Security Pension

Old Age Security, or OAS, pension is a monthly public pension payment. It is available to most Canadians aged 65 and over — even if they no longer live in Canada. The amount is adjusted quarterly for increases in the cost of living as measured by the Consumer Price Index (CPI). The maximum monthly OAS pension payment for July to September 2006 was $487.54. The OAS is administered by Human Resources and Social Development Canada (HRSDC).

You must apply for OAS!

Non-resident recipients of OAS

OAS payments can be made to addresses outside Canada. If you are not a resident of Canada, a "non-resident tax" may be withheld from your payment of OAS. The maximum withholding is 25 percent. HRSDC will not withhold any non-resident tax on payments of OAS if you are a resident of the United States or the United Kingdom.

Speed up the receipt of your OAS! Have your OAS payment deposited in any bank account in Canada or the United States.

OAS eligibility criteria

Eligibility for an OAS pension is based on two criteria: age, and years resident in Canada. OAS pension is not affected by your employment history, and you are entitled to receive it whether or not you have retired. Two categories of people are eligible for OAS:

- ✔ People living in Canada who
    - • Are 65 or older,
    - • Are Canadian citizens or legal residents, and
    - • Have lived in Canada for at least 10 years while adults.
- ✔ People living outside Canada who
    - • Are 65 or older,
    - • Are Canadian citizens or legal residents at the time they cease to live in Canada, and
    - • Had lived in Canada for at least 10 years as adults.

Don't fall into either of these categories? You still may be eligible to receive OAS! Canada has a number of social security agreements with other countries. If you lived in one of these countries or contributed to its social security system, you may qualify for a pension from that country, Canada, or both. Need more information to determine whether you qualify? Contact HRSDC at 1-800-277-9914.

HRSDC's Web site at www.sdc.gc.ca contains a wealth of information as well. You can also drop into a regional HRSDC office; addresses can be found on the Web site.

Are you entitled to full or partial OAS?

The main criterion in determining whether you're entitled to a full or partial OAS pension is the length of time you've been in Canada. You should qualify for full OAS if the following criteria apply to you:

- ✔ Lived in Canada for at least 40 years after your 18th birthday, or
- ✔ Were born on July 1, 1952, or earlier, and
  - Lived in Canada on July 1, 1977
  - Between your 18th birthday and July 1, 1977, lived in Canada for some period of time, or
  - Lived in Canada for 10 years prior to your OAS application being approved.

Don't qualify because you haven't lived in Canada for the past 10 years? Don't fret! You should still qualify for full OAS if

- ✔ You lived in Canada for the year immediately before your application was approved.
- ✔ Prior to those past 10 years, you lived in Canada as an adult for a period of at least three times the length of your absences during the past 10 years. (Go ahead; be confident — do the math!)

If you don't qualify for a full OAS pension, a partial pension may be available to you. The amount you would receive is based on the number of complete years you lived in Canada after turning 18.

Applying for OAS

To ensure your OAS payments start on time, you should apply six months before your 65th birthday. A registration kit (ISP3000) is available from any HRSDC office, or you can call 1-800-277-9914. The kit can also be downloaded from the HRSDC Web site at www.sdc.gc.ca. You cannot apply online. You need to download the form ISP3000, complete it, and send it to the address noted on the Web site.

Is my OAS pension taxable?

You bet. Reporting OAS on your tax return, however, is very simple. If you received OAS payments in 2006, you will receive a T4A(OAS) information slip summarizing the amount paid. You should expect this slip to arrive in January 2007. If you are computer savvy, you can also see your slip online. Follow the links on the Web site at www.sdc.gc.ca.

Include the amount noted in box 18 on line 113 of your tax return. Some tax may have been held back on the OAS pension payment to you (see below). If so, this amount will be noted in box 22 of the T4A(OAS). Be sure to include the withheld tax on line 437 of your return.

If you want to reduce the amount of taxes that come due on April 30 each year, you can request that more taxes be withheld from your OAS pension payments.

OAS repayment ("clawback")

The government giveth, and the government taketh away! Much to the chagrin of seniors, our government believes that those with income in excess of $62,144 do not need to receive a full OAS pension. When a taxpayer has received OAS higher than his or her calculated maximum OAS entitlement, the excess amount must be repaid. The amount that must be repaid is equal to 15 percent of net income in excess of $62,144 — stay tuned for an example.

The clawback works by reducing monthly OAS payments to take into account an individual's expected repayment. High-income individuals do not receive any OAS at all. This withholding of OAS adds a measure of complexity to tax return preparation, as we explain below.

Once it is determined that you have to make an OAS repayment, the CRA (based on information on your tax return) tells HRSDC, which in turn adjusts your future monthly OAS payments. Assuming you file your 2006 tax return by April 30, 2007, the CRA should assess you by the end of June 2007. Based on the assessment of your income on your 2006 return, HRSDC will adjust your next 12 monthly OAS payments beginning with the July 2007 payment. (Your July 2007 payment may be significantly different from your June 2007 payment!) In other words, HRSDC expects that you will have to repay all or a portion of your 2007 OAS in an amount that is approximately what you had to repay in respect to the 2006 OAS. Rather than paying you the OAS and then waiting for you to repay OAS as part of your 2007 tax return, HRSDC simply reduces the amount of your monthly OAS cheque.

What if your 2007 net income is *lower* than your 2006 net income? Are you losing out? No worries . . . the government pays any difference between what you receive and what you are entitled to by decreasing your tax liability (or increasing your tax refund) on your 2007 tax return.

Calculation of OAS repayment

Say Jim turned 65 on January 1, 2006. He applied for OAS six months before his 65th birthday. (We have purposely made Jim's income exceed $62,144 to detail the calculation and impact of the OAS repayment on his tax return and tax liability.)

Let's work through an illustration of how the OAS repayment (or clawback) is calculated.

Old Age Security (OAS) pension (estimate)	$5,800
Other pension income	$65,000
Interest income	$2,000
Deduction for support payments made to former spouse	($5,000)
Net income before deduction for OAS repayment (line 234 on tax return)	$67,800
Net income before deduction for OAS repayment (as above)	$67,800
Less base amount	$62,144
Excess net income	$ 5,656
Net income before deduction for OAS repayment (as above)	$67,800
Less repayment — 15 percent on excess net income (line 235 on tax return)	$848
Net income after OAS repayment (line 236 on tax return)	$66,952

The amount of repayment owing is included on line 422 of the tax return as part of the calculation of your total tax liability or refund for the year. Depending on your tax position, the OAS repayment may increase your tax owing for 2006 — or decrease your refund!

Protect your OAS! Once your net income is $100,031, you repay all your OAS (or it is clawed back). Use the tips in this book to minimize your income and the OAS clawback.

Guaranteed Income Supplement (GIS)

The GIS provides low-income seniors in Canada with supplementary public pension payments in addition to the regular OAS pension. The GIS is based on the taxpayer's income and marital status. The maximum monthly GIS from July to September 2006 was $597.53 for a single person and $392.01 for an individual married to an OAS recipient. The GIS payment is included in the monthly OAS pension cheque.

Is the GIS taxable?

No, but the amount must be reported on your tax return. The T4A(OAS) slip will note the amount of GIS you received in box 21. First include this amount in your income on line 146 and then deduct it on line 250.

The Allowance

The allowance is an additional amount paid to low-income seniors aged 60 to 64 with a spouse or common-law partner who receives the OAS and GIS. It is like an early OAS pension. To receive it, you must meet some residency tests.

If you are receiving the allowance, you will get an annual T4A(OAS) slip. The amount received will be noted in box 21. The allowance is not taxable but must be reported on your tax return in the same fashion as the GIS. You apply for the allowance using form ISP3008.

Applying for the GIS and yearly renewal

As with OAS pension, you must apply for GIS to begin receiving it. Use form ISP3025 (2006-2007), "Application for Guaranteed Income Supplement," which you can get from the HRSDC Web site (www.sdc.gc.ca) or by calling 1-800-277-9914. The GIS is renewed annually, since it is based on your income from the previous year. You do not need to reapply each year — just be sure to file an income tax return each year. (Sometimes, the government will still send you a renewal form. If you receive a form, complete it right away to ensure your GIS payments are not held up.)

Allowance for the Survivor

Additional money is paid to low-income seniors aged 60 to 64 if their spouse or common-law partner has died and they meet residency requirements. Like those receiving the allowance, recipients of the allowance for the survivor will receive an annual T4A(OAS) slip. It is not taxable, although it is still reported on your tax return. Again, enter the amount received as noted in box 21 and deduct the same amount on line 250. Form ISP3008 is used to apply for the allowance for the survivor.

To continue receiving the GIS, the allowance, or the allowance for the survivor, ensure you file a tax return by April 30 each year. Without a tax return on file, your payments will stop!

See Table 5-1 for a summary of the tax implications of these items.

Table 5-1	Taxation of Old Age Security (Line 113)
Type of Receipt	*Taxable?*
Old Age Security (OAS) pension	Yes — and it can be taxed up to 100 percent. (See "OAS repayment (clawback)" earlier in this chapter.)
Guaranteed Income (GIS)	No — but it must be reported on your Supplement tax return.
The allowance	No — but it must be reported on your tax return.
Allowance for the survivor	No — but it must be reported on your tax return.

Line 114: Income from the Canada Pension Plan (CPP) and Quebec Pension Plan (QPP)

The CPP and its Quebec counterpart the QPP are a second level of public pension available to certain Canadians. However, unlike the OAS pension, which is available to all Canadians who meet certain residency requirements, you receive a CPP/QPP pension only if you've paid into the plan. If you earned employment or self-employment income during your working days, you most likely paid into one (or both) of these plans and can reap some benefits in your retirement years.

Table 5-2 lists the variety of benefits you can receive CPP and the QPP and whether or not they're taxable.

Table 5-2   Summary of CPP/QPP Benefits and Taxation

Type of Receipt	Taxable?
CPP/QPP lump-sum benefit	Yes — but a portion may be taxed in a prior year
CPP/QPP retirement pension	Yes
CPP/QPP disability pension	Yes
CPP/QPP child disability benefit	Yes — but taxed in child's tax return
CPP/QPP survivor benefit	Yes
CPP/QPP child survivor benefit	Yes — but taxed in child's tax return
CPP/QPP death benefit	Yes — but taxed in estate

CPP versus QPP

The Quebec government administers the QPP on behalf of the residents of Quebec. HRSDC administers the CPP for the remaining nine provinces and three territories. With respect to most issues, the two plans operate in a similar fashion. For simplicity and conciseness, most of this chapter deals with CPP issues.

Reporting your CPP/QPP income on your tax return

Each January, HRSDC sends CPP recipients a T4A(P) tax slip. You can also go online at www.sdc.gc.ca to see your slip electronically. Enter the amount noted in box 20 on line 114 of your tax return. Amounts in the other boxes on the slip provide a breakdown of your sources of CPP. You do not need to report these amounts on your tax return, with the exception of box 16 — the disability benefit. Enter this amount on line 152 of your return, which is just to the left of line 114. Do not add box 152 when calculating your total income; the amount is already included in box 114.

Lump-sum CPP/QPP benefit

If you receive a lump-sum benefit in 2006, all or part of it may be in respect to a prior year. You need to report the amount in your 2006 tax return. However, you may qualify for preferential tax treatment. If the amount related to a previous year is $300 or more, you can have that portion taxed in the year to which it relates. Doing so is beneficial if the tax in the relevant year would be lower than your 2006 tax would be if the amount were included in your 2006 return — for example, if you were in a lower tax bracket in that previous year. The CRA, based on information from HRSDC, will reassess your 2006 return and that of the other year, and advise you of the results in a Notice of Reassessment.

CPP retirement pension

The CPP is a monthly pension paid to individuals who have contributed to

- ✔ The CPP, or
- ✔ Both the CPP and Quebec Pension Plan (QPP), if you live outside Quebec.

Like OAS, you must apply to receive a CPP retirement pension.

Once you qualify to begin to receive CPP you are permitted to work as much as you like and your pension amount will not be affected. However, you can no longer contribute to the CPP.

Applying for Your CPP Retirement Pension

You can apply for your CPP retirement pension online at www.sdc.gc.ca/en/isp/common/rtrinfo.shtml. You can fill out this application up to one year before you wish to begin receiving your pension. If you choose this method, keep in mind that there is still some information that you need to send to the government to prove you are you, like a signature form and proof of birthdate. If you don't want to apply online, you can also fill out the form by hand and mail it in. The form you need is called ISP1000 and can be found on the forms area of the HRSDC Website at www.sdc.gc.ca/cgi-bin/search/eforms/index.cgi?app=list&group=all&lang=e. You can also pick one up at any HRSDC office, or call 1-800-277-9914 and they'll send you a copy. HRSDC suggests you apply six months before you want your retirement pension to begin (much like the OAS).

To find out how much CPP you are entitled to at different start dates, you can contact HRSDC. Simply fill out form ISP1003, "Estimate Request for Canada Pension Plan (CPP) Retirement Pension," with alternative start dates. The closer you are to the date you want your pension to begin, the more accurate the estimate will be. The form is available at any HRSDC office or via the Web site (www.sdc.gc.ca).

 As with the OAS, you may qualify for a CPP retirement pension that is based not only on contributions you have made to the plan, but also on contributions you have made to another country's social security system. This is good news if you were in Canada for only a short while before you retired but had previously worked and paid social security taxes to another country. See the International Benefits section on the HRSDC Website (www.sdc.gc.ca) for further information.

Taking your CPP retirement pension early

The retirement pension is designed to be paid starting when an individual turns 65. However, you have the option of taking a discounted payment at any time between the ages of 60 and 64. If you decide to start your CPP retirement pension before you are 65 years of age, the payments are reduced by 6 percent for each year (actually 0.5 percent per month) that you are under 65.

To choose this option, you must have stopped working, or you must be earning less than the monthly maximum CPP retirement pension. In 2006 this was $844.58 per month.

Increasing your CPP retirement pension

If you elect to start receiving your CPP retirement pension after you are 65 years of age, you are entitled to an increased amount — again, 6 percent per year (or 0.5 percent per month). If you wait until your 70th birthday, your entitlement increases by 30 percent! (The amount cannot be increased more than 30 percent — so, waiting until you are 71 or 72 will not get you a bigger CPP pension.)

How do you decide when to start taking your CPP retirement pension?

HRSDC suggests that in making your decision of when to start collecting CPP benefits, you consider the following:

- Whether you are still working and contributing to the CPP
- How long you have contributed
- How much your earnings were
- What your other sources of retirement income are
- How your health is
- What your retirement plans are, including desired lifestyle

In general, if you are still working or don't need the extra cashflow the CPP will provide you, you might want to wait to get a bigger CPP pension later. On the other hand, if your health is poor or the extra cashflow will come in handy, you might opt to take your CPP pension early in order to maximize your situation.

Other benefits offered by the CPP

In addition to the retirement pension, the CPP also provides the following:

- CPP disability benefits
- CPP survivor benefits

CPP disability benefits

The CPP will provide you with a monthly pension if you have been a CPP contributor and are considered mentally or physically disabled according to its guidelines. Payments can also be made to dependent children. Your disability must be "severe and prolonged." HRSDC considers "severe" to mean that you cannot work regularly at any job, and "prolonged" to mean that your condition is long-term or may lead to death. The benefit comprises a flat amount plus a second amount based on the number of years you have contributed to the CPP. The maximum monthly disability benefit in 2006 was $1,031.05.

If you become disabled, your child under 18 can also qualify for a benefit. Even if your "child" is between ages 18 and 25, he or she will still qualify if enrolled in what HRSDC considers a recognized institution — usually a school providing post-secondary education. The maximum amount paid in 2006 was $200.47 per month per child.

You must apply for both CPP disability benefits — the regular benefit and the children's benefit. Application forms are available from HRSDC offices or from HRSDC's Web site. You should apply as soon as you consider yourself to have a long-term disability that prevents you from working at any job. The government will require you to provide a medical report from your doctor.

CPP survivor benefits

CPP survivor benefits are paid to your estate, surviving spouse or common-law partner, and dependent children. There are three types of survivor benefits.

Death benefit

The death benefit is a one-time payment to your estate. The maximum amount for this benefit is $2,500.

Survivor's pension

Your surviving spouse or common-law partner can receive a monthly pension. The amount of the payment depends on how long you paid into the CPP, your spouse or common-law partner's age when you die, and whether he or she is receiving a CPP retirement or disability pension. The calculation is based on what your CPP retirement pension would have been if you had been 65 at the time of death. This amount is then adjusted to take into account the age of your survivor. The maximum amount that can be received is 60 percent of what your retirement pension would have been (the 2006 monthly maximum is $506.75, or 60 percent of $844.58). To receive this amount, your survivor must be aged 65 or over at the time of your death. If your survivor is younger, the payments are lower.

If your surviving spouse or common-law partner is under 35 and is not disabled or raising your dependent child, the amount is deferred until he or she is 65 or becomes disabled. The survivor will continue to receive the pension even if he or she remarries.

Prior to a change to the rules in 1987, a surviving spouse who remarried would lose the pension. If this happened to you, contact HRSDC to find out whether you are now eligible.

Children's benefit

The children's benefit is a monthly payment to a deceased contributor's dependent children. At the time of the contributor's death, the child must be under 18, or between the ages of 18 and 25 and enrolled full time in a recognized educational institution. The maximum monthly amount in 2006 was $200.47. At least one of the child's parents must have been a contributor to the CPP. A child may get two benefits if both parents are deceased or disabled.

You must apply for CPP survivor benefits. Applications are available at HRSDC offices and on the HRSDC Web site.

Splitting CPP benefits with your significant other

You and your spouse or common-law partner can apply to receive an equal share of the CPP retirement pension you both earned during the years you were together. You must both be at least 60 years of age, and must request that your CPP be shared or "split" at the time you apply for CPP. CPP sharing or splitting is also referred to as an assignment of your CPP retirement pension. Splitting your CPP does not increase or decrease the overall retirement pension to which you and your spouse or common-law partner are entitled.

Why would you split?

The main reason for CPP splitting is to reduce the combined tax you and your spouse or common-law partner pay. This can be done when you are in different income tax brackets. Let's take a look at an example to make this a little clearer. Assume your income, before your CPP retirement pension, is about $120,000. This puts you into the top tax bracket. The actual tax you pay will be based on the province or territory you live in. Let's say you live in a province or territory where the top tax rate is 45 percent. Let's further assume that your spouse makes $10,000, excluding his or her CPP retirement pension. At this level of income, let's say the tax rate is 23 percent. Your CPP retirement pension is $5,000 and your spouse's is $2,000. As illustrated in the following table, you and your spouse will pay an aggregate of $2,710 in income tax on your combined CPP retirement pension.

	You	*Spouse*	*Total*
CPP retirement pension	$5,000	$2,000	$7,000
Tax rate	45%	23%	
Tax	$2,250	$460	$2,710

Let's improve the situation. You and your spouse agree to split your CPP retirement pension.

	You	Spouse	Total
CPP retirement pension	$3,500	$3,500	$7,000
Tax rate	45%	23%	
Tax	$1,575	$805	$2,380

You can see that the tax is reduced to $2,380 — a $330 saving, just by filling out a form! This result is optimal when one spouse is in the highest tax bracket (taxable income in excess of $118,285), and the other spouse is in the lowest tax bracket (taxable income of less than $36,378). The saving is enhanced further when the high-income-earning spouse also receives a CPP retirement pension significantly higher than that received by the lower-income spouse.

CPP and marriage breakdown — Splitting CPP credits

CPP credits are used to determine the amount of your entitlement to a CPP retirement pension. Since spouses and common-law partners build up credits during a marriage or common-law relationship, both can share in the CPP entitlements earned while they were together. CPP credits can even be split if only one spouse or common-law partner paid into the CPP. You or your ex or one of your lawyers can apply to HRSDC.

CPP/QPP overpayments

If you were required to repay a CPP or QPP amount that was paid to you in error and included in your income, you can deduct the amount repaid on line 232 of your tax return.

Line 115: Other Pensions

The dollar amounts of your various pension incomes are to be aggregated and reported on line 115 of your return. This is fairly straightforward — most pension income will be reported on T4A slips or other tax information slips.

Types of pension income

Here are descriptions of the various types of pension income:

- ✔ **Payments from a former employer's or union's registered pension plan (box 16 of T4A slip).** If you transferred a lump sum from a pension plan to your RRSP, see "Transferring Pension Income" later in the chapter.

- ✔ **Payments from an RRIF — a Registered Retirement Income Fund (T4RIF slip) and payments from an annuity (T4A slip).** If you are *under* age 65, report these amounts on line 130 of your return — not on line 115. This is so the income will *not* qualify for the pension income credit. The pension income credit is discussed briefly in this chapter and then in detail in Chapter 12.

- ✔ **Certain annuity income.** If you have purchased an annuity with non-RRSP funds, the annuity payments you receive are considered to be part interest and part capital. The capital portion is not subject to tax because it represents a partial return of the purchase price that you funded with tax-paid dollars. The interest portion is usually taxed as interest (hey, this makes sense!). However, if you are aged 65 or older and have receipts from a "mixed annuity" (an annuity payment in which the interest and capital portion are determined by the tax rules), the interest portion is considered pension income and is reported on line 115.

Foreign pension income

Foreign pension income refers to any pension income that is received from a source outside Canada. A common type is U.S. social security paid to a resident of Canada. To receive this you would have worked in the U.S. at some time in your life. If you worked in the U.S. or any foreign country you may have been part of a foreign employer's pension plan. When you retire you are entitled to receive your pension even though you are no longer resident in the country that is making the pension payments. You also may have served in a foreign country's armed forces. If so, you may be entitled to a pension from the respective country. Most foreign pension income is subject to tax — but not all! Immediately below, we discuss various sources of foreign pension income. We also comment on the respective tax issues of each source.

U.S. social security income

Include the full amount of U.S. social security income you receive on line 115. Of course, you will need to translate the U.S.-dollar amount received into a Canadian-dollar amount!

To convert to Canadian dollars, use the exchange rate as of the day you received the social security payment. Alternatively, you can use the annual average U.S.–Canada exchange rate that the CRA provides. These exchange rates can be found on the CRA Web site at www.cra-arc.gc.ca/tax/individuals/faq/exchange_rate-e.html. Choose the method that is most beneficial to you — that is, the method that translates into the lowest Canadian-dollar equivalent.

On line 256 of your return, you can take a 15 percent deduction of the amount you received in U.S. social security. This results in only 85 percent of your U.S. social security being subject to tax!

Other foreign pension income

The CRA suggests that you include foreign pension income on line 115 of your tax return after applying the appropriate exchange rate, and then attach a note to your return indicating the type of pension and its country of origin. If the foreign country withheld tax from your pension payment, do not deduct the tax, but report the gross pension receipt. The foreign tax paid may qualify as a tax credit (referred to as a foreign tax credit) in calculating your tax liability (see Chapter 13).

Canada has a number of tax treaties with other countries. A treaty may adjust the amount of a foreign pension that is taxed in Canada. The CRA can assist you in determining if any of your foreign pension is partially or completely exempt from Canadian tax. The number to call is 1-800-267-5177. In order to make this determination, the CRA will ask for details about your pension, so you should keep any documents sent to you from the pension plan. If you determine that an amount is not taxable in Canada, it can be deducted on line 256 of your return.

Non-Taxable Pension Income

The following pension payments should not be included in your tax return:

- Capital element of an annuity. If you are receiving annuity payments, a portion is interest and a portion is capital (in other words, a portion is part of your original purchase price or investment). Since you invested after-tax funds, you are not taxed again.

✔ Military and civil pensions paid under the

- *Pension Act* (pension on death of a Canadian armed forces member)

- *Civilian War Pensions and Allowances Act* (pensions for civilians injured in the Second World War)

- *War Veterans Act* (pension for veterans, spouses, and dependent children)

✔ War service pension from other countries allied with Canada

✔ German compensation in respect of Nazi persecution

✔ Halifax disaster pension

Pension Income Credit

You can claim a pension income credit amount if you receive certain types of pension income (schedule 1, line 314 of the tax return).

The maximum pension credit has been increased to $2,000 (from $1,000) of eligible pension income. If your eligible pension income is less than $2,000, your credit amount will be equal to the amount of eligible pension income. For complete details, see Chapter 12, line 314.

If you incur legal fees to establish your right to a pension benefit, the fees may be fully or partially deducted on your tax return. If so, deduct fees paid on line 232 of your return.

Transferring Pension Income

The tax rules let you transfer lump-sum pension amounts (within limits) from one registered pension plan (RPP) to another RPP or to your registered retirement savings plan (RRSP). The transfer is tax-free if the funds are transferred directly from one plan to the other. By "directly," we mean that you don't actually see the money — only the financial institutions do!

If the funds are directly transferred, there will be no income inclusion in your tax return and no need for you to take an offsetting deduction. The institutions involved should not issue you a T4A slip or any kind of tax information slip.

You may want to transfer funds when you change jobs or take early retirement. In these cases, you may be given the choice of leaving the funds where they are or moving them elsewhere — usually to your RRSP. You may also choose to transfer the funds to a new employer's pension plan, although in practice, we find this form of transfer rare.

Your decision to move the funds will rest on the confidence you have in the pension plan, where you have no say in how your pension funds are invested, versus the confidence you have in your ability to take control of the funds (likely with your own investment adviser's help) through a self-directed RRSP. But be forewarned: if you transfer the funds from an RPP to an RRSP, don't expect to be able to take the funds out of the RRSP (even if you want to pay tax on the RRSP withdrawal). Most provincial pension rules require the funds to be put in a "locked-in" RRSP. This often means you can't get at the funds until you are at least age 60.

The value of the portion of your employer's RPP that you plan to transfer to an RRSP is often referred to as the "commuted value."

Chapter 6

Tax Tips for Investment Income

So you might glance at the topics above and think that this chapter will be really light reading — well, as light as it gets for a tax book, that is. Only two lines on your tax return? How much can there be to know! Don't kid yourself: tonnes of important information is tied to lines 120 and 121.

In this chapter we will look at the taxation of dividends (which has changed this year), interest, and other types of investment income, along with the tax treatment of loans from corporations to their shareholders and employees and the implications of distributions from a registered education savings plan. Let's dive right in!

Line 120: Dividends

A *dividend* is a distribution of a corporation's profits to its shareholders. Investors receive dividends being paid on the stocks that they purchase in their investment portfolios, and small business owners may also receive dividends from their own companies. Either way, a dividend comes from the earnings of a company after all expenses and income taxes have been paid. The important thing for you to remember here is the after-taxes part!

Canadian-source dividends

Canadian-source dividends — that is, dividends from a Canadian corporation — receive special tax treatment when paid to residents of Canada.

Although all Canadian dividends receive special tax treatment, the treatment differs depending on the type of corporation paying the dividends. This is because different types of Canadian corporations pay different rates of tax. For example, a small corporation running a business would normally pay a very low rate of tax, while a large publicly listed company or a private investment holding company would normally pay tax at a very high rate. On an overall basis, the Canadian tax rules try to even the playing field, so to speak, so that the corporate tax plus the personal tax the shareholder pays on the dividends would be about the same amount paid by the individual if he or she had earned the corporate income personally. This is known as the theory of integration and we talk about this in more detail below.

How does this all affect the taxation of Canadian dividends in 2006? In recognition that different types of Canadian corporations pay different tax rates, starting this year, all Canadian dividends must be classified as either "eligible" or "non-eligible" "Eligible for what?" you might ask. The easy answer is, more tax credits! Why? Because (in the case of eligible dividends) the company paying you those dividends has already paid a lot of tax on its income — in recognition of that the government is allowing you to pay less tax on that company's dividends. Trust us when we say, it's a good thing.

Eligible dividends generally include dividends paid any time after December 31, 2005, by public corporations. Non-eligible dividends are generally those paid by private companies to their shareholders — but there may be exceptions if your small business has active business income higher than $300,000. If you don't own shares of your own business, but rather invest in publicly traded stocks, your dividends will be classified as eligible dividends.

Don't worry, it's not up to you to determine whether dividends you received are eligible or non-eligible. Your T5 slip will indicate the classification for you. What's the difference? If you receive eligible dividends, you will receive even more tax credits than you have in the past. Read on for more details.

The special tax treatment for Canadian dividends involves including the entire dividend in income and then "grossing up" or adding an additional amount of the dividend into your income. For eligible dividends, the gross-up is 45 percent. For non-eligible dividends the gross-up is 25 percent. So, if you receive $10,000 in eligible dividends this year, you'll have to include $14,500 in your income. If that dividend was non-eligible, you would include $12,500 in income.

Does it seem like you are being penalized for investing in public companies in Canada? At first glance, it might. However, the calculations don't stop there. You are entitled to a dividend tax credit, which reduces your tax bill. In fact, although it seems like you are exposing yourself to more tax if you earn eligible dividends, the tax credit on these dividends works so that you will pay less tax on eligible versus non-eligible dividends. Confused yet? Read on and we will explain it all.

The concept that drives most of the complicated rules in tax is the concept of "tax integration." We alluded to this concept earlier in this section. At its core is the idea that the total tax paid by a corporation and its shareholders should be the same amount of tax paid by an individual who carries on the same business directly without a corporation. By using a separate tax entity — a corporation — and passing the profits to the shareholder, tax is paid once at the corporate level and again at the individual shareholder level. The theory of tax integration says that although there are two levels of tax, the total tax bill is no higher than if the shareholder had earned all the profits personally. Tax integration works to both avoid "double tax" on the same dollar of income — always a good thing! — and to ensure there is no tax benefit in earning income in different ways.

Without an integrated tax system, one could retain more cash after tax by running a business through a sole proprietorship versus earning income in a corporation and then paying the after-tax profits out as a dividend. Since it is not the government's intention to put corporate shareholders at a disadvantage when it comes to earning income, it created an elaborate system to level the playing field.

Calculations, calculations

To avoid unjustly penalizing shareholders in terms of the tax they pay both personally and through the corporation's shares they own, the tax rules work as follows:

- ✔ Eligible dividends, that is, dividends from public corporations resident in Canada (along with a few other types of dividends that are much less common) must be included in the taxable income of an individual shareholder and grossed up by 45 percent (that is, multiplied by 1.45, or 145 percent). The grossed-up dividend represents an estimate of what the dividend would have been if the corporation had not been subject to tax.

- ✔ Non-eligible dividends, that is, dividends from Canadian-controlled private corporations (generally small, privately held companies), must be included in the taxable income of an individual shareholder and grossed up by 25 percent (that is, multiplied by 1.25, or 125 percent). The grossed-up dividend represents an estimate of what the dividend would have been if the corporation had not been subject to tax.

- ✔ A federal and provincial/territorial dividend tax credit is then calculated.

Why the difference in the rates between eligible and non eligible dividends? Canadian controlled private corporations generally pay about 20 percent tax on their income, while public corporations in Canada pay tax at a much higher rate. Had the public corporation not paid any tax on its income, it would have had much more to pay out in dividends to its shareholders, thus the higher gross-up.

The dividend tax credit is designed to reflect the tax paid by the corporation. Put another way, you as a shareholder receive a tax credit for the tax the corporation paid on your behalf. The federal dividend tax credit is 13.33 percent of the grossed-up non-eligible dividend, and 19 percent of the grossed-up eligible dividend paid. (Don't you just love all the math?)

Prior to 2006, all Canadian dividends were taxed the same way. That is, they were grossed-up by 25 percent and then 13.33 percent of the grossed up amount could be claimed as a dividend tax credit.

Say Tom receives a $10,000 eligible dividend from IM Canadian Corporation, a publicly listed Canadian corporation. He also runs his own business through his corporation, Tom Incorporated and receives $10,000 in non-eligible dividends from that company. Assume Tom has a high taxable income (above $118,285), and therefore will pay federal tax of 29 percent on the dividend. Further, assume Tom is subject to a provincial tax rate of 14 percent and a provincial dividend tax credit of 5 percent of the grossed-up non-eligible dividend and 6.5 percent eligible dividend (refer to Table 6-1). How is tax calculated on each type of dividend that Tom receives?

Table 6-1	Integrated Tax System	
	Eligible Dividend	Non-Eligible Dividend
Actual dividend received	$10,000	$10,000
Taxable dividend (grossed-up dividend)	$14,500	$12,500
Federal tax (at 29%)	$4,205	$3,625
Less federal dividend tax credit	($2,755)	($1,667)
Net federal tax payable	$1,450	$1,958
Provincial tax (at 14%)	$2,030	$1,750
Less provincial dividend tax credit	($942)	($625)
Total tax	$2,538	$3,083

As you can see, the net result of this calculation is that Tom pays about 25 percent tax on the eligible dividend from IM Canadian Corporation and about 31 percent tax on the non-eligible dividend from Tom Incorporated. When these taxes are added to the tax the corporations have already paid, the total tax equals the tax Tom would have paid if he had earned the money directly instead of through the corporation.

When you receive a T3 or T5 slip reporting your dividend income, you will notice that the slip has boxes that contain both the actual amount of dividends and the taxable amount of dividends paid. Be sure to include only the taxable amount of dividends on your tax return. The T3 or T5 slip will also note the federal dividend tax credit you are entitled to. (Phew!)

In some cases it is possible to pay no personal tax on dividends received because of the basic personal exemption (line 300, Chapter 12) and the dividend tax credit. Federally, you can receive about $66,000 in Canadian eligible dividends and not pay any tax. Of course, this assumes that you have no other sources of income, and there are also provincial taxes to consider. The amount of tax-free dividends you can receive will depend on your province/territory of residence, since tax rates differ. A tax professional can assist you in finding out the maximum amount you can receive in dividends and still manage to avoid the tax collector.

Stock dividends and stock splits

A *stock dividend* is a dividend that a corporation pays to its share-holders by issuing new shares instead of cash.

The rules for a stock dividend mirror those for a cash dividend. The only difference, of course, is that you owe tax, but you have not received any cash to pay the tax! The corporation paying the stock dividend will issue you a T5 slip showing you the amount of dividend to report on your tax return. The value or amount of the stock dividend in dollars will be determined by the corporation's board of directors. If the corporation is a Canadian resident, the gross-up and dividend tax credit rules discussed above will apply.

Be aware that a stock dividend and a stock split are not the same thing. A *stock split* is simply dividing your shares into more shares with no change to the company's share capital. No tax is owed on stock splits, while substantial tax can be owed on stock dividends if the board of directors places a high value on the stock issued via the stock dividend.

Foreign dividends

Foreign dividends are dividends received from non–Canadian resident corporations. The most common foreign dividends we see here in Canada are dividends received on shares of U.S. corporations. It may come as no surprise that foreign dividends are treated in a different manner than dividends received from Canadian resident corporations. Here are the details:

- Foreign dividends are not subject to the dividend gross-up and dividend tax credit calculations.

- Foreign dividends are included in income at their full amount. Even if the originating country withheld tax on the dividend, the full amount — not the dividend minus the tax withheld — is included in income.

- The dividends must be converted to Canadian dollars. The CRA publishes foreign exchange rates on its Web site each year.

- Tax withheld on a foreign-source dividend can be recovered by claiming a foreign tax credit. (Foreign tax credits are discussed in Chapter 13.)

- All foreign dividends are included in calculating your taxable income. Even if the dividend you received is not taxable in the country of origin, it is still taxable here!

- If you own shares of a foreign corporation or have interests in foreign property with a cost of more than $100,000 Canadian (in total) at any time in the year, you will need to file form T1135, the "Foreign Income Verification Statement," with your tax return. On this form you indicate the cost of your foreign shares and the amount of the income earned in the year.

Claiming dividends received by your spouse on your tax return

Say your spouse or common-law partner receives dividends from a Canadian resident corporation but has income, and a resulting tax liability, that is too low to make full use of the dividend tax credit. If this is the case the dividend tax credit may go partially or fully unused — a tax credit being wasted! (A dividend tax credit in excess of a tax liability does not result in a tax refund.)

To avoid "wasting" part or all of the dividend tax credit, the spouse with the lower income can transfer the dividends to the higher-income spouse to claim on his or her own tax return. Once transferred, the dividends will be grossed up and the dividend tax credit can be claimed.

Why in the world would you want to do this? At first glance, you'd think it would result in *more* tax, since the higher-income spouse is paying tax at a higher rate. But by transferring income out of the lower-income spouse's hands, you may be increasing the spousal credit amount (line 303, Chapter 12) that the higher-income spouse can claim. The increase in the credit, together with the fact that the higher-income spouse can use the full dividend tax credit, will more than offset the higher tax rate paid. If it doesn't, you simply do not make the transfer!

This transfer has a few restrictions:

- ✔ Only dividends received by your spouse or common-law partner can be transferred. Dividends received by other dependants are not eligible.

- ✔ Only dividends received from taxable Canadian corporations (that is, dividends eligible for the 45 or 25-percent gross-up) may be transferred. Foreign dividends do not qualify.

- ✔ All the spouse's eligible dividends must be transferred. Partial transfers are not allowed.

- ✔ This transfer is allowable only if it creates or increases the spousal credit amount you are entitled to.

If you are 65 or older, transferring your spouse's dividends to your return could reduce your age credit if it brings your net income above $30,270.

Non-taxable dividends

Believe it or not, there are such things as non-taxable dividends. Really, there are. Read on.

Dividends paid from a private corporation's "capital dividend account" are non-taxable in the hands of Canadian-resident shareholders. What is a capital dividend account? Well, it's a special tax account where private corporations accumulate income that is non-taxable. Sources of non-taxable income received by a corporation include:

✔ The non-taxable portion of net capital gains earned in the corporation. (Only 50 percent of capital gains are subject to tax for Canadian taxpayers, whether that taxpayer is a corporation, trust, or individual — we provide more details in Chapter 7.)

✔ Capital dividends received from other corporations.

✔ The untaxed portion of gains on the disposition of eligible capital property (i.e., goodwill).

✔ Proceeds of life insurance less the adjusted cost base of the policy received by the corporation.

If you have your own investment holding corporation, check with your accountant to see if your corporation has a capital dividend account. Since investment holding companies generally earn some capital gains over the years, you may have an opportunity to pay yourself tax-free dividends from your corporation! Your accountant can help you fill out the special paperwork required to ensure the dividend is in fact recognized as non-taxable.

Don't confuse a capital dividend with a capital gains dividend. Capital gains dividends are *taxable* dividends paid by mutual funds or investment corporations.

The capital dividend account is another tool of tax integration — just like the dividend gross-up and dividend tax credit discussed above. The capital dividend account works to ensure that tax-free income in a corporation remains tax-free in the hands of the shareholders of private corporations.

Line 121: Interest and Other Investment Income

Interest is the consideration paid for the use of money belonging to someone else. The problem with interest is that it is taxed at the same high rate as employment and business income. This rate, as you know from Chapter 1, is much higher than the dividend or capital gains rate. Therefore, many individuals and businesses have spent time and effort to structure transactions to make it appear that the income reported is of a capital or dividend nature rather than interest. To combat these efforts the *Income Tax Act* rules deem many transactions to involve interest, and have brought in requirements on when and how these transactions are to be included in income.

How to report interest income

The *Income Tax Act* requires taxpayers to include in income "any amount received or receivable by them in the year as, on account or in lieu of payment of, or in satisfaction of, interest." Simple, eh? Actually, what this means is that taxpayers can't get away with not reporting interest income just because they haven't received any payment.

Furthermore, the *Income Tax Act* specifies that individuals must report interest on debt obligations using the accrual method. *Accrual* (perhaps better spelled "a cruel") simply means that interest is included in income as earned, not as received. Take Sarah, for example. She owns a $1,000 bond that earns interest of 10 percent, or $100, every year. However, Sarah receives the interest only every three years. Unfortunately, the tax laws don't care when Sarah receives the money. Each year, in her tax return, Sarah must report the $100 earned and pay tax on that $100.

Types of interest income

Interest income falls into one of two broad categories: regular interest or compounded interest. *Regular interest* is interest earned on a regular basis during the term of the investment. This interest is reported annually to the investor on a T5 slip. *Compounded interest* is interest that is reinvested throughout the term of the investment. Once earned, the interest is added to the principal so you can earn "interest on interest." Again, compounded interest earned is reported to the investor on a T5 slip.

Methods of reporting interest income

Depending on when you purchased your investments, how you record and report the interest can vary dramatically. The following section outlines the different reporting methods for interest income.

Interest on investments made after 1989

This is the easy one. All interest earned on debt must be accrued and included in income on an annual basis, based on the anniversary date of the investment. For example, if you purchased a three-year compounding guaranteed investment certificate (GIC) on September 3, 2005, you would include the interest earned from September 3, 2005 to September 3, 2006 (the anniversary date) on your 2006 tax return — even though the interest was not actually received and won't be received until the GIC matures on

September 8, 2000. The financial institution would issue you a T5 slip each year to document the interest earned to the anniversary date.

Interest on investments acquired after 1981 and before 1990

Interest earned on investments between 1981 and 1990 can be reported in several different ways at the option of the investor:

- ✔ You can elect to accrue and report interest on an annual basis, as above.

- ✔ If you do not elect to use the annual method, interest must be accrued and reported on a three-year basis — that is, you need to report interest earned on a compounding investment only once every three years from the acquisition date. The acquisition date is considered to be December 31 of the year the investment was acquired. For example, if you bought a compounding investment on June 4, 1989 (or anytime in 1989), you would have reported interest earned to December 31, 1992 on your 1992 tax return, and the next time you would have reported interest would have been in your 1995 tax return.

Interest on investments acquired before 1982

Interest-bearing investments acquired before 1982 are deemed to have been issued on December 31, 1988, provided the investor has held them continuously since 1982. The first three-year anniversary for reporting the interest income earned was the year ending December 31, 1991.

Investments requiring special reporting methods

Certain investments have their own special methods for reporting interest income. Be sure to consider these interest reporting methods when making investment decisions, as they may have a significant impact on the investment's after-tax return.

Annuity contracts

Annuity contracts acquired after 1989 are subject to annual interest accrual reporting. If you acquired the annuity before 1990 and the premiums paid were fixed, then you can use the three-year basis of reporting interest income. If the payments were not fixed, you are required to use the annual reporting method.

Investments acquired at a discount

The difference between the face value of the investment (value at maturity) and the purchase price is generally considered interest, and will be included in income at maturity. Investments that sell at a discount include Treasury bills. If you cash in the investment prior to maturity, you may have a capital gain or loss in addition to interest income. See Chapter 7 for further info.

Stripped bonds

For investments in stripped bonds, you must report a portion of the total interest earned in income over each year of ownership. The interest must be accrued and reported at its anniversary day (the day the stripped bond was initially issued and each one-year anniversary thereafter). For example, if you purchased a four-year stripped bond on August 1, 2006, and will earn $1,000 of interest in total on the stripped bond, you are not required to report any interest income in 2006, but in 2007 you report $250 (interest from August 1, 2006 to July 31, 2007 — the anniversary date).

Indexed debt obligations

Indexed debt obligations contain a provision that adjusts the interest return up or down depending on the effect of inflation — that is, if you are to receive 6 percent interest and inflation is running at 3 percent, the obligation will pay 9 percent to compensate for the effects of inflation. So, you pay tax on 9 percent.

Canada Savings Bonds

Canada Savings Bonds have their own unique reporting rules.

- ✔ **R bonds:** Interest on the R bond is paid and reported annually on a T5 slip (issued by the federal government) until the bond matures or is disposed of.

- ✔ **C bonds:** Interest on C bonds (compounding bonds) is not received until the bond is cashed. However, all interest must be reported annually and is taxable each year. Again, the federal government will issue a T5 slip to report the interest earned.

 If you purchase Canada Savings Bonds using the payroll purchase plan, the interest charged by your employer is deductible in calculating your taxable income. You'll find more comments on interest deductibility in Chapter 10 — line 221.

Other special rules

✔ Banks and investment companies generally will not issue a T5 slip if interest earned is less than $50. You must determine how much interest was earned and report it yourself. You can't use the excuse "I didn't get a slip!"

✔ Interest earned on tax refunds must be included in income in the year it was received.

✔ You must report interest income on joint accounts in the same proportion as your contributions to the account, regardless of whose name appears on the T5. For example, if you and your spouse have a joint account, and you contributed 60 percent of the funds, you are to report 60 percent of the interest income.

Interest on foreign-source income

Interest from foreign sources is subject to the same rules as dividends from foreign sources we talked about earlier in this chapter.

✔ The interest income must be converted to Canadian dollars when received.

✔ The full amount of the interest must be included in your income regardless of whether you received all the funds (for example, because tax was withheld at the source country).

✔ A foreign tax credit can be claimed for taxes withheld by the source country.

✔ For investments made after 1989, interest earned but not paid on a regular basis must be accrued and included in income on an annual basis.

✔ For investments made before 1990, you may use the three-year basis to report the interest income earned.

Shareholder and employee loans

Shareholder and employee loans have been the focus of numerous court challenges and legislative changes over the years. The primary concern the government has with these arrangements is that, if structured correctly, they can become vehicles for corporations to distribute all their profit and retained earnings to shareholders and employees on a totally tax-free basis. By extending no-interest indefinite loans, the corporations could give you all the money you wanted with no tax implications to you or the corporation. Banning these loans altogether is not the answer. The government recognizes that in certain situations loans from a corporation to an employee or shareholder are necessary — so corporations are allowed to extend loans in certain situations, but there are *very* restrictive rules on them.

Loans made to a shareholder who is not an employee of the corporation

Generally, all loans to shareholders or persons related to a shareholder are included in the income of the shareholder or the related person in the year the loan was made. The same rules apply if a shareholder (or person related to a shareholder) becomes indebted to a corporation in some manner — for example, if a shareholder buys a vehicle from the corporation and pays for it with a promissory note. This being tax, there are exceptions to this general rule.

Shareholder loans are not included in income of the shareholder when:

✔ The loan is made in the ordinary course of the business of loaning money, provided that bona fide repayment arrangements are made at the time of the loan. For example, banks and other financial institutions can make loans to shareholders without the shareholder being concerned that the loan will be included in their taxable income since a bank is in the business of loaning money to begin with.

✔ The loan is repaid within one year from the end of the corporation's taxation year. For example, if the loan is made in 2006 and the corporation's year-end is December 31, 2006, the loan must be repaid by December 31, 2007 to avoid the entire amount of the loan being included in the shareholder's 2006 income.

The loan cannot be part of a series of loans and repayments. This means you, as a shareholder, can't repay the loan, then take out another loan — in theory, you really haven't paid back the original amount. The tax laws state that if you use this strategy, you will be required to report the amount of the loan in income.

If a shareholder is also an employee of the corporation making the loan, further exceptions to the general income inclusion rules discussed above apply. The shareholder/employee can avoid an income inclusion if the loan was made in these specific circumstances:

✔ The loan is made to an employee who is not a "specified employee" — that is, an employee who owns fewer than 10 percent of the shares of the corporation;

✔ The loan was made to an employee to acquire a home for occupation;

✔ The loan was made to an employee to purchase shares of the employer corporation from the corporation itself — not from another shareholder; or

✔ The loan was made to an employee to acquire an automobile needed to perform duties of employment.

For the shareholder/employee to take advantage of these exceptions, two additional conditions must also be met:

✔ The loan arose because of the employee's employment and not because of shareholdings. In simpler terms, the loan must be available to all employees, or at least all employees of a particular class (for example, management), not just shareholding employees; and

✔ There are bona fide repayment terms. An agreement must be in place for the loan to be repaid within a reasonable period of time.

For corporations where a significant shareholder is also the day-to-day manager of the corporation's activities, it can be difficult to prove that the loan was made because the person was an employee, not a shareholder. The CRA has said that loans made to a person will be considered as by virtue of shareholdings where the shareholder can significantly influence business policy. Nevertheless, an employee-shareholder may be able to have the loan excluded from income if he or she can establish that other employees who perform similar duties and responsibilities for a similar-sized employer — but who are not shareholders in that employer-corporation — received loans or other indebtedness of similar amounts under similar conditions.

Loans made by a corporation to an employee who is not a shareholder

A loan made by a corporation to an employee who is not a shareholder of the corporation or related to a shareholder of the corporation is *not* included in the employee's income.

However, the employee does not fully escape some tax! The employee is considered to have received an imputed interest benefit, which is subject to tax. The imputed interest benefit rules are discussed below.

Imputed interest on shareholder and employee loans

If you receive a no-interest loan or low-interest loan because of your shareholding or your past, present, or future employment (there's a catch-all!), and the loan was not included in your income by virtue of the exceptions detailed above, you will be considered to have received a taxable benefit referred to as an *imputed* or *deemed* interest benefit. This benefit is equal to the difference between the interest paid in the year (or within 30 days after the year-end), if any, and the interest determined by the CRA using its prescribed rates of interest. CRA's prescribed rates of interest are updated every three months and can be found on the CRA Web site at `www.cra-arc.gc.ca/tax/faq/interest_rates/menu-e.html`. For the first quarter of 2006, the prescribed interest rate was 3 percent, it increased to 4 percent for April through to the end of September, and then increased to 5 percent for the remainder of the year.

If the loan was made by virtue of your employment, the imputed interest benefit is considered employment income and will be included in your T4.

Let's say that Dale receives a non–interest-bearing loan from his employer for $100,000 at the beginning of the year. Dale is not a shareholder. The loan is outstanding until the end of the year. Assuming a prescribed rate of 5 percent, what is Dale's interest benefit? Dale will be deemed to have an interest benefit of $5,000 ($100,000 times 5 percent is $5,000). This amount should be added to Dale's T4'd employment income for the year. Any interest Dale paid on this loan during the year (or the first 30 days of the next year) would reduce the imputed interest benefit.

 If you receive a loan from your employer and are required to pay interest on the loan, try to arrange to pay the interest portion on January 30 (not 31) of the following year. This will let you keep your cash as long as possible and still reduce or eliminate the deemed interest benefit for the current year.

 Where possible, convince your employer to make your loan interest-free. You will have an imputed interest benefit added to your employment income, but the tax cost of a benefit is cheaper than actually paying interest. For example, if you are at a marginal tax rate of 40 percent, a 5-percent deemed interest benefit costs you only 2 percent (5-percent benefit times 40-percent tax rate = 2 percent in tax payable). Effectively, you have a 2-percent loan — cheaper than actually paying interest at 5 percent!

Forgiven loans

If a shareholder or employee loan or debt is forgiven, the forgiven amount is a taxable benefit and is added to the income of the shareholder or employee.

Employee loans with special treatment

Employee loans for the purchase or relocation of a home are given special treatment when it comes to calculating the imputed interest benefit.

- ✔ **Home purchase loans:** Where the loan is made to you as an employee home purchase loan, the interest rate used to calculate the imputed interest benefit for the first five years will never be greater than the CRA-prescribed interest rate at the time the loan was made. (However, you can take advantage of a lower imputed interest benefit should the prescribed rates decrease!) When the five years are over, the continuation of the loan is considered a new loan, and the prescribed rate in effect on that day will be the maximum rate charged for the next five years. For example, Maureen receives an interest-free employee home purchase loan on January 1, 2006. On January 1, 2006, the CRA prescribed interest rate was 3 percent. Over the next five years, Maureen's taxable benefit will be calculated using a prescribed rate that could be less than 3 percent but will never be more.

- ✔ **Home relocation loans:** If the loan is an employee home relocation loan — that is, a loan to help you purchase a home that is at least 40 kilometres closer to a new work location — you receive a special deduction in the calculation of the interest benefit. See line 248, Chapter 11 for more information on this deduction.

Registered Education Savings Plan (RESP) Income

RESPs are one of the most popular ways for Canadians to save for a child's education. In a nutshell, here's how they work: A person (usually a parent or grandparent, but it could be someone else) places funds in the plan for a child's benefit. Although there is no tax deduction for RESP contributions (like there is for RRSP contributions), funds within the plan can grow tax-sheltered. Plus, the government provides and extra bonus, the Canada Education Savings Grant to help pump up the savings!

Contributions to an RESP

Contributions to an RESP can be made at a bank, through your investment advisor or through companies that specialize in these types of plans. A "subscriber", usually a parent, grandparent or other individual will make the contribution into the plan where the funds will be invested. The maximum allowable annual contribution is $4,000 per child, with a maximum lifetime limit of $42,000.

The federal government currently "kicks in" an additional 20 percent of the amount contributed to an RESP, to a maximum of $400 per year per child. The extra 20 percent is called the Canada Education Savings Grant, or CESG. Don't miss out on free money for your child's education!

The CESG will increase to 40 percent for the first $500 contributed by families with income up to $36,377. Where family income is between $36,378 and $72,755 the CESG will be 30 percent of the first $500 contributed. Whatever the income level, the maximum CESG a child is eligible for is $500 per year and $7,200 per lifetime.

The investment income earned by an RESP is not taxable in the hands of the contributor. Instead, the income becomes taxable income of the student when he or she removes the money for educational purposes. The advantage of having the tax paid by the student is that the student probably has little or no other income, and can claim the tuition and education amount.

It is not until funds are withdrawn from the plan that tax is payable, and it's important to note that only the *growth* (including growth derived from the CESG) in the plan is taxable. Since no deduction is available for contributions it does not make sense that the withdrawal of your contributions would be taxable.

Even if you do not have the funds to contribute to your child's RESP you might be eligible for a Canada Learning Bond to help you get a kick start on education savings. If your child was born after December 31, 2003, and you get the National Child Benefit Supplement (baby bonus), the government will deposit $100 each year for up to 15 years into an RESP for your child. For free brochures on RESPs and the Canada Learning Bond call 1-800-O-CANADA.

Distribution from an RESP to the contributor

If the beneficiary of the RESP does not attend an institution of higher education, the contributions and the income earned from these contributions (accumulated income payments) can be returned to the contributor. The initial contributions can be withdrawn tax free, but the accumulated income can be withdrawn only under certain circumstances:

- ✔ The plan must have existed for at least ten years, and
- ✔ The beneficiary is at least 21 years of age and will not be attending an institution of higher learning.

If these requirements are met, the contributions and the accumulated income can be withdrawn, although the CESGs received by the RESP must be paid back to the federal government. Any growth in the RESP due to the CESGs being invested can be withdrawn.

Any income returned to the contributor is taxable, and there is a special penalty surtax of 20 percent on top of the regular tax payable on this income. The surtax can be completely or partially avoided when the accumulated income is transferred directly to the contributor's RRSP. The maximum amount that can be transferred is subject to a lifetime limit of $50,000. Sufficient RRSP contribution room must be available to transfer funds to an RRSP. If the contributor passes away, the contributor's spouse can make use of the RRSP transfer option instead.

Other Investment Income

Line 121 of your income tax return is designed to capture all interest and other investment income. Believe it or not, there are still other forms of investment income we haven't yet touched on. In this section we highlight some of the more recognizable forms of other investment income you may have to claim on your tax return.

Mutual funds

Mutual funds are pools of assets managed by professionals. The assets managed range from real estate to mortgages to stocks and bonds. As the mutual fund earns income, or sells some of its underlying assets, income and capital gains may be generated. These income and gains, net of fund expenses, are distributed to the fund's investors. Investors in mutual funds receive T3 or T5 slips to report their share of those income or gains.

If you invest in mutual funds, you will find that most income distributed to you retains its identity in your hands. This means that income earned as capital gains or Canadian dividends by the fund is still regarded as capital gains or dividends to you.

Investors can take advantage of the low rate on Canadian dividends due to the dividend tax credit and pay tax on only 50 percent of capital gains, just like they could if they owned the underlying assets directly. Interest income retains its identity only if you purchase a mutual fund trust and you receive a T3 slip. If you own a mutual fund corporation investment (which you do if you receive a T5 slip), you'll notice that you'll never get an interest distribution — it's just not possible (trust us on this one).

Very often, funds automatically reinvest distributions to the fundholders in new units of the fund. In these situations, although you never see any of the cash, you will be taxed on the income distributed. This is why you may have received a tax slip this year even though you didn't see any cash coming into your account. Be sure to keep track of the reinvestments, since they will increase your adjusted cost base and can help minimize capital gains when you eventually redeem your mutual fund units.

Royalties

Royalties are payments you receive for the use of your property. This income can be classified as business or investment income, depending on its nature. Royalties received for writing a book are business income, while royalties received for the use of property you purchased are investment income.

Annuities

Annuities are amounts payable on a periodic basis according to a contract, will, or trust. Report the interest income earned from an annuity at line 121, unless you are 65 years of age or older and receiving retirement income, in which case you report the interest at line 115: "Other pensions or superannuation." Pension income is discussed in Chapter 5.

Labour-sponsored venture capital corporations

Labour-sponsored venture capital funds are sponsored by organized labour to provide venture capital to startup businesses. Investments in the funds generally offer special tax credits both federally and provincially. Investments can be withdrawn at any time, but penalties (i.e., repayments of the tax credits received) usually apply if money is withdrawn before eight years.

Exempt life insurance contracts

Offered by insurance companies, exempt life insurance contracts allow you to pay life insurance premiums and make deposits to a tax-sheltered investment account (up to certain limits). The investments grow tax-free inside the plan and can be withdrawn tax-free if they form part of the death benefit paid to the beneficiary.

Chapter 7

Tips for Capital Gains and Losses

● ●

In This Chapter

▶ Calculating a capital gain or loss

▶ Calculating a taxable capital gain and a net capital loss

▶ Sorting out capital gains versus ordinary income

▶ Understanding types of capital property

▶ Understanding capital gains exemptions

▶ Getting a handle on the capital gains reserve

● ●

*I*n this chapter we provide you with the general information you need to report a capital gain or loss. You'll be treated to tonnes of definitions and savvy tips to minimize your tax liability. What is a capital gain or loss, you ask? Well, read on.

Line 127: Taxable Capital Gains

When you sell a *property*, meaning any asset to which you have legal title — you can end up with a gain or loss on the sale (well, you could also break even). This gain or loss is referred to as a capital gain or a capital loss. To calculate a capital gain or loss, you need to know the following three amounts:

1. The proceeds of disposition (total funds to be received from the sale of an asset)

2. The *adjusted cost base* of the property (book value adjusted for changes or improvements) — often referred to as simply "the ACB" or the "tax cost" of a property

3. The costs related to selling your property — often referred to as "selling costs" or "outlays and expenses" — e.g., legal fees and real estate commissions

A capital gain or loss is calculated as the proceeds of disposition less the adjusted cost base of the property less the costs incurred in selling the property — or (1) minus (2) minus (3) equals the capital gain or loss.

Only 50 percent of the capital gain is taxable. The amount of the capital gain subject to tax is referred to as your *taxable* capital gain. Did you incur a capital loss? We get to this later! We also look at what is meant by property and capital property later in this chapter.

As noted, you can have a capital gain or loss when you sell a capital property. A capital gain or loss can also occur when you have a "deemed sale" or "deemed disposition" for tax purposes. What does "deemed" mean? In certain situations, such as death or emigration, the tax rules consider you to have sold or disposed of something when in the true economic sense you have not. A capital gain can be triggered, along with a tax liability on the gain. This can be quite harsh in terms of cash flow — remember, it's only a disposition for tax purposes, so it doesn't mean you have received any cash, which you could use to pay your tax bill.

When you die, you are considered to have sold all your property at market value immediately before your death — so any accrued gains can be subject to tax. (An exception to this rule is when assets are bequeathed to a spouse.) Also, when you cease to be a resident of Canada you are considered to have disposed of all your property (with a few exceptions), and tax would be payable on the accrued gains. Leaving Canada can be expensive!

Here are some other examples of cases in which you are "deemed" to have disposed of capital property:

- ✔ You exchange one property for another.

- ✔ You give or donate property (other than cash).

- ✔ You transfer property to a trust (exceptions to this include transfers to an *alter-ego* — set up by an individual acting on his or her own — and joint spousal/partner — set up by a couple in partnership — trusts).

- ✔ Your property is expropriated, stolen, or destroyed.

- ✔ An option that you hold to buy or sell property expires.

- ✔ You change all or part of a property's use (for example, the change of use of your residence to a rental property, or vice versa).

Proceeds of disposition

The "proceeds of disposition" is the amount you received or *will receive* in consideration for the sale of your property. In most cases, it is the selling price of the property.

You may think that just because you haven't received any proceeds from a sale, you have no capital gain (or loss) to report. A common example of this occurs when you give property to a family member. The problem is that for tax purposes you are deemed to have received proceeds of disposition equal to the market value of the property at the time the gift. It doesn't matter how much cash — if any — actually changed hands.

Many individuals think they can sell a property, such as a cottage, to a friend or family member for $1 so no capital gain is incurred. Well, the selling individual may receive only $1, but for tax purposes he or she is considered to have received proceeds equal to the market value of the property at the time of the sale.

Adjusted cost base (ACB)

The adjusted cost base of a property is usually the purchase price of the property plus any expenses incurred to acquire it, such as real estate commissions and legal fees. However, in many situations figuring out the adjusted cost base is a little more complicated. Here are some examples:

- ✔ If you make improvements to a property, such as a major overhaul of your family cottage, the cost of these improvements will increase the property's adjusted cost base.

- ✔ If you inherit property, or perhaps receive property as a gift, your adjusted cost base of the property will be the market value of that property on the day you took ownership of it (although special rules apply if you inherited the property from your spouse).

- ✔ If you are a newcomer to Canada, your adjusted cost base is the market value (not your purchase price) of your property on the day you became a Canadian resident for tax purposes.

- ✔ If you reinvest distributions — such as dividends in a dividend reinvestment program (DRIP), or mutual funds allocations where you received additional units rather than cash — these reinvestments increase your adjusted cost base. Think of it as having received the cash and then used the cash to purchase additional shares or mutual fund units. The amount of your investment has increased, so your adjusted cost base should increase as well!

✔ If you elected to crystallize — or lock in — a capital gain back in 1994 to use your lifetime capital gains exemption, your adjusted cost base is likely higher than the purchase price of the property. We discuss the 1994 capital gains election near the end of this chapter.

Identical properties

You may have "identical properties" if over time you've purchased shares of the same class of a corporation's capital stock or units of the same mutual fund. If you own identical properties, you have to do a special calculation to figure out your adjusted cost base.

To determine your adjusted cost base you have to calculate the average cost of each property in the group at the time of each purchase. You determine the average cost by dividing the total cost of identical properties purchased (usually the cost of the property plus costs involved in acquiring the property) by the total number of identical properties owned (that is, the number of shares or mutual fund units).

Partial dispositions of capital property

When you sell only part of a property, you have to divide the adjusted cost base of the property between the part you sell and the part you keep.

Graeme owns 100 hectares of vacant land with an adjusted cost base of $100,000. He decides to sell 25 hectares of this land. Since 25 is ¼ of 100, Graeme calculates ¼ of the total ACB as follows:

Total ACB	$100,000
The ACB of the part sold ($100,000 × ¼) =	$ 25,000

Graeme's adjusted cost base for the 25 hectares he sold is $25,000. The adjusted cost base of the remaining hectares is $75,000.

Outlays and expenses (selling costs)

As we note above, you deduct the costs incurred in selling a property (referred to as "outlays and expenses") in calculating a capital gain or loss. These costs will cause the capital gain to be lower and the capital loss to be greater. They include fixing-up expenses, finders' fees, commissions, brokers' fees, surveyors' fees, legal fees, transfer taxes, and advertising costs.

Calculation of taxable capital gains

You have a capital gain when you sell, or are deemed to have sold, a capital property for more than its adjusted cost base and the selling costs. You include 50 percent of your capital gains on your return as part of your calculation of taxable income. Once capital gains are reduced to their 50 percent inclusion amount, they are referred to as *taxable* capital gains.

Say that in 2006 Lynne sold 1,000 shares of Public Corporation Limited for $7,500. She received the full proceeds at the time of the sale and paid a selling commission to her investment advisor of $80. The adjusted cost base of the shares is $3,500 (equal to the original purchase price of the shares plus her buying commission). Lynne calculates her capital gain — and taxable capital gain — as follows:

Proceeds of disposition	$7,500
Less: Adjusted cost base	($3,500)
Less: Outlays and expenses	($ 80)
Capital gain	$3,920

Because only 50 percent of the capital gain is taxable, Lynne reports $1,960 ($3,920 × 50 percent) as her taxable capital gain on line 127 of her tax return.

Lynne enters the actual calculation of the capital gain (proceeds of disposition, adjusted cost base, and outlays and expenses) and the 50 percent calculation to arrive at her taxable capital gain of $1,960 on schedule 3 of the tax return package, "Capital Gains (or Losses) in 2006." Note that if you have "net capital loss" at the bottom of schedule 3 you do not carry the amount to line 127 of your return because you report only taxable capital gains, not losses, on line 127. We discuss losses in the next section.

What about capital losses?

Unfortunately, not everything goes up in value. You have a capital loss when you sell, or are deemed to have sold, a capital property for less than its adjusted cost base and the selling costs. A capital loss reduced to the 50 percent inclusion amount is referred to as an *allowable* capital loss because this is the amount you're allowed to offset taxable capital gains with.

Capital losses offset capital gains

As you would expect, in calculating the amount of capital gains subject to tax you can deduct capital losses.

Let's continue the example of Lynne's sale of shares. As we note earlier, Lynne has incurred a capital gain of $3,920 on her sale of 1,000 shares of Public Corporation Limited. Let's say she also sold 1,000 shares of Private Corporation Limited for $4,000. Her adjusted cost base of these shares was $5,000 and she paid selling commissions of $50. Lynne would calculate her total capital gains and taxable capital gains as follows:

Capital gain on sale of 1,000 shares of Public Corporation Limited (as above)		$3,920
Capital loss on sale of 1,000 shares of Private Corporation Limited		
Proceeds of disposition	$4,000	
Less: Adjusted cost base	($5,000)	
Less: Outlays and expenses	($ 50)	
Capital loss		($1,050)
"Net" capital gain		$ 2,870

Lynne enters her taxable capital gains — 50 percent of the "net of her capital gains and losses in the year — at the bottom of Schedule 3 and on line 127 of her tax return.

(50 percent of $2,870)	$ 1,435

What if a taxpayer has only capital losses?

So, what happens if the only share sale Lynne had in the year was the sale of the 1,000 shares of Private Corporation Limited? She would report the $1,050 capital loss on Schedule 3, and at the bottom of Schedule 3 she would report a net capital loss of $525 (50 percent of $1,050).

Can Lynne carry the loss to line 127 of her return so the loss is effectively deducted against her other sources of income (employment income, interest income, etc.) in calculating her taxable income? Would it not be logical that if 50 percent of capital gains are subject to tax, then 50 percent of capital losses should be deductible in computing taxable income? (We think it would!)

Sadly, it doesn't work that way. Lynne cannot carry the net capital loss of $525 to line 127 because line 127 is for taxable capital gains only. However, Lynne has other options. She cannot get any tax relief in 2006 from the loss as she has no gains to offset the loss against. However, if she has reported taxable capital gains on her tax return in any or all of the prior three years (2005, 2004, and 2003), the net capital loss can be "carried back" to those years to be applied against the taxable capital gains reported previously. Doing this will result is a tax refund for the year or years Lynne has carried the net capital loss back to.

Say Lynne reported taxable capital gains of $300 in 2003, $2,500 in 2004, and none in 2005. In preparing her 2006 return, Lynne could prepare form T1A, "Request for Loss Carryback," indicating she wished for $300 of her 2006 net capital loss of $525 to be carried back or applied against the $300 of taxable capital gains she reported in 2003, and the remaining $225 to be applied against the taxable capital gains in 2004. The CRA will reassess Lynne's 2003 and 2004 returns and issue her a refund cheque for these years, as the loss application reduces the capital gains that were subject to tax in those years.

You must use form T1A to request net capital loss carry backs. Do not file amended tax returns for the years in which the taxable capital gains were reported!

Losses can be carried back to a previous year only to the extent they cannot be used to reduce gains realized in the current year.

In most circumstances, you should request that net capital losses be carried back to the third previous year if you reported taxable capital gains in that year. This will be your last chance to recoup taxes paid on capital gains from that year since losses can be carried back for only three years. By the time the 2007 tax year rolls around, those 2003 gains will be off the table.

What if a taxpayer has not reported taxable capital gains in the last three years?

Can Lynne get any tax relief from her 2006 net capital loss if she has not reported any taxable capital gains in the last three years?

The answer is, hopefully, yes! Any net capital loss that cannot be carried back to a prior year can be carried forward to a subsequent year and be applied against taxable capital gains reported in those years. There is no time limit in using the losses.

If Lynne does not incur a taxable capital gain until 2011 she can still apply her 2006 net capital loss against the taxable capital gain reported in that year. The 2006 net capital loss would be reported on line 253, "Net capital losses of other years," on Lynne's 2011 return. The loss carry forward would not impact the schedule 3 filed with Lynne's 2011 return, or the amount she would report on that year's line 127.

 If a taxpayer dies with unused net capital losses of earlier years, these losses can be deducted against any type of income, such as employment income, interest income, or pension income reported in the year of death. The amount deductible may be restricted if the taxpayer had ever claimed the capital gains exemption.

Capital Gains versus Ordinary Income

Usually, you have a capital gain or capital loss when you sell or are considered to have disposed of a *capital property*. The question of whether a property is a capital property can be difficult to answer. If it is not considered a capital property it is considered an *income property*.

The judgment depends on both the nature of the property and the manner in which the owner manages the property. If the owner intends to realize a profit from the property (e.g., a speculator in real estate) versus holding the property for the income it produces (e.g., a landlord of a rental property), the gain or loss realized on the sale is treated as an ordinary income gain (fully taxed) or loss as opposed to a capital gain or loss (only 50% taxed).

 In an ideal situation, you would treat your gains as capital and your losses as income. The reason for this is twofold: one, capital gains are only 50 percent taxable, while business income is fully taxable; and two, capital losses can be applied only against capital gains, while a business loss can be applied against any source of income to reduce tax. For the average stock and mutual fund investor, doing this will be difficult. However, if you are planning to sell other types of capital property, it is something to think about.

To understand the difference between capital and income in relation to the taxpayer's intention, think about the scenario of a tree and its fruit. If you bought the tree with the intention of selling the fruit, then any subsequent sale of the tree would be on account of capital. If, however, you purchased the tree intending to sell it and make a quick buck, then you would treat the proceeds of the sale as income — and 100 percent of any gain would be taxable.

In deciding whether the gain or loss is on account of income or capital, tax courts have used the following tests:

✔ **The period of ownership:** If property has been held for only a short period, it may be considered to have been purchased to be resold and therefore the profits may be treated as income. A property held for a longer period is more likely to be treated as capital.

✔ **Improvement and development:** Where a systematic effort has been made to make a property more marketable, it may indicate a business of selling properties.

✔ **Relationship of the transaction to the taxpayer's ordinary business:** The more similar the transaction is to the taxpayer's ordinary business, the more likely it is that the transaction will be treated as income (for example, the sale of a renovated home by a general contractor).

✔ **Reasons for and nature of sale:** If the sale of a property is the result of an active campaign to sell it as opposed to the result of something unanticipated at the time of purchase, the profits may be considered on account of income.

✔ **The frequency of similar transactions:** A history of buying and selling similar properties, or of quick turnovers, may indicate the taxpayer is carrying on a business.

Even if your transaction does not satisfy one of these tests, that does not mean the transaction will automatically be considered capital or income. The courts look at the larger picture, and you may have the opportunity to argue either way.

Types of Capital Property

Report capital gains and losses on schedule 3 of your tax return. Schedule 3 is divided into a number of sections, as we explain below.

Real estate

Use the real estate section of schedule 3 to report a capital gain or loss if you sell any of the following types of property during the year:

- ✔ Vacant land
- ✔ Rental property (both land and buildings)
- ✔ Farm property, including both land and buildings (other than qualified farm property)
- ✔ Commercial and industrial land and buildings

Do not use this section to report the sale of personal-use property, such as your home or cottage. We discuss personal-use property later in the chapter.

If you sell a property that includes land and a building, you need to determine how much of the proceeds of disposition (selling price) and cost (adjusted cost base) relate to each of the land and the building. The sales of these items are to be reported separately on schedule 3.

If the building was used in a business or rental activity and you claimed capital cost allowance on the building in any past tax year, your situation is slightly more complex. In addition to a potential capital gain, you may also have recapture or a terminal loss to deal with. See "Depreciable property" later in this chapter for more info.

Mutual fund units and shares

Use this section to report a capital gain or loss when you sell shares or securities that are not described in any other section of schedule 3. These shares or securities include the following held in a non-registered (or open) investment account

- ✔ Publicly traded shares
- ✔ Units of a mutual fund
- ✔ Shares issued by private corporations that are not qualified small business corporation shares or qualified family farm corporation shares
- ✔ Shares of foreign corporations

Also use this section if you make a donation to a registered charity of publicly traded shares and/or mutual fund units.

If you donate publicly traded shares or mutual fund units to public charities, you'll be deemed to have disposed of them at their current market value. The good news is, if you made the donation on or after May 2, 2006, any capital gain triggered will no longer be taxable. You'll still receive a donation slip equal to the market value of your shares or mutual fund units on the day of donation. Report the dispositions on Form T1170, "Capital Gains on Gifts of Certain Capital Property."

Thanks to the 2006 federal budget, capital gains are no longer triggered when ecologically sensitive land is donated to conservation charities.

If you own shares or units of a mutual fund, capital gains can arise in two ways:

- ✔ When you sell your shares or units of the mutual fund, a capital gain (or loss) will result from the difference between your proceeds of disposition and the adjusted cost base of the investment. Report capital gains and losses on dispositions in part 3 of schedule 3.

- ✔ Capital gains realized by the mutual fund from its investment portfolio are usually "flowed out" to you as distributions. You should receive information slips from your investment dealer (a T3 or T5 slip) detailing the amounts to be reported in this situation. Report these amounts on line 174 (T5 slips) and line 176 (T3 slips) of schedule 3.

Bonds, debentures, promissory notes, and other properties

In this section of schedule 3, report capital gains or losses from the disposition of bonds, debentures, Treasury bills, promissory notes, bad debts, foreign exchange transactions, and options, as well as discounts, premiums, and bonuses on debt obligations.

Treasury bills (T-bills) and stripped bonds

When a T-bill or a stripped bond is issued at a discount from its face value and you keep it until it matures, the difference between the issue price and the amount you cash it in for is considered interest income that accrued to you — not a capital gain. However, if you sell the T-bill or stripped bond before it matures, in addition to the interest accrued at that time a capital gain or capital loss comes into play. Before you calculate your capital gain or loss, you have to determine the amount of interest accumulated to the date of disposition. Subtract the interest from the proceeds of disposition, and calculate the capital gain or loss in the usual manner, as we explain earlier in the chapter.

Foreign currencies

Use the foreign currencies section of schedule 3 to report capital gains or capital losses realized by virtue of fluctuations in foreign currencies on investments you've sold. Provided that the foreign currency transactions are capital in nature (which they generally are if the underlying investment was capital, such as a share), they are treated in the same way as any other capital gain or loss. The only difference is that the first $200 of gain realized is not taxable and the first $200 of loss cannot be claimed as a capital loss.

Before deducting the $200 amount from the capital gain or loss determined, all capital gains and losses from foreign currency must be netted and the $200 exemption applied against the net foreign-exchange gain or loss for the year.

There is no place on schedule 3 to report your reduction for exchange gains or losses. Therefore, a reduction in the gain can simply be reflected as a reduction in the proceeds of disposition. If the foreign-exchange gain or loss is $200 or less you do not need to report it on schedule 3.

For example, suppose Oscar bought 2,500 shares in a U.S. company for US$20 (Cdn. $30) per share in 2003. The shares grew to a value of US$25 ($28.75). Selling those shares in early 2006 would result in a capital loss of $3,125 (2,500 x $1.25). Oscar would report a capital loss (relating to foreign exchange) for tax purposes of $2,925 ($3,125 – 200) on Schedule 3.

Mortgage foreclosures and conditional-sale repossessions

If, as a mortgagee, you repossess a property because the mortgagor failed to pay you the money owed under the terms of the mortgage, you are considered to have purchased the property. At the time of repossession, you do not have a capital gain or a capital loss. Any gain or loss will be postponed until you sell the property.

If you are the mortgagor and your property is repossessed because you do not pay the money owed under the terms of the mortgage, you are considered to have sold the property. Depending on the amount you owed at the time of repossession, you may have a capital gain, a capital loss, or, in the case of depreciable property, a terminal loss. However, if the property is personal-use property (such as your principal residence), you cannot deduct the loss. (More on this later.)

A *mortgagee* is a person who lends money under a mortgage on a property. A *mortgagor* is a person who borrows money under a mortgage.

Personal-use property

Personal-use property is an asset that you hold and use for your own personal enjoyment. Common examples of personal-use property include your home (see discussion on the principal residence exemption below), family vacation properties (that are not rented out), cars, boats, furniture, artwork, jewellery, and the like. It is not the asset itself that makes it qualify as a personal-use property, but your use of the asset.

In most cases, people are not affected by the capital gains rules when they own assets for their personal use. When you sell such property usually you do not end up with a capital gain. This is because these types of property generally do not increase in value over the years. In fact, because many personal-use assets depreciate in value, you may actually end up with a loss.

Although you have to report a capital gain on the sale of personal-use property on your tax return, you are not ordinarily allowed to claim a capital loss. (We agree that this seems unfair.) However, you can claim a loss under the following circumstances:

✔ If you disposed of personal-use property such as art or jewellery that is considered "listed personal property" (see next section); or

✔ If a bad debt is owed to you from the sale of a personal-use property to a person with whom you deal at arm's length (in other words, a third party). In this case you can claim the bad debt owed to you as a capital loss; however, your claim cannot be more than the capital gain previously reported on the sale of the property.

To calculate any capital gain or loss realized when you dispose of personal-use property, follow these rules:

✔ If the adjusted cost base of the property is less than $1,000, its adjusted cost base is considered to be $1,000.

✔ If the proceeds of disposition are less than $1,000, the proceeds of disposition are considered to be $1,000.

✔ If both the adjusted cost base and the proceeds of disposition are $1,000 or less, you do not have a capital gain or a capital loss. Do not report the sale on schedule 3 when you file your return.

If you sell your home — your principal residence — for more than it cost you, you usually do not have to report the sale on your return or pay tax on any capital gain (see the "Sale of a Principal Residence" section later in this chapter for more details).

Listed personal property

Listed personal property (LPP) is a type of personal-use property that usually increases in value over time. Listed personal property includes the following capital properties:

✔ Rare manuscripts or rare books

✔ Prints, etchings, drawings, paintings, sculptures, or other similar works of art

✔ Jewellery

✔ Stamps and coins

Report capital gains or losses from selling such items in the special section of schedule 3.

To determine the value of many of these items, you can have them appraised by book, art, jewellery, stamp, or coin dealers. Because listed personal property is personal-use property, the $1,000 minimum proceeds of disposition and adjusted cost base rules apply. See the previous section, "Personal-use property," for more information about these rules.

There is one very important difference, for tax purposes, between personal-use property that *is not* listed personal property and personal use property that *is* listed personal property. If you have a loss when you dispose of listed personal property, these losses are not, well, lost. In fact, the losses can be used to offset gains generated on listed personal property this year, in the previous three years, or in any of the seven subsequent tax years.

Keep a record of your listed personal property losses that have not expired, so you can apply these losses against listed personal property gains in other years. A listed personal property loss expires if you do not use it by the end of the seventh year after it was incurred.

Depreciable property

Depreciable property is a special kind of capital property on which capital gains must be calculated. Common examples are buildings used as rental properties, computer equipment, or office furniture. Depreciable property can be considered capital property used to earn income from a business. You can write off the cost of the property as capital cost allowance (CCA, depreciation for tax purposes) over a number of years — meaning that at the time the asset is sold, undepreciated capital cost (UCC) will likely be less than the original purchase price.

When you dispose of depreciable property, you may have a capital gain but not a capital loss — capital losses on depreciable property are simply considered to be nil. But the tax implications don't end there. You may also be required to add a recapture of prior-year CCA deductions to your income, or you may be allowed to claim a terminal loss. See Chapter 9 for details.

Sale of a Principal Residence

When you sell your home, you may realize a capital gain — that is, you may make money on it. Congratulations! If the property was your only principal residence for every year you owned it, you don't have to report the sale or the capital gain on your tax return. However, if at any time during the period you owned the property it was not your principal residence, or you owned more than one property, you may have to report all or a portion of the capital gain and pay tax on it. In this section we'll explain the meaning of a principal residence, how you designate a property as such, and what happens when you sell it.

If after reading this section you need more information, read the CRA's Interpretation Bulletin IT-120R6, "Principal Residence."

What Is your principal residence?

Your *principal residence* can be a house, cottage, condominium, apartment, trailer, mobile home, or houseboat. A property qualifies as your principal residence for any year if it meets the following conditions:

- ✔ You own the property alone or jointly with another person.

- ✔ You, your spouse, your former spouse, or any of your children 18 years of age or younger lived in it at some time during the year.

- ✔ You designate the property as your principal residence for the year. (You do not need to make this designation until you sell, or are deemed to have sold for income tax purposes, a property that can qualify for the principal residence exemption.)

The land on which your home is located can also be part of your principal residence. Usually, the amount of land that you can consider as part of your principal residence is limited to one-half hectare (about one acre). However, if you can show that you need more land to use and enjoy your home, you may consider more than this amount as part of your principal residence — for example, this may happen if the minimum lot size imposed by a municipality at the time you bought the property was larger than one-half hectare.

Can you have more than one principal residence?

For 1982 and later years, you can designate only one home as your family's principal residence for each year. If you are married or are 18 or older, your family includes you, your spouse (unless you were separated for the entire year), and your children (other than a child who was married during the year or who was 18 or older). If you are not married or are not 18 or older, your family also includes your mother and your father, and your brothers and sisters (who were not married or 18 or older during the year).

For years before 1982, more than one housing unit per family could be designated as a principal residence. Therefore, for these years a husband and wife can designate different principal residences (for example, a house and a cottage) to help minimize capital gains (and taxes) on a sale. After 1982, only one residence per family can be named the principal residence. Therefore it is important to calculate the potential capital gains on each property you own so you can take maximum advantage of the principal residence exemption.

Did you and your spouse have two properties before 1982? If so, you can still double up on principal residence exemptions for growth in value of the properties prior to 1982!

Disposition of your principal residence

When you sell your home, usually you do not have to report the sale on your return and you do not have to pay tax on any gain from the sale. This is the case if the home was your principal residence for every year you owned it. For many Canadians, this is a no-brainer because they have only one home.

However, for those fortunate enough to have a family cottage, or even more than one home, the principal residence exemption is not quite as straightforward. Things are complicated further if you didn't actually live in the home, cottage, or whatever during a particular year. If your home was not your principal residence for every year you owned it, you have to report the part of the capital gain on the property that relates to the years when you did not designate the property as your principal residence.

If you have a loss when you sell you are not allowed to claim the loss because your home is considered personal-use property.

If only part of your home qualifies as your principal residence and you used the other part to earn income, you may have to split the selling price between the part you used for your principal residence and the part you used for other purposes (for example, rental or business purposes). You can do this by using square metres or the number of rooms, as long as the split is reasonable. Report only the gain on the part you used to produce income. Don't worry, however, if the income-earning activity was ancillary to the main use of the residence (i.e., say you rented out a small portion of the house) and you have not claimed capital cost allowance on the income-producing portion of the home in the past. In these cases, the whole residence can still be considered your principal residence and no portion of any capital gain on sale will be taxable to you.

If you are renting out a portion of your home, avoid claiming capital cost allowance (CCA) on that portion of the home. If you do, you won't be able to shelter the entire gain using the principal residence exemption, when you eventually sell the home.

If the principal residence exemption does not completely shelter the capital gain on the sale of a property, form T2091, "Designation of a Principal Residence," will help you calculate the number of years for which you can designate your home as your principal residence, as well as the part of the capital gain, if any, that you have to report and pay tax on.

Include form T2091 with your return only if you have to report a capital gain. If your gain is fully sheltered by the principal-residence exemption, you don't have to report anything on your tax return.

Calculation of the exempt portion of a capital gain on your principal residence

If you sell a property on which all of the capital gain is not fully tax-exempt, the following formula calculates what portion of the gain is tax-exempt.

$$\text{Exempt gain equals } \frac{1 + \text{The number of years the home was designated as principal residence}}{\text{total number of years you owned the home after 1971}} \times \text{gain}$$

Since an individual can designate only one home as a principal residence for any given year, the 1 + in the formula allows you to protect the principal-residence exemption when you sell and purchase a home in the same year.

Let's say Tiffany is in the process of moving from Toronto to Vancouver and must sell both her city home and her cottage. She primarily uses the cottage on the weekends to get away from the city smog and traffic. She purchased her city home in 1992 for $120,000, and anticipates that she can sell it for $200,000. She purchased her cottage in 1995 for $100,000, and her real estate agent assures her that she will get $150,000 for it.

She knows about the principal residence exemption, but isn't sure how it will apply to her since she has owned two homes since she purchased the cottage in 1995.

The first thing Tiffany needs to do is calculate the "capital gain per year" from the sale of each property.

	City Home	*Cottage*
Proceeds	$200,000	$150,000
Adjusted cost base	$120,000	$100,000
Capital gain	$ 80,000	$ 50,000
Number of years	15	12
Capital gain per year	$5,333	$4,167

Since the city home has a larger gain per year, Tiffany should designate as many years as possible to the city home. Now, initially you would think she should designate 15 years to the city home and none to the cottage. However, remember the formula's 1 + rule. Because of that rule, she should designate 14 years to the city home and 1 to the cottage. The result is as follows:

	City Home	*Cottage*
Gain	$80,000	$50,000
Principal residence exemption	($80,000)[1]	($8,333)[2]
Capital gain	$0	$41,667

Notes:
1. $(1+14)/15 \times \$80,000 = \$80,000$
2. $(1+1)/12 \times \$50,000 = \$8,333$

Sale of Qualified Small Business Shares

You may be eligible to shelter all or a portion of your capital gain (up to $500,000, in fact!) from the disposition of qualified small business corporation (QSBC) shares. The next obvious question is, what is a qualified small business corporation share? A share of a corporation will be considered to be a *qualified small business corporation share* if all of the following conditions are met:

- ✔ At the time of sale, it was a share of the capital stock of a small business corporation, and it was owned by you, your spouse, or a partnership of which you were a member; *and*

- ✔ At least 90 percent of the corporation's assets at market value were used by the corporation in an active business (i.e., a non-rental, non-investment type of business) — called the "900 percent rule"; or

- ✔ At least 90 percent of its assets are shares or debts in related corporations that meet the 90 percent rule; or

- ✔ A combination of assets and shares meet the 90 percent rule; *and*

- ✔ Throughout the 24 months immediately before you disposed of the share, it was a share of a Canadian-controlled private corporation and more than 50 percent of the market value of the assets of the corporation were the following:

  - • Used mainly in an active business carried on primarily in Canada by the Canadian-controlled private corporation, or by a related corporation;

  - • Certain shares or debts of connected corporations; or

  - • A combination of these two types of assets; and

- ✔ Throughout the 24 months immediately before the share was disposed of, no one other than you, a partnership of which you were a member, or a person related to you owned the share.

You report the capital gain or loss realized on the sale of qualified small business corporation shares in section 1 of schedule 3. A $500,000 capital gain would become a $250,000 taxable capital gain and be reported on line 127 of your return. If the full $500,000 capital gain qualifies for the $500,000 capital gains *exemption,* you would be able to claim a $250,000 capital gains *deduction.* Claim it on line 254 or your return and include form T657, "Calculation of Capital Gains Deduction." The line 254 deduction in computing taxable income would offset the line 127 inclusion in taxable income.

You may find it difficult to determine whether your shares qualify for the capital gains exemption. Be sure to visit a tax professional if you think your shares may qualify. Even if they don't currently qualify, it is possible to "purify" the corporation of assets not

considered to be active business assets, such as cash or investments, so that you will be eligible for this exemption when the time
arises to sell the shares.

If you own qualified small business shares, consider crystallizing —
or locking in — your qualified small business corporation capital
gains exemption now. You never know when the government might
repeal the exemption, or when the rules listed above may no longer
apply to your corporation.

Sale of Qualified Farm Property

A special $500,000 capital gains exemption is also available if you
sell qualified farm property. The property will qualify if it meets
either of these tests:

- ✔ The property must be used by you, your spouse, child, or
  grandparents in the 24 months immediately before you sell,
  and your gross revenue from the farming business for a minimum of two years exceeds your income from all other sources.

- ✔ The property must be used by a corporation or partnership
  where the principal business is farming for a minimum of
  24 months prior to the sale.

Qualified farm property includes the following:

- ✔ An interest in a family-farm partnership that you or your
  spouse owns.

- ✔ A share of the capital stock of a family-farm corporation that
  you or your spouse owns.

- ✔ Real property, such as land and buildings; and eligible capital
  property, such as milk and egg quotas.

You, your spouse, or a family-farm partnership must own the farm
property. If a corporation or partnership carries on the farming
business, the property will qualify if you, your spouse, or your child
is an active participant in the business and more than 50 percent of
the market value of the property is used in the business of farming.
Generally, when you dispose of qualified farm property, you report
any capital gain or loss realized in the special section of schedule 3.
If you dispose of farm property other than qualified farm property,
report any capital gain or loss in the section "real estate and depreciable property" on schedule 3.

If you transfer farm property to a child it may be possible to completely avoid tax on the disposition. Consult a tax professional, who can determine whether you can take advantage of a "tax-free intergenerational transfer."

Determining whether your farm property qualifies for the $500,000 capital gains exemption is not a do-it-yourself project. The tax rules surrounding farm property are quite complex (definitely not bedtime reading material), so a visit to a tax professional is a must.

Capital Gains of Fishers

After May 1, 2006, the $500,000 lifetime capital gains exemption is also available for dispositions of qualified fishing property. In addition, a tax-deferred intergenerational rollover is also available for transfers of qualified fishing property to a child or grandchild.

The Lifetime Capital Gains Exemption

Prior to February 23, 1994, everyone had a $100,000 personal capital gains exemption. This meant that every Canadian could generate up to $100,000 of capital gains during their lifetime (up to this date) and not pay tax on those gains. As the saying goes, all good things must come to an end; therefore, in order to get a final benefit from this exemption, in 1994 many people elected, on form T664, to use up their exemption and trigger a capital gain.

If you used this election, you effectively sold capital property to yourself. The sale price chosen was usually a price between the adjusted cost base and the market value of the property — the idea was to trigger a capital gain that could be fully offset by the remaining amount of the $100,000 exemption. You were then considered to have repurchased the capital property at the same price, effectively increasing the adjusted cost base of the capital property so that when the property was actually sold, the capital gain would be that much less.

As noted, for *most* capital properties the chosen sale price in making the election determined both the amount of capital gain that was triggered and the "new" increased adjusted cost base of the capital property. However, special rules existed for capital assets referred to as "flow-through entities" like mutual funds.

If you elected to trigger a capital gain on a mutual fund in 1994, and you sold that mutual fund this year, be sure to seek the help of a tax professional. There are a few rules specific to this situation that make calculating the adjusted cost base of the fund a bit tricky.

If you sold capital property during 2006, be sure to check back to your 1994 tax return to see if you elected to trigger any gain. Your adjusted cost base may be higher than you think it is — and your capital gain, and tax bill, lower!

The Capital Gains Reserve

When you sell a capital property, you usually receive full payment at that time. However, sometimes you receive the amount over a number of years. For example, you may sell a capital property for $50,000, receiving $10,000 when you sell it and the remaining $40,000 over the next four years. When this happens you can claim a *reserve,* which allows you to shift or differ reporting a portion of the capital gain to a later year (or years). In other words, if you have not received the full selling price for your capital property in the year of sale, you do not need to pay all the tax on the capital gain right away!

To claim a reserve, you still calculate your capital gain for the year as the proceeds of disposition minus the adjusted cost base and the outlays and expenses involved in selling the property. (We tell you how to do this at the beginning of this chapter.) From this amount, you deduct the amount of your reserve for the year to arrive at the amount of capital gains that will be subject to tax in the current year. What you end up with is the part of the capital gain that you have to report in the year of disposition. This is the part of the gain that will be taxed in the year.

The amount of reserve you can take in any particular year is the lesser of the following:

(Proceeds still to be paid/Total proceeds) × Gain
⅕ of the gain × (4 – # of preceding taxation years ending after disposition)

Did you catch all that? Let's take Finlay, for example. In 2006, Finlay sold capital property for $200,000. However, he received only $20,000 up front. The remaining $180,000 is not due until 2007. The adjusted cost base of the property was $150,000. The total gain from the sale of the property is $50,000 ($200,000 proceeds less cost base of $150,000). However, since Finlay did not receive all the proceeds in 2006, he is eligible to claim a reserve.

In 2006 his reserve is the lesser of the following:

($180,000/$200,000) × $50,000 = $45,000
(⅕ × $50,000) × (4 − 0) = $40,000

Therefore, in 2006 he can shelter a portion of the $50,000 gain with a $40,000 reserve. He will report only $10,000 of the gain in 2006.

In 2007, he must include in his income the $40,000 reserve he claimed in 2006. His 2007 reserve is the lesser of the following:

0/$200,000 × $50,000 = 0
(⅕ × $50,000) × (4 − 1) = $30,000

Therefore, in 2007 Finlay cannot claim any reserve and must include in his income the remaining $40,000 of the capital gain. This makes sense since he received all the proceeds by the end of 2007, so no further reserve should be permitted.

To deduct a reserve in any year, you have to complete form T2017, "Summary of Reserves on Dispositions of Capital Property." The information provided on the back of the form explains the limits on the number of years for which you can claim a reserve, and the amount of the reserve you can deduct. The calculations work such that you report the full capital gain by the end of the fourth year after the year you dispose of the capital property. Therefore, you pay the tax on the capital gain over a maximum period of five years, whether or not money is still owed to you after the five-year period.

If you claimed a reserve last year, include that reserve when you calculate your capital gains for the current year. For example, if you claimed a reserve in 2005, you have to include it in your capital gains for 2006. If you still have an amount payable to you after 2006, you may be able to calculate and deduct a new reserve, which you include in your capital gains for 2007.

Capital Gains Deferral on Eligible Small Business Investments

Have you sold shares of a small business corporation during the year? If so, then read on. It is possible to defer tax if you sell certain share investments and then replace those investments with new eligible small business investments.

To be eligible for this deferral, the shares you dispose of or repurchase must be of a Canadian-controlled private corporation that used at least 90 percent of the market value of its assets in an active business in Canada.

Time limits apply to this tax deferral. First, you must have held the original shares for more than 185 days. In addition, you must acquire the replacement shares at any time in the year of disposition or within 120 days after the year-end.

If you manage to defer your capital gain because of this rule, you must remember to decrease the adjusted cost base (ACB) of your investment. You must do a number of calculations to come up with the exact ACB reduction. Take a look at the CRA's guide *Capital Gains* (T4037) and the beginning of this chapter for more information.

The rules for calculating the actual amount of gain you can defer are quite complex (trust us, you don't want us to go into it here). If you need to use this deferral, we strongly recommend you consider getting a professional accountant involved.

Chapter 8

Tips for Other Types of Income

* *

In This Chapter

▶ Entering Employment Insurance benefits

▶ Earning limited and non-active partnership income

▶ Tallying taxable rental income

▶ Computing taxable alimony or separation allowances

▶ Recording RRSP and RRIF income

▶ Accounting for other income

▶ Entering workers' compensation benefits

▶ Understanding the tax treatment of social assistance

▶ Receiving the Universal Child Care Benefit

* *

*I*n this chapter we will examine sources of income that are generally classified under that ominous title of "other income." Far from being unusual, taxpayers encounter some of these sources on a regular basis. So hold on tight as we dive headfirst into the not-so-weird world of Other Income.

Employment Insurance Benefits (EI): Line 119

Employers in Canada are required by law to deduct Employment Insurance (EI) premiums off the pay of most employees. The employer must also kick in premiums on the employee's behalf. All of these premiums are kept aside by the government so that if the employee becomes unemployed, funds will be available to help weather the financial blow that unemployment so often brings.

This brings us to the income part of EI. Amounts received as EI benefits are taxable and must be reported on line 119 of your tax return. These benefits are usually the result of unemployment, sickness, or maternity leave.

Perhaps to the surprise and chagrin of EI recipients, the government holds back part of your cheques as "tax withheld." The government generally assumes you will be in the lowest tax bracket and calculates how much to withhold accordingly. Enter the amount in box 14 of the T4E, "Total benefits," at line 119 of your tax return. Deduct the tax withheld, shown in box 22, at line 437.

Some EI benefits are not included in income. These benefits are payments for a course or retraining program to facilitate re-entry into the labour force, and will not appear on the T4E slip. You do not have to enter them anywhere on your tax return.

EI clawback

If you have collected EI benefits in the year, and your net income as determined from line 234 of your income tax return is greater than $48,750, you may be required to pay back a portion of the benefits you've received. The repayment rate is 30 percent of the lesser of

- Your net income in excess of $48,750; or
- The total regular benefits you were paid in the year.

If you receive maternity, parental, or sickness benefits, you will not have to repay those benefits. This ensures that parents who stay home with their newborn children or workers who are too sick to work are not penalized.

If you are a first-time claimant, you will not have to make any repayments.

If you are required to repay part of your EI benefits, you can deduct the repayment at line 235, "Social benefits repayment." (This is so you're not taxed on the amount in addition to having to pay it back!) Also report the repayment itself on your tax return, at line 422.

EI premiums

As we explained above, employers in Canada are required to deduct EI premiums off the pay of most of their employees to help protect them from financial hardship should they become unemployed. The government sets the required premium rate each year. For 2006, the premium rate of 1.87 percent, up to a maximum of $39,000 of earnings. That means if you earn $39,000 or more, your employer will withhold the maximum premium of $729.30 ($39,000 × 1.87 percent). If you earn less than $39,000, your premiums are simply your gross earnings times 1.87 percent.

All EI premiums paid entitle you to a 15.25-percent non-refundable tax credit on schedule 1 of your tax return, plus a provincial credit on your provincial tax forms. This credit directly reduces your taxes payable for year. So, if you paid the maximum $729.30 of EI premiums (because you earned at least $39,000 of employment income in 2006), you will have a tax credit of $111.22 to claim against your tax bill. See Chapter 12 for more on non-refundable credits on EI benefits.

If your EI-insurable earnings fall below $2,000 for the year, you will receive a full refund of premiums paid. If you over contribute to EI because your employer withheld too much or because you had more than one job in the year and both employers withheld the maximum, you will likewise receive a refund of your over contribution.

If you are self-employed, you are not required or permitted to pay EI premiums. Unfortunately, you are also not eligible to collect EI if you find yourself out of work.

Limited and Non-Active Partnership Income: Line 122

In a regular partnership, each partner can be held personally responsible for any of the partnership's liabilities. The term "limited or non-active partnership" describes a business relationship where, as the minority or limited partner, you can avoid being held personally responsible for any of the partnership's liabilities. You simply invest a sum of money and leave the day-to-day running of the business to others. Limited partnerships are often used for tax shelters promoting real estate, oil and gas, films, and so on.

At-risk amount

Tax shelters usually mean tax losses. Be warned, however, that the losses that you can claim as a limited partner are restricted to your "at-risk amount" (the amount you paid to purchase the limited partnership, plus any further capital contributions you made to the partnership) unless you've owned an interest in the partnership since before February 26, 1986. We talk about the "at-risk amount" in more detail in Chapter 11.

In the past, investors in limited partnerships had to worry not only about the denial of their loss deductions if they didn't have enough at-risk room, but also the complete denial of the losses if the partnership had no "reasonable expectation of profit" (REOP). Talk about a double whammy! Many taxpayers fought the government on this rule, and following rulings in the Supreme Court of Canada (*Stewart* and *Walls*), the REOP rule will no longer apply if there is clearly no personal element to the loss.

But it doesn't end there. The government doesn't like to be one-upped, so it proposed legislation that brings back the old concept of REOP. Specifically, if you expect more losses than income on your limited-partnership investment (or even a business) on a cumulative basis, you might find your losses denied after all. This proposed legislation, although slated to apply in 2005, is still in draft form.

Slip T5013: "Statement of Partnership Income"

When a limited partnership earns a profit, or produces deductions or credits that you can claim on your personal tax return, the information is reported to you on a T5013 or a separate statement of income.

Rental Income: Line 126

Rental income is earned from renting properties such as a building, a house, a room in a house, an apartment, office space, machinery, equipment, vehicles, and so on. Most types of rental income are considered to be "income from property" and therefore are reported on line 126, although if you rent out properties as a business, you report it as self-employment income (see Chapter 9).

On the line for rental income on your tax return there is a line for "gross" income (line 160) and a line for "net" income (line 126). Gross income is the full amount of rental income you received in the year, before taking into account expenses you incurred to earn that income. Net income is the amount left over after expenses. If you have real estate rental income and expenses, you should fill out form T776 and file it with your tax return so that all of your expenses are clearly spelled out for the CRA to see. It will also help you remember all the types of expenses you might be able to claim. We'll talk about those in a minute.

Rental income is always reported on a calendar-year basis — that is, January to December. If you co-own a rental property, your share of the rental income or loss will be based on your percentage of ownership. Arbitrary allocations are not acceptable.

Reasonable expectation of profit

The primary motivation of any business should be to earn profit. If you don't earn profit, why are you in business? As we discuss above under limited partnerships, the reasonable expectation of profit (REOP) principle was the standard the taxman used in examining your business to determine if it was a legitimate business or simply a tax shelter. If after examining your rental business the CRA determined that the business had no REOP, it was concluded to be not legitimate and denied the rental losses.

Due to two precedent-setting cases heard in the Supreme Court of Canada during 2002 (*Stewart* and *Walls*), the REOP test was found to be an invalid reason for the CRA to deny losses in certain situations. The Court determined that so long as there is no personal or hobby element to an activity, losses cannot be denied if there have never been profits, or there may not be profits in the future.

The fact that the courts ruled in favour of *Stewart* and *Walls* does not mean the REOP test cannot be used against you. Say you own a cottage that you and your family regularly use, but you also rent out to others a few weeks a year. In this case, you are supposed to report the rental income you receive on your tax return and you are also entitled to deduct some of your cottage expenses. However, there is a personal element to these activities and since you are essentially deducting some costs as rental expenses that you would have incurred even if you hadn't rented out part of your premises (think of property taxes, insurance, maybe even mortgage interest), if you claim losses on that rental activity, the REOP test can still be used to deny your losses. As well, REOP may be returning, although its current status is uncertain. We talk about this in the limited partnership section earlier in this chapter.

If you had rental losses denied in prior taxation years because the CRA said you had no REOP, fight it. You will have to file a Notice of Objection (see Chapter 15) or, if you missed the cut-off date to object, you could ask the CRA to reassess your tax return for the year(s) in question to allow the losses based on the *Stewart* and *Walls* cases. You have three years from the date on your Notice of Assessment for the tax year(s) in question to ask for a reassessment before your return is statute-barred, or in other words, before you are out of time to be allowed any further legal recourse. (see Chapter 15).

Undeveloped land

The tax treatment of undeveloped land is a tricky issue. If you rent out this undeveloped land (or even if you don't!), you need to ensure that you do not run afoul of the rules.

Deductibility of interest and property taxes

If you rent out vacant land, you will be allowed to deduct any interest and property tax only to the extent of the net rental income earned on the land (that is, income after other expenses are deducted). In other words, you cannot use the interest and property tax to create a loss on vacant land not used to produce income.

If, on the other hand, the land is used or held to carry on a business, or if the land is held primarily for the purpose of gaining or producing income, the interest and property tax can be deducted in excess of earned income. This distinction allows land under buildings and land used in a business (for example, a parking lot) to avoid the interest and property tax restrictions.

Capital assets

If the vacant land is considered a capital asset (which it would normally be if you purchased it to hold as a long-term investment), the non-deductible interest and property tax will be added to the cost of the land. This will reduce the capital gain (or increase the capital loss) on sale when the land is eventually disposed of.

Real estate rentals — What's deductible, what's not

If you are renting out real estate, you likely incur a variety of costs in order to earn that income. You can deduct many of these costs for tax purposes. You will need to keep track of your deductible expenditures during the year and then list them on form T776

when you file your tax return. You do not have to send in your receipts for rental expenses when you file your tax return, but you should keep them on file in case the CRA asks to see them.

Here is a list of the most common expenses incurred that may be deducted against rental income:

- ✔ Mortgage interest
- ✔ Property tax
- ✔ Insurance
- ✔ Maintenance and repairs
- ✔ Heat, hydro, water
- ✔ Accounting fees
- ✔ Condo fees
- ✔ Landscaping
- ✔ Office supplies
- ✔ Fees paid to find tenants
- ✔ Advertising
- ✔ Management and administration fees
- ✔ Salaries or wages paid to take care of property
- ✔ Legal fees to collect rent or prepare rental documents
- ✔ Lease cancellation fees (amortized over the remaining term of lease to a maximum of 40 years)
- ✔ Mortgage application, appraisal, processing, and insurance fees (deducted over five years)
- ✔ Mortgage guarantee fees (deducted over five years)
- ✔ Mortgage broker and finder fees (deducted over five years)
- ✔ Legal fees related to mortgage financing (deducted over five years)

Unlike vacant land, real estate rentals can create losses for tax purposes. These losses can be used to offset other types of income you report on your tax return, thereby reducing your overall tax payable in the year.

If you own one rental property in addition to your principal residence, you can deduct motor vehicle or travel expenses to conduct repairs and maintenance or to transport tools and materials to the rental property provided the property is located in your general area of residence. If you own only one rental property (and no other residence), you cannot deduct travel expenses to collect rent; this is considered a personal expense. Also, you cannot deduct travel expenses for a property outside your area of residence.

If you own two or more rental properties, you can deduct all of the above expenses plus travel to collect rents, supervise repairs, and generally manage the properties. The properties can be located anywhere, not just your area of residence.

Real estate commissions or legal fees paid in connection with the purchase or sale of the property are not deductible as incurred. Instead, they must be added to the cost base of the property.

Renting out your own residence

When renting out a residence that you also use personally, you have to determine which expenses relate solely to the rental activity and which ones are shared with the whole house. The ones that are shared need to be reasonably allocated between the rental and personal portions of the residence. This is because your personal portions of expenses are not deductible.

- ✔ **Expenses of the rental activity:** Expenses such as advertising, cleaning, and cutting keys are incremental costs of owning and renting the property. These expenses are 100-percent deductible against rental income.

- ✔ **Expenses shared with rest of house:** Expenses such as taxes, insurance, water, hydro, heat, maintenance, and mortgage interest would have been incurred even if a portion of the house were not rented out. These expenses are allocated between the rental and the rest of the house.

The CRA accepts two ways of allocating expenses:

- ✔ Based on the number of rooms in the house. If the house has ten rooms and two are rented, allocate $\frac{2}{10}$th of the household expenses to the rental units.

- ✔ Based on the square footage. If the house is 2,000 square feet and the rental is 400 square feet, allocate $\frac{400}{2000}$th of the house expenses to the rental portion.

As tempting as it might be, do not claim capital cost allowance (CCA) when renting out part of your home. The reason? Once you claim CCA against your rental income, the part of your home that is rented stops being your principal residence. This means that

when you sell your home, part of your proceeds will be taxable
because they are no longer exempt under the principal residence
exemption. See Chapter 7 for more information on this exemption.

Capital versus current expenditures

Unless you're a slumlord, you're likely going to incur some expenditures on your rental property. The question is, can you deduct
these expenses against your income?

Expenses of a property can be divided into two main categories: current expenditures and capital expenditures. Current expenditures
are the operating or recurring expenses that provide short-term benefits. These expenditures tend to maintain or keep the property in
the same shape. Examples are repairs and maintenance, landscaping, window cleaning, heat, hydro, property tax, and interest
expense on the mortgage. Capital expenditures, on the other hand,
are the expenses of purchasing the property or substantially
improving it. Capital expenditures are expenses that give lasting
benefits that improve the property beyond its original condition.
Examples of capital expenditures include major repairs to the property such as a new roof, additions to the property, new windows,
new plumbing or electrical wiring, and a new furnace or coalscuttle.

The key concept in determining if a repair is a capital or current
expenditure is the concept of betterment. If a repair improves what
was initially there, it will be classified as a capital expenditure. If
the repair only restores what was there initially, it is a current
expense.

Capital expenditures are not expensed in the year of occurrence;
rather, they are amortized or deducted over time using the capital
cost allowance system, which we discuss in the next section.

Capital expenditures to assist the disabled are fully deductible in the
year of occurrence. These expenses are given current expense treatment in an attempt to encourage landlords to install them, and may
include the following: installing hand-activated power door openers;
installing ramps; modifying bathrooms, elevators, or doorways to
accommodate wheelchairs; modifying elevators to assist the blind;
and installing telephone devices for the hearing impaired and computer equipment or software to assist people who have disabilities.

Capital cost allowance

Capital cost allowance is a method of writing off the cost of a capital item over time since the cost of capital assets cannot be

deducted all at once in the year of acquisition. The length of time that the tax laws permit you to "write off" the asset is supposed to represent the time it takes for the asset to wear out or become obsolete. The amount that you are allowed to deduct each year is called the capital cost allowance (or CCA).

How do I determine how much CCA I can claim?

The amount of CCA you are permitted to claim on a yearly basis depends on the type of asset you own and when the asset was purchased. The *Income Tax Act* puts each type of asset into a specific asset group, or "class." Each class has a predetermined amortization rate. For example, office furniture and equipment are Class 8 assets, and therefore the cost of any new purchase of office furniture or equipment gets added this class. Think of it as a running total of the value of like-assets you own.

How do you know what class to put your capital asset in? The CRA's *Rental Income* guide has a good discussion of CCA classes. See the CRA Web site at www.cra-arc.gc.ca.

Various CCA classes also have different rules with regard to the treatment of assets in the first year that their costs are added to the class. Most classes require you to use the "half-year rule" for new additions. This rule allows you to claim only half the normal CCA in the first year an asset is added to a class. This rule was designed to prevent individuals from buying assets on the last day of the year and claiming a full year of amortization (too bad!).

Suppose Andrea buys a building that costs $500,000 and a fashionable chaise longue that costs $1,000. The building is added to class 1. This class has an amortization rate of 4 percent per year, and the half-year rule applies. The fashionable chaise longue is added to class 8. This class is amortized at 20 percent per year, and the half-year rule applies.

	Building	*Chaise Longue*
Year 1		
CCA rate	4%	20%
Cost of assets in class	$500,000	$1,000
CCA	($500,000 × 4%) × ½ = $10,000	($1,000 × 20%) × ½ = $100

	Building	*Chaise Longue*
Year 2		
Cost	$500,000	$1,000
Less: Prior year's CCA	$10,000	$100
(Undepreciated capital cost)	$490,000	$900
CCA	($490,000 × 4%) = $19,600	($900 × 20%) = $180
Undepreciated capital cost at end of second year	($490,000 – $19,600) = $470,400	($900 – $180) = $720

You do not have to claim the maximum CCA every year. This is a discretionary deduction, meaning you can choose to claim any amount from zero to the maximum allowed. If you do not owe tax in a particular year, for example, you may not wish to claim CCA that year and instead preserve your deduction for other tax years when you might need it. Remember, though, there is a maximum amount you can claim each year even if you forgo deductions in previous years. No double-dipping!

Separate classes

Normally, assets of the same type are put into the same class, or pool, for CCA purposes. What this means is that you basically add together the costs of all like types of assets in order to depreciate them together on your tax return. This makes it much easier than having to calculate CCA separately on each and every asset you buy.

Rental buildings costing $50,000 or more acquired after 1971 must be placed in separate CCA classes. This means that if you buy two class 1 buildings and they cost more than $50,000 each, they must not be combined into one class 1 group of buildings; instead, they must each be in a separate class 1 group. The reason for this rule is that when buildings are disposed of (usually for a gain), the government wants to recapture (or reverse) the CCA claimed on the building. (If the building was sold for a gain, it obviously did not depreciate, so why allow CCA?) The rules of recapture do not permit the reversal of CCA on an asset if there is still another asset in the same class. By forcing each building into its own class, there is usually guaranteed recapture when the building is sold.

Combining rental income to calculate CCA

You cannot use CCA to create a loss on rental income. The government requires you to combine all rental income and losses from all properties before calculating CCA. In this way, you are prevented from using CCA to create or increase net rental losses.

Let's say Jack owns two buildings. Both buildings are in class 1. The income and loss on the rental buildings are as follows:

	Building 1	*Building 2*
Net income before CCA	$10,000	($15,000)

Since Jack has to combine the income of both buildings, he has a net rental loss of $5,000. Since Jack is in a net rental loss position, he cannot claim CCA on either building without increasing the rental loss. If this rule did not exist, he could claim CCA on Building 1 to bring income to zero and claim no CCA on Building 2. The result would be a net rental loss of $15,000.

Recapture and terminal loss

Recapture and terminal loss are adjustments that you must make when you dispose of assets and find (based on your selling price) that the assets either were not depreciated enough over time, or depreciated too much. To recapture means to reclaim CCA taken in excess of actual depreciation. To claim a terminal loss means to claim additional CCA when actual depreciation exceeds the allowed capital cost deductions. Neither recapture nor terminal losses can be claimed while assets are still in a CCA class (that is, if you had more than one asset of the same type being depreciated). When all assets in a class have been disposed of, you will be able to determine if you over- or underdepreciated assets.

Let's say that Lisa sells her class 1 building for $1,000,000. She originally bought the building for $500,000. Over the years, she has claimed $300,000 of CCA. Since this building is the last asset in the class, we can calculate recapture or terminal loss. At the time of sale, Lisa's undepreciated capital cost balance was $200,000 ($500,000 – $ 300,000 = $200,000).

Since the building increased in value and did not depreciate, Lisa had been entitled to CCA tax deductions in prior years that did not reflect the actual wear and tear of the building. Although the CCA deductions were valid at the time she took them (since the tax laws state how much you are entitled to deduct as CCA), now that Lisa is disposing of the asset she will be required to include $300,000 of recapture in her income for the year of disposition.

For more information on the capital cost allowance rules, see Chapter 9.

Foreign rental income

For tax purposes, you must include in your Canadian income any rental income that you receive on property located anywhere in the world. The same rules and restrictions apply to foreign-source rental income as apply to Canadian-source rental income, including the CCA rules.

All foreign transactions must be converted to Canadian dollars at the exchange rate in effect on the transaction date. You can use the average exchange rate for the year if you have income and expense transactions that take place throughout the year.

The Bank of Canada has some handy currency conversion calculators on their Web site. Check them out at: www.bankofcanada.ca/en/rates/exchange.html.

If you also had to pay tax to another country on your foreign rental income, you may be eligible for a foreign tax credit when you calculate your rental income for Canadian tax purposes. This system helps to ensure you're not paying double the tax on the same income. See Chapter 13 for more information.

Support Payments: Line 128

The tax rules surrounding support payments have undergone significant changes in the last decade. The catalyst for these changes was the high-profile *Thibaudeau* case. This case argued that the rules on support payments severely disadvantaged the receiving spouse and children since these payments were fully taxable. The court agreed and changed the rules, effective May 1, 1997. Since some taxpayers are still receiving support payments under the old rules, we'll summarize them all below.

Old rules (before May 1, 1997)

Under the old rules, alimony, child support, and separation allowances paid pursuant to a court order are deducted from the payer's income and included in the recipient's income. Once included, this payment makes up part of the recipient's taxable income and is taxed at that person's marginal rate. Obviously, because of this additional tax burden the amount available to the recipient is reduced.

New rules (after April 30, 1997)

For court orders or written agreements made after April 30, 1997, **child support** payments are not deductible from the income of the payer or included in the income of the recipient. The net result is that tax does not reduce the amount intended for child support. On the other hand, **spousal support** payments are still deductible from income by the payer, and are taxable to the recipient. The new rules go on to say that if a court order or written agreement specifies that an individual must make both child support and spousal support payments, payments are allocated first to child support and second to spousal support. This additional provision ensures that all child support must be paid before the payer can claim a deduction for spousal support, and the recipient has to include spousal support in income.

If child support is in arrears, the government will not consider any of the future payments from the payer to be spousal support — at least, not until all back child support is paid. This ensures that the recipient will not be taxed on back child support even if the payer calls it spousal support.

If the court order or agreement does not specify separate amounts for child support and spousal support, all payments will be considered child support and will not be taxable to the recipient or deductible to the payer.

Luckily, you and your former spouse can elect to use the new rules even if your court order or agreement predates May 1, 1997. By using form T1157, "Election for Child Support Payments," the recipient and the payer can agree to treat the child support portion of the payments as non-deductible to the payer and not included in the recipient's income. After this election is filed, however, you cannot return to the old rules.

If you had a pre–May 1, 1997, agreement but make changes to it, you will fall under the new rules, making the child support portion of payments non-taxable and non-deductible. Discuss any changes you make to your agreement with a lawyer to ensure the tax conse-quences are taken into account.

 Taxable support payments qualify as earned income for RRSP purposes.

Specific-purpose payments

Instead of making payments directly to a former spouse, some tax-payers choose to make specific-purpose payments to third parties for the benefit of a former spouse or child. Common third-party payments include rent, tuition fees, medical expenses, or mainte-nance payments on a residence.

Unlike regular support payments, specific-purpose payments may not take place at regular intervals, and often are not at the discretion of the beneficiary. Regardless, if the payments are made pursuant to a court order or written agreement, the tax treatment will generally be the same as for payments made directly to the spouse for spousal or child support. In other words, if a payment is made pursuant to a pre–May 1, 1997, agreement, the full payment made to the third party is taxable to the former spouse (benefici-ary) and deductible to the payer. If the agreement was made after April 30, 1997, specific-purpose payments that benefit the child (for example, the child's medical bills or tuition) are not deductible or taxable, although payments that benefit the former spouse are.

RRSP and RRIF Income: Line 129

Registered retirement savings plans (RRSPs) are government-sanctioned plans that Canadians can use to save for their retire-ment. Setting up an RRSP is easy. You can do so at any financial institution or with a financial adviser in your area.

Why use an RRSP? You get a tax deduction for contributions you make to the plan (within limits), and earnings within the plan grow free of tax — that is, until you make withdrawals. You might have guessed that at the point you make withdrawals you have income to report on your tax return.

A registered retirement income fund (RRIF) is created when you convert your RRSP — usually in the year you turn 69 (although you could do it earlier). Once your RRSP is converted to an RRIF, you are **required** to make annual taxable withdrawals (withdrawals from an RRSP are optional). RRIF withdrawals, like RRSP withdrawals, are taxable.

Withdrawals from an RRSP

Once you've placed funds in an RRSP you are generally able to withdraw those funds whenever you want. However, we don't normally recommend you make withdrawals prior to retirement because your RRSP assets are supposed to help fund your retirement and you will be taxed on the withdrawals.

You may choose to withdraw funds on a tax-preferred basis, though, using the Home Buyers' Plan or the Lifelong Learning Plan. We talk about these plans later in this chapter.

Different withdrawal rules exist where you have a "locked-in RRSP." A locked-in RRSP is created when you transfer funds from a registered pension plan to an RRSP. Withdrawals from locked-in plans are legislated in each province and may be limited.

Mature RRSP

An RRSP matures when you reach 69 years of age. At this time, the government requires you to convert your RRSP to an annuity or an RRIF. Taxable retirement payments must commence the following calendar year.

Withdrawals prior to RRSP maturity

Whenever you withdraw amounts from your RRSP, the amount of the withdrawal is included in your income. In addition, these withdrawals will be subject to *withholding tax at source.* This means that the financial institution where you hold your RRSP is obligated to take some tax off the payment being made to you, and then remit that tax to the CRA on your behalf. You will receive a T4RSP at tax time outlining the amount of taxable payment made to you, as well as the amount of tax withheld. Report the full RRSP withdrawal amount on line 129 of your tax return, and the withheld tax on line 437.

In many cases the amount of withholding tax will not be enough to cover your actual tax liability when you file your tax return. Therefore, be sure to calculate how much tax you will actually owe (based on your marginal tax rate) to ensure that if the withholding tax taken off is not enough, you keep enough money on hand to pay the taxman in April. For the mathematically inclined, you can calculate this by figuring out what federal tax bracket you are in (see Table 1-1 in Chapter 1) and then what provincial tax bracket you are in (Table 14-1, Chapter 14). For example, say you live in British Columbia and you expect your total income for the year to be $40,000. You want to take $5,000 out of your RRSP this year to go on a vacation to Mexico (not that we recommend a withdrawal for this purpose!). From Table 1-1, we see that you are in the second tax bracket so you will pay 22% of federal tax on this withdrawal. Then, we see from Table 14-1 that you will pay 9.15% of provincial tax. So, in total, we can estimate that the total tax you will have to pay on this withdrawal is 31.15%, or $1,557. If only 10% of tax was withheld for taxes when the withdrawal was made (which is the required amount in all provinces but Quebec), you will have just over $1,000 to come up with when you file your tax return next year. Something to ponder over your margarita.

Normally, you should withdraw money from an RRSP only when you really need the income, so you can defer the resulting tax for as long as possible. If you do have to make a withdrawal, use these few simple strategies to save tax in the process:

- **Low-income withdrawals:** Try to withdraw amounts during a year in which you anticipate having a lower income. This will reduce the tax bite when the amounts are eventually included in income.

- **Take out small quantities:** Don't take all the money out at once. Take the funds out in increments of $5,000 or less. This will reduce the withholding tax to 10 percent (if you reside outside of Quebec) and give you more money to use when you need it. When filing your return, you will, of course, need to pay tax at your marginal rate for the income inclusion. If you urgently need the money, however, better to have it in your hands than in the taxman's (as withheld tax).

- **Withdraw over two tax years:** Try to take the money out in two different tax years. By taking funds out at the end of December one year and in January of the next year, you will be splitting the withdrawal over two tax years, thus reducing the tax hit in any one year. In addition, tax will not be payable on the January withdrawal until April 30 of the following year — so, if you withdraw money from an RRSP in January 2006, additional tax will not be payable on this amount until April 30, 2007.

- **Withdraw RRSP cash from low-income earners:** If you are married, remove money from the RRSP of the lower-income earner first. This will reduce the tax paid by the family, since the lower-income earner probably has a lower marginal tax rate and will pay less tax on the withdrawal.

Withdrawals of unused contributions or overcontributions to an RRSP

Sometimes taxpayers are a little overzealous when it comes to contributing to their RRSPs. However (as you can imagine), we're not allowed to put unlimited amounts into our retirement savings plans. When you put more then you are allowed into your RRSP, you are said to have *overcontributed.* (We discuss these contribution limits in Chapter 10.)

Other taxpayers contribute within the allowable limits, but decide for one reason or another not to deduct the contribution on their tax return. This is referred to as having an *unused contribution.*

It may make sense to create an *unused contribution* when you find yourself in an unusually low tax bracket. If you save the RRSP deduction for a year when your marginal tax bracket is higher, your tax deduction will be worth more. To do this, you should still include the contribution on the RRSP deduction workchart (line C), but then simply choose to not claim the deduction this year (line D). This will result in the calculation of an undeducted contribution on line G of the workchart. By including the contribution on this year's tax return, you will ensure that the CRA knows the contribution was made, and avoid problems in future years when you actually want to claim the deduction.

Generally, any withdrawals of contributions to your RRSP, even those that exceed your contribution limit, are reported on line 129 and taxed as income. This is the case even when you withdraw any undeducted contributions to the RRSP! Luckily, there are relieving provisions that allow you an offsetting deduction against these income inclusions. (After all, you didn't get a deduction for the contribution, so why should you pay tax on the withdrawal?)

There are time limits in place, however. Specifically, you must withdraw the overcontribution in the year the contribution was made or in the following year, or in the year an assessment is issued for the year the contribution was made or the following year. For example, if you made the overcontribution in 2006, you have to take it out of your RRSP in 2006 or 2007 to be entitled to the offsetting deduction. If your 2006 tax return is assessed in 2007 (as it probably will be), you then have the added option of removing the overcontribution by the end of 2008 in order to take advantage of the tax relief. These tight timeframes make it very important to remove the overcontribution from your RRSP as soon as you find out about it. If you wait too long, you will be taxed on the withdrawal or will face penalties for the overcontribution. Neither is a very positive outcome.

If you are going to withdraw your RRSP overcontribution, use form T3012A, "Tax Reduction Waiver on the Refund of Your Undeducted RRSP Contribution." When you submit this form to the CRA, it will direct your financial institution not to withhold tax on the withdrawal of funds. If you withdraw funds without form T3012A, the issuer of the plan will withhold tax. In this case, use form T746, "Calculating Your Deduction for Refund of Undeducted RRSP Contributions," to calculate the amount of your tax deduction given that you have already paid withholding tax.

Home Buyers' Plan

Although the general rule is that withdrawals from your RRSP are taxable, in some special circumstances the government allows you to withdraw funds with no tax. The first situation is when you withdraw money from your RRSP to purchase a home under the Home Buyers' Plan. Of course, your tax obligations aren't over yet. You are required to repay the amount you withdrew for your Home Buyers' Plan to your RRSP. If you don't? You guessed it — the shortfall will be added to your income at line 129. Read Chapter 10 to learn more about the Home Buyers' Plan.

Lifelong Learning Plan

As is the case with the Home Buyers' Plan, you can withdraw funds from your RRSP on a tax-free basis to help you go back to school. This program is called the Lifelong Learning Plan.

If you do not pay back funds withdrawn under the Lifelong Learning Plan according to the required schedule, they are included in your income at line 129 every year that the payment is missed. Also, if you withdraw the money but do not use it for education, and if you do not return the funds to the RRSP by the end of the calendar year following your withdrawal from the educational institution, the entire amount will be included in income. For more on the Lifelong Learning Plan, see Chapter 10.

Spousal RRSPs

A spousal RRSP is an RRSP you have contributed to but that names your spouse as the "annuitant." This means that all retirement funds out of this RRSP will belong to your spouse and not to you, the contributor (although you do get the up-front tax deduction). A spousal RRSP is usually used by individuals who have much higher incomes than their spouses and wish to "split" their retirement income rather than have the entire amount included in their income. For more about spousal RRSPs, see Chapter 10.

A withdrawal from a spousal RRSP has very special rules that seek to dissuade individuals from placing money in a spousal RRSP and then withdrawing it soon after, to take advantage of the spouse's lower marginal tax rate. If these rules are violated, the income will be attributed back to the contributing spouse, which means it will be added to his or her income and taxed at that person's marginal tax rate instead. This would be the same outcome had that person contributed to his or her own RRSP and then withdrawn the funds.

If your spouse withdraws money from a spousal RRSP that you have contributed to in the year or in the previous two years, the withdrawal will be taxed in your hands and must be included on line 129 of your return. It does not matter if your spouse's name is on the T-slip! For example, if your spouse withdraws money from a spousal RRSP in 2006 that you contributed to in 2006, 2005, or 2004, the withdrawal will be included in your income, not your spouse's.

If the contributor is separated from his or her spouse, or was deceased at the time funds were withdrawn, the government will not attribute the income back to the contributor.

Contribute to a spousal RRSP at the end of the year (instead of on January 1) to reduce the waiting time on withdrawals from three years to just over two.

RRIF income

When you reach age 69 the tax laws require that you convert your RRSP to a registered retirement income fund (RRIF) or an annuity. You can choose to do this conversion early if you wish to earn a retirement income. In either case, the transfer of the assets in your RRSP to your RRIF can take place without triggering any current tax. You simply need to contact the financial institution where your RRSP is held, or your financial adviser, to request your RRSP be converted to an RRIF. They will take care of the required paperwork.

Like the RRSP, the RRIF earns income tax-free inside the plan. An RRIF is different from an RRSP, however, in that you can no longer contribute to the plan, and you must make a minimum income withdrawal from the plan each year following the year in which the RRIF was established. These withdrawals are considered taxable income.

Conversion from an RRSP to a RRIF must take place when you reach age 69, however, you might choose to do this conversion early. Some reasons include:

✔ You need the income

✔ You are at least 65 and want to take advantage of the pension credit (Chapter 12, line 314) on the first $2,000 of pension income

✔ You are currently in a low tax bracket and expect to pay very little tax on your withdrawals

Of course, if you can afford to, it generally makes sense to keep the funds in your RRSP for as long as possible in order to defer the tax hit on withdrawal.

 If you are 65 years of age or older, report your minimum required RRIF withdrawal at line 115. Starting in 2006, income reported at line 115 is eligible for the $2,000 pension credit at line 314 (this credit used to be just $1,000). If you are under 65, report income from an RRIF at line 130.

 Minimum required withdrawals from an RRIF are not subject to withholding tax, except in Quebec. However, if you withdraw more than the minimum amount, these withdrawals will be subject to withholding tax and must be reported at line 130. Any tax withheld is reported on line 437.

 In order to defer the tax hit from your RRIF for as long as possible, and if your spouse is younger than you, consider basing your minimum withdrawals on your spouse's age. This will reduce the amount you are required to withdraw each year, allowing you to defer tax and leave more assets in your RRIF for future growth.

 You don't have to make any withdrawals from your RRIF in the year you set up the plan. In fact, you can (and should, if you are financially able) defer making a withdrawal until December of the year after your RRIF is set up, in order to defer tax for as long as possible.

Other Income: Line 130

Line 130 is called the "catch-all," since it's basically used to report income that does not belong anywhere else on the tax return. This section covers some of the most common types of income to be reported on line 130.

Retiring allowances

Don't be confused by the term *retiring allowance* — it doesn't apply only to payments you receive when you retire. In fact, it also includes what people normally refer to as "severance" or "termination" pay, as well as to a court award or settlement for wrongful dismissal. Legal awards are discussed in more detail below.

Portion of retiring allowance eligible for RRSPs

Retiring allowances are taxable. However, when you leave your employer and receive a retiring allowance, you might be able to pay a portion of your payment into your RRSP. This portion is called your "eligible" retiring allowance. If you choose to do this, you include the full amount of the allowance on line 130, but a deduction is given on line 208 for the amount paid to your RRSP. If those two amounts are the same, you will effectively receive the retiring allowance tax-free — or at least tax-free until the time you make withdrawals out of your RRSP.

Not all retiring allowances are eligible for transfer into your RRSP. In fact, the *Income Tax Act* sets limits on the amount of retiring allowance you can have paid into your RRSP. The limit is calculated as follows:

- ✔ $2,000 per year or part year of employment service prior to 1996, plus

- ✔ $1,500 per year or part year of employment service prior to 1989 in which you had no vested interest in any employer's contributions to a registered pension plan or deferred profit-sharing plan.

So, if you worked for an employer from say, 1997 to 2006, any retiring allowance paid to you would not be eligible for the special transfer into your RRSP. Too bad!

Let's suppose Susan left her employer in 2006 and received a $50,000 termination payment. She had started working there in 1985 and joined the pension plan in 1987.

The amount she can have paid to her RRSP is calculated this way:

$2,000 × 11 years (1985 to 1995)	$22,000
$1,500 × 2 years (1985 to 1987)	$3,000
Eligible portion of retiring allowance that can be paid to her RRSP	$25,000

The amount of a retiring allowance that can be paid to your RRSP and deducted on your personal tax return is over and above your regular RRSP contribution (or "deduction") limit. You can still make your regular RRSP contribution in addition to this special contribution. It's not critical that the retiring allowance be paid directly to your RRSP. However, you must contribute the funds to your RRSP within 60 days following the end of the year in which you receive the payment. For allowances received in 2006, this means the contribution must be made by March 1, 2007, or you lose your right to this special contribution.

The eligible portion of a retiring allowance can be rolled into an RRSP of which only you are the annuitant. It cannot go into a spousal RRSP.

Ineligible portion of retiring allowance

Any allowance received in excess of the amount you can have paid to your RRSP under the rules outlined above is considered an ineligible retiring allowance. In other words, the ineligible retiring allowance is any portion paid to you that relates to your employment from 1997 on. This amount is reported in box 27 of your T4A, and must be reported on line 130 of your income tax return. The ineligible portion of a retiring allowance does not open up new RRSP room for you.

Here are some things that may help ease the tax burden on any ineligible portion of a retiring allowance:

- ✔ If you have regular unused RRSP contribution room, consider making an RRSP contribution with your ineligible retiring allowance. In fact, you can have your employer send the portion that you are going to contribute directly to your RRSP and avoid any withholding tax. To do this you must show your employer that you have the RRSP contribution room available.

- ✔ Ask to receive the retiring allowance payment over a number of years. You do not have to pay tax on a retiring allowance until it's received, so this can help to defer tax to a year when you may be in a lower tax bracket.

What is not a retiring allowance?

Obviously, eligible retiring allowances can be very beneficial since they can be paid on a tax-free basis to an RRSP. This is one reason that Canadians want to receive retiring allowances when they leave a job. However, it's important to note that not all amounts will qualify as a retiring allowance. A retiring allowance does not include the following:

- ✔ A superannuation or pension benefit
- ✔ An amount received as a result of an employee's death
- ✔ Payments for accumulated vacation leave
- ✔ A payment made in lieu of earnings for a period of reasonable notice of termination
- ✔ Payments made for human rights violations under human rights legislation

Scholarships, Fellowships, Bursaries, and Research Grants

Did you receive a scholarship, fellowship, bursary, or prize for achievement in your field of endeavour this year? First off, congratulations! Second, starting this year, these amounts are not taxable. So, congratulations from the Department of Finance as well!

The amount received is not taxable if the program you are enrolled in entitles you to claim the education tax credit (line 323, Chapter 12). If the program does not qualify for purposes of the education tax credit, only the first $500 is exempt.

What are scholarships and bursaries?

Scholarships and *bursaries* are amounts given to students to help them pay for school — generally a university, college, or similar educational institution. Normally, a student is not expected to do specific work for the payer in exchange for a scholarship or bursary.

A scholarship from your employer given with the condition that you return to work after completing your studies is not a scholarship at all! In fact, you must report the amount received as employment income on line 104. Sorry! However, as we discuss in Chapter 4, if the courses you take are for your employer's benefit, the amount paid on your behalf could be a non-taxable benefit.

What is a fellowship?

Fellowships are like scholarships or bursaries in that they're given to students to help them pursue their education. The difference is that in most cases they are given to graduate students by a university, charity, or similar body. However, when the primary purpose of the fellowship is not education and training but rather carrying out research, the award is considered to be a research grant.

If a student receives a genuine loan to assist in financing education, the loan is not considered to be a scholarship, bursary, or fellowship. In other words, the loan is not taxable. For a genuine loan to exist, provisions must generally be made for repayment within a reasonable time.

What is a "prize in my field of endeavour"?

A *prize in your field of endeavour* sounds pretty impressive, right? Although we're not talking about the Academy Awards, prizes do come in all shapes and sizes. Prizes that fall under this heading are awarded for success in an area of effort. It is a result of accomplishment, rather than luck. For example, if you achieve the highest mark on your bar exam, the $1,000 you receive will qualify as a prize. In this case, you wouldn't have to report anything on your tax return because prizes in your field of endeavour are tax-free. Take the $1,000 and enjoy it.

A *prescribed prize* is a prize recognized by the public and awarded for achievement in the arts, sciences, or for public service. These prizes are also exempt from tax altogether, as long as the amount cannot be considered compensation for services rendered or to be rendered. Although this exemption is aimed at high-profile awards, such as the Nobel Prize, the definition is general enough for other prizes, such as those in recognition of community service, to be exempt from tax.

What is a research grant?

Did you receive a *research grant,* money given during the year to help pay expenses necessary to carry out a research project? If so, you must report as income any amount you received in excess of expenses. Research grants do not qualify for the tax exemption. Grant money received in excess of expenses is classified as employment income and is reported on line 104 of your tax return (not line 100). If you've been given a research grant this year, you should receive a T4A. The amount you receive is reported in box 28, and the bottom of the slip should indicate the amount related to a research grant.

Want more info on scholarships, fellowships, bursaries, prizes, and research grants? Go to the CRA's Web site and take a look at Interpretation Bulletin #IT-75R4, "Scholarships, Fellowships, Bursaries, Prizes, Research Grants, and Financial Assistance": www.cra-arc.gc.ca/E/pub/tp/it75r4/README.html.

Tuition Assistance Payments

Tuition assistance payments received from the Employment Insurance Commission (EIC) or Human Resources and Skills Development Canada (HRSDC) are taxable. The amounts are reported on T4E or T4A slips.

An offsetting tax deduction (reported on line 256) is available to recipients of tuition assistance for adult basic education (ABE). ABE includes primary- and secondary-level education or other forms of training that do not qualify for the tuition tax credit. This includes courses taken to:

- Finish high school
- Develop stronger literacy skills
- Upgrade secondary-school credentials to prepare an individual for specific occupations or fields of higher learning

Your T-slip should indicate whether your tuition assistance payment is taxable or non-taxable.

Death Benefits

A death benefit is an amount paid on the death of an employee to a spouse or other beneficiary in recognition of service in an office or employment. The first $10,000 of a death benefit paid in respect of any one employee is exempt from tax.

Death benefits paid under the Canada or Quebec Pension Plans do not qualify for the $10,000 exemption.

Legal Awards

It's a common misconception that legal awards, such as payments for damages, are not taxable. Although it is possible that the payment is not taxable, this is not always the case. Take, for example, a retiring allowance.

A retiring allowance is taxable and includes an amount received *as a result of loss of office or employment.* Some individuals, after losing their jobs, hire a lawyer in order to seek additional compensation. Payments received from a lawsuit or out-of-court settlement in relation to employment, for whatever reason, are taxable as a retiring allowance. This may even include amounts paid on account of or in lieu of damages — that is, damages for loss of self-respect, humiliation, mental anguish, hurt feelings, and so on — if the payment arose from a loss of office or employment. The easiest way to look at it is like this: If you sue your employer and you receive payment, it's taxable. If you continue to work, it's included in employment income; otherwise, it's a retiring allowance.

If you win a lawsuit and receive payment that's classified as a retiring allowance, you can deduct any legal expenses incurred. But you can deduct only up to the amount of the allowance you include in income. That is, if you can have the entire retiring allowance paid to your RRSP (as we describe earlier in the chapter), you can't deduct any legal costs. Any legal costs you can't deduct can be carried forward for the next seven years, to offset any taxable retiring allowance you may receive in the future as a result of the lawsuit.

Some specific legal payments are excluded from income altogether. For example, all amounts received by a taxpayer or the taxpayer's dependants that qualify as special or general damages for personal injury or death are excluded from income, regardless of the fact that the amount of such damages may be determined with reference to the loss of the taxpayer's earnings. Examples of amounts received as a result of personal injury or death include the following:

- ✔ Out-of-pocket expenses such as medical and hospital bills

- ✔ Accrued or future loss of earnings

- ✔ Pain and suffering

- ✔ Shortened expectation of life

- ✔ Loss of financial support caused by the death of the supporting individual

Foreign Income

Keep in mind that if you're a Canadian resident, you're taxable on your entire worldwide income. So if you received money from another country, and no other line numbers are appropriate for reporting your income, you can include the amount on line 130. Make sure you remember to convert it to Canadian dollars first!

More "Other Income"

Many T-slips you receive will indicate amounts paid to you as "other income." Fortunately, you don't have to remember to include these other types of income on your tax return, since you'll have the slips to remind you. Simply follow the instructions on your T-slips, and you can't go wrong.

Workers' Compensation Benefits (WCB): Line 144

WCB received as a result of injury, disability, or death must be included in income. This amount is found in box 10 on the T5007 sent to you by the Workers' Compensation Board. This income inclusion is then deducted at line 250, with the net result that no tax is payable on this income. You might wonder why you have to go through all this trouble to end up in a tax-neutral position. By including the benefit at line 144, you increase your net income, thus reducing your entitlement to certain credits and deductions, such as the Child Tax Benefit and the GST credit. This higher income will also reduce the spousal amount that your spouse can claim for you.

If you receive money from your employer as an advance of WCB, the employer will usually put the amount in box 14 of your T4. You should subtract this from your T4 and include it at line 144. Be sure to get a letter from your employer explaining the amount. Submit this letter with your return.

Social Assistance: Line 145

Social assistance payments (box 11 on the T5007) are included in your income at line 145 and deducted at line 250 in calculating taxable income. Just as with workers' compensation benefits, the net result of social assistance payments is no tax. But (again, just as with WCB) since the social assistance payments form part of your net income, you could have a reduced entitlement to certain tax credits and deductions. By the way, if your spouse has a higher income than you do, the social assistance payments should be included and deducted on your spouse's return instead of yours.

Universal Child Care Benefit

Starting in July 2006, the government pays families $100 per month for each child under the age of 6 in a household. This Universal Child Care Benefit is meant to provide financial support for child care for preschool children, although there is no requirement that the child actually attend preschool for this benefit to be paid.

The Universal Child Care Benefit is taxable to the lower-income spouse (or the recipient where there are not two parents living together). You must include the payments you received for July to December 2006 on your 2006 income tax return. These payments will not affect your entitlement to Old Age Security, Employment Insurance, or the child care expense deduction, where applicable.

You must apply to receive the Universal Child Care Benefit. An application can be found at www.cra-arc.gc.ca/E/pbg/tf/rc66/README.html. With payments of up to $1,200 per year, per child, it is worth your while, even if it is taxable!

Chapter 9

Tips for Self-Employment Income

In This Chapter

▶ Understanding the tax realities of self-employment

▶ Using the accrual method of accounting

▶ Reporting various types of self-employment income and expenses on your tax return

▶ Using capital cost allowance as a tax deduction

*S*elf-employment means running your own business. You are an entrepreneur — someone who accepts the risks and enjoys the rewards of business. There are many advantages to self-employment, including the tax savings component. While the tax savings are attractive, most people become self-employed because they want to "be their own boss."

The Tax Implications of Being Self-Employed

You are required to report your business profits (or losses) on your personal tax return if you are unincorporated. This is because a sole proprietorship is not a separate legal entity — it is simply treated as an extension of the owner (the proprietor). On the other hand, if you own shares in a corporation, your corporation is required to report its income or loss on its own tax return. In that case your corporation should issue you a T4 for income and a T5 for any dividends paid to you in the year.

It is usually easiest to set up any new business as a sole proprietor-ship. However, once the business starts becoming profitable, you may want to consider incorporating. This is because corporations can benefit from some tax savings (so long as you actually leave profits in the company).

How does self-employment save taxes?

The tax "win" from self-employment is that any expense you incur to build and run the business is generally deductible in calculating your business income subject to tax. This is logical since every dollar you earn from the business will be taxed, so every dollar you spend on the business should be tax deductible. If you are run-ning a business and incur a loss, the loss is deducted from other sources of income on your tax return. (An exception to this may be a loss incurred in operating a farm. We discuss farming near the end of this chapter.)

If your business produces a loss this year but you don't have any other sources of income to use the loss against, consider filing form T1A, "Request for Loss Carryback," to offset income you paid tax on in the previous three years. The CRA will then send you a cheque for some or all of the taxes you paid.

If you have a loss that arose in 2003 or earlier, you can carry for-ward the loss for *seven* years and deduct it against any type of income. If you incur a loss in 2004 or 2005, that loss can be carried forward for *ten* years to offset income.

Thanks to the 2006 federal budget, the carry-forward period for business losses incurred in 2006 and subsequent years has been extended to 20 years.

Generally, self-employment offers you the opportunity to deduct more expenses than if you were employed, since only certain employees can deduct expenses they incur to do their job. Even when an employee has the opportunity to deduct a lot of expenses, the self-employed person can usually deduct more.

We've all heard stories about self-employed individuals taking advantage of their status for so-called tax savings. Just because you don't receive T4s, T5s, and so on, reporting the income of your business does not mean you can understate your actual income when you prepare your tax return (even if you were paid in cash).

You also cannot deduct personal expenses in calculating your business's net income.

Choosing a taxation year-end for your business

As of 1995, all businesses must either adopt a calendar year-end (that is, December 31) or make a special election to have an alternative date apply. If you ask us, adopting the calendar year-end will save you a lot of hassle.

Most businesses operate on a January 1 to December 31 taxation year. This is the simplest solution in terms of the complexities of reporting your business's income and expenses. If your business is cyclical or seasonal, it may make sense for you to elect to have a non–December 31 year-end.

Once you have filed a tax return with your business's taxation year-end noted, the taxation year becomes fixed. Though it is possible to change a taxation year-end, it can be difficult: first, you must have a pretty good reason for doing so, and second, you have to ask the CRA for permission. Our advice is that you take your time in determining the appropriate taxation year-end for your business.

The Accrual Method of Accounting

Most self-employed individuals must use the *accrual method* of accounting in reporting their income and expenses earned from self-employment. (As we note elsewhere, some people prefer the spelling "a cruel method of accounting.") As we discuss near the end of the chapter, self-employed individuals who earn commission income or are involved in farming and fishing have the option of using the cash method of accounting.

Here is how to use the accrual method of accounting:

  ✔ Record income as it is *earned* — not when your customer pays you. In most cases you are considered to have earned your income when an invoice is issued. Where at the end of your business's taxation year you have invoiced customers but not yet received payment, the sale would be recognized as being earned in the year. The unpaid amount would be considered an "accounts receivable" at the end of the taxation year.

✔ Record expenses as they are *incurred* — whether or not you actually paid for the expense in the taxation year. Often, the invoice date is used to indicate when the business has incurred an expense. If you received an invoice from a supplier that was dated for a purchase made prior to the taxation year-end, the expense would be recorded in your business's taxation year as it was incurred in the year. The unpaid amount at the end of the taxation year is considered an "accounts payable."

If you purchase an item that you are going to sell as part of your business, do not account for it as an expense or cost until the item is actually sold.

The Cash Method of Accounting

Another method of accounting is the *cash method*. Income is reported when cash is received. Expenditures are recorded when cash is *paid*. The recording of inventory is usually irrelevant when the cash method of accounting is used. (Again, you will see that a farm business is an exception. A farmer's "inventory" may need to be valued — even when the cash method is used. More on this near the end of the chapter.)

Lines 135 and 162: Business Income

Business income is the first line on the portion of your return dealing with self-employment income. (Refer to the self-employment section about one-third of the way down on page 2 of the tax return.) You report the gross income from your business on line 162 and the net income or loss of the business on line 135.

Form T2124, "Statement of Business Activities"

Most self-employed individuals should complete the T2124 tax form, "Statement of Business Activities." The form serves as an income statement for the self-employed person. All income and expenses of the business are reported on the form. The "net" amount of income (income less expenses) is what the self-employed person pays tax on.

You will see that Form T2124 is broken down into a number of sections. Obviously the first step is to fill in the identification section. We think you can handle that. Next, you'll have to fill in the details of your sales and expense amounts for the year. Here are some tips for dealing with these items.

> ✔ **Sales, commissions, or fees (line c, lines 8000 to 8299):** Record your self-employment sales, commissions, or fees earned in the year on line 8299. You are responsible for ensuring the amount recorded is correct. You may not receive any T-slips from your customers indicating how much you have billed them in the year; it is up to you to track and report the correct amount on your tax return.
>
> The gross income you report should not include any Goods and Services Tax (GST at 6 percent — 7 percent prior to July 1, 2006), Harmonized Sales Tax (HST at 14 percent — 15 percent prior to July 1, 2006), and/or provincial retail sales tax charged to customers. These taxes are excluded because they do not represent the income of your business — you simply collect these taxes on behalf of the federal and provincial governments.
>
> If a customer provides you with a deposit for goods or services to be provided after the taxation year-end, do not include the deposit in your gross income. The deposit is not yet considered income because the goods or services for which the deposit was received have not been provided as of the end of your business's taxation year.
>
> ✔ **Cost of goods sold (lines 8300 to 8518 and line d):** If you purchase goods for resale, the calculation of your cost of goods sold is detailed on lines 8300 to 8518 of form T2124. If your business provides only services, your cost of sales is zero.
>
> ✔ **Expenses of your business (lines 8521 to 9270):** You simply detail your expenses on these lines. If your business is registered for GST/HST, do not include GST/HST in the amounts noted on these lines. If your business is not registered for GST/HST, include the GST/HST you have paid in connection with these expenses in the expense totals.

The CRA requests on form T2124 that in reporting your business's expenses, you "enter business part only." This is the CRA's way of saying, "Do not deduct any personal expenses in computing your self-employment income because it is against the law and you will pay dearly if we catch you — so watch out." Many of your business expenses will be 100-percent business use. If you advertise your business in the Yellow Pages, it would be fairly difficult to argue that a part of your advertising cost was personal in nature. However, you probably use your car for both business and personal use. Perhaps you operate your business from your home or apartment. If so, the costs of maintaining your home office need to be tracked. Only the "self-employment" or business-use portion of your car and home office expenses can be claimed on form T2124. We take a look at deducting a portion of your car and home expenses later in the chapter, along with more details on some specific expenses you can deduct.

Doing your taxes will be much less onerous if you keep good records throughout the year. You can use a computer program to help, or even just get a bunch of envelopes and label each with the various expense categories noted on form T2124. As you pay for items throughout the year, simply place your receipts in the envelope — and at the end of the year, add them all up!

✔ **Partnerships (your share of line g above — line h):** If you are operating as a partnership, you put your share of line g on line h. For example, say you have a 33 ƒ ⅓ percent interest in a contracting business that is operated by you and a couple of partners. If line g on your tax return reported $90,000, your 33 ƒ ⅓ percent share would be $30,000. You would enter $30,000 on line h.

✔ If your partnership has five or more partners, the reporting of your share of the partnership's income is very simple. There is no need for you to detail the income and expenses of the whole partnership. On behalf of all the partners, the partnership should have sent the CRA a copy of the partnership's financial statements detailing the partnership's income and expenses. The partnership will simply issue you a T5013, "Statement of Partnership Income," indicating your share of the partnership's net income. If you receive a T5013, simply report your share of the partnership's net income at line 9369 (net income [loss] before adjustment) on the T2124.

Some of the expenses you can deduct

As we will see, most business expenses are fully deductible in calculating your self-employed income subject to tax. But, tax being tax, it is not always that straightforward. In this section, we comment on some of the more interesting rules dealing with the deductibility of expenses.

Overall deductibility

The general rule is that any expense incurred to operate a business is deductible. To be deductible, the amount of the expense must be "reasonable" in the circumstances. For example, if the business pays your spouse a salary that is in excess of what you may have paid someone not related to you, the excess may be considered "unreasonable" and the CRA may disallow the deduction.

Salary and payroll costs

In computing the total expenses of your business or partnership, a deduction cannot be taken for salaries, wages, or fees paid to yourself, or amounts you have taken as "drawings." Sole proprietors simply pay tax on the amount of business income that remains after all other expenses have been recorded. If you are in a partnership, the bottom-line income is shared among the partners on a basis as agreed to by the partners.

Self-employed individuals are permitted to deduct one-half of the Canada Pension Plan or Quebec Pension Plan contributions paid for their own coverage as a business expense. The non-deductible half will continue to qualify as a tax credit. See Chapter 12 for more details.

Prepaid expenses

As we note earlier in the chapter, under the accrual method of accounting you recognize an expense when it is incurred, not when it is paid. Sometimes the benefit, or a portion of the benefit, of something you pay for will be in a future taxation year. Take a look at your business insurance for example. Before the "insurance year" commences, you receive a bill for the full premium. Say your business taxation year was January 1 to December 31. In September 2006 you arranged to purchase business insurance for the first time. You receive a bill for $1,200 to cover your business for the period October 1, 2006 to September 30, 2007. You make the full $1,200 payment in October 2006.

In preparing the T2124 for your business's 2006 taxation year, you can deduct only $300 for the insurance. This is because only one-quarter (the three months of October through December) of the insurance coverage falls into 2006. The remaining nine months (January to September 2007) of coverage falls into the business's next taxation year — January 1, 2007 to December 31, 2007. You will deduct the remaining $900 of the premium on your 2007 tax return.

Meals and entertainment expenses

Generally, only 50 percent of the amount of meals (including beverages) and entertainment expenses is deductible. Why 50 percent? 'Cause that's the rule! So, say you purchased tickets to a Calgary Stampeders game to take some clients to — only 50 percent of the cost of the tickets would be tax deductible. The same rule applies if you purchase restaurant gift certificates to give away.

Premiums for health-care coverage

If self-employment income is your main source of income, your business can probably take a deduction for the cost of a health-care plan. Claim this expense as part of the "other" category at line 9270 of the T2124.

Automobile expenses

Line 9281 is where you report the automobile expenses of your business. If your business needs a car or van that is used 100 percent of the time in the business — say, to make deliveries — the amount included on line 9281 is simply the total of the expenses to keep the vehicle on the road, such as gas and oil, repairs and maintenance, and insurance. As you'll see below, however, some of your automobile expenses will be restricted — even if the entire use of the vehicle is business related.

Reporting automobile expenses gets a little more complicated when you use your own car, since you likely drive your car for both business and personal reasons.

You can deduct only the "self-employment use" or "business use" portion of your automobile expenses in computing your net income from self-employment. It is essential that you track the kilometres you drive for self-employment and the total kilometres driven in the year so that, come tax time, you will know what proportion of your car expenses can be deducted. In other words:

$$\frac{\text{Total car expenses} \times \text{self-employment kilometres}}{\text{\# of total kilometres}}$$

If the CRA has questions regarding the portion of your car expenses claimed on your T2124, it will want to see a log of your kilometres driven for purposes of operating your business. Get in the habit of having a log in the car, documenting where you are going, where you have been, and the kilometres travelled. It will make things much easier if you ever need to respond to a CRA query.

Car expenses deductible for tax purposes include the following:

- ✔ Fuel (gas, propane, and oil)
- ✔ Repairs and maintenance
- ✔ Insurance
- ✔ Licence and registration fees
- ✔ Leasing costs (within limits)
- ✔ Interest incurred on a loan to purchase a car (within limits)

If you own your car (versus leasing it) and you use it at least partially to carry out business activities, you will also be able to claim capital cost allowance, or CCA. We discuss CCA in detail in a section later in this chapter titled "Capital Cost Allowance (CCA)."

Restrictions on certain automobile expenses

As noted above, where you are entitled to deduct a portion of your automobile costs you deduct only the "business use" portion of the expenses. However, certain automobile expenses have a cap on how much you can use in calculating the business-use portion (even if the business-use portion is 100 percent!).

Specifically, the government has placed restrictions on automobile lease and interest costs because it does not want to permit tax deductions that it considers to be excessive. So if you lease or finance an expensive vehicle, you will find the amount you can deduct for your lease and interest costs restricted to maximum amounts. See Table 9-1 for details.

Table 9-1	Maximum Amounts Deductible for Lease and Interest Costs	
	Leased/Purchased in	
	2001–2006	*2000*
Monthly lease cost	$800	$700
Monthly interest cost	$300	$250

Notes

1. The government reviews these limits annually and announces any changes prior to the end of the year so that taxpayers are aware of the rules in advance of the year in which they apply. The rates are set by Finance Canada and released by press release.

2. All limits are before sales tax. The limits are actually slightly higher when provincial and territorial retail sales tax and GST/HST are added.

The maximum amounts apply *before* you prorate your passenger vehicle expenses between business use and personal use.

Let's look at Angie. Angie is a self-employed commission agent working out of Regina. She sells hair-care products to beauty salons. She sells a number of lines for a variety of hair-care product manufacturers.

On January 1, 2006, Angie leased a BMW. Her monthly lease cost is $875. Angie uses the BMW 75 percent for her self-employment. The effective tax deduction she will have is the $800 per month maximum (see Table 9-1 above) multiplied by her 75 percent self-employment use. This results in a tax deduction equal to $600 per month, or $7,200 for all of 2006.

We have simplified things here. So don't think you can get around the lease restriction rules by making a big deposit before the lease commences or guaranteeing the car will have a higher value than normal at the end of the lease. Both these tactics would bring your monthly lease costs down. However, the actual calculation to determine the maximum lease costs takes these tactics into account. In fact, one of the calculations focuses on the manufacturer's list price of the car. If the car is considered expensive in the government's eyes, you simply have to live with the restrictions on the amounts you can deduct!

Home office expenses

If you operate your business from your home or apartment (a home office), you can deduct a portion of the expenses related to maintaining the home office workspace. This deduction is particularly attractive because you will find that you can get a tax deduction for a portion of the expenses you must incur anyway, such as monthly utilities, rent, and mortgage interest. However, for the costs to be deductible, you must ensure your workspace meets either one of these two tests.

Under the first test, the workspace must be the chief place where your business is carried out. The CRA offers the example of the contractor who runs his own business. A contractor spends a great deal of time fulfilling contracts at customer locations. However, the business functions of receiving work orders, bookkeeping, purchasing, and preparing payrolls may be done at home. In this case, the workspace would qualify as a home office and the contractor could deduct related expenses.

Under the second test your workspace must be used exclusively to carry out your business activities. (Note that the word *exclusively* was not used in the first test.) In addition to using the space exclusively for these activities, you must use the space on a "regular and continuous" basis for meeting customers or others associated with carrying out your business. In the CRA's opinion, infrequent meetings or frequent meetings at irregular intervals are not regular and continuous.

You cannot claim home office expenses to "create or increase a loss" from your business. Say your 2006 business expenses (excluding home office expenses) are greater than your 2006 business income: you have a loss from self-employment. You cannot claim home office expenses to increase the loss. If your non–home office business expenses do not exceed your income, you can claim home office expenses only to the extent that they bring your "net" self-employment income to nil — you cannot create a loss. Any home office expenses that can't be used this year can be carried forward for use in future tax years.

Deductible home office expenses

Subject to the restrictions on deducting home office expenses just mentioned, you can deduct the following expenses:

- ✔ Electricity, heat, and water (utilities)
- ✔ Maintenance costs, condo fees
- ✔ Rent
- ✔ Property tax
- ✔ Insurance on your home or apartment
- ✔ Mortgage interest (but not mortgage principal)

You can deduct only the portion of these expenses that directly relates to your workspace. In most cases you can simply take the square footage of your home office space divided by the total square footage of your home to come up with a reasonable percentage.

Capital Cost Allowance (CCA)

The money you spend in operating your business can be classified in one of two ways:

- ✔ **Day-to-day expenditures of running the business:** These expenditures are not considered to have a future value and are therefore "expenses" of your business. Most of these expenses are noted on lines 8521 to 9270 on form T2124. Examples of day-to-day expenditures include salaries paid to employees, office rent, lease payments, bank charges, travel, and telephone.

- ✔ **Capital expenditures:** Capital expenditures are made when you purchase a capital asset — an asset that has an expected useful life that will extend beyond the end of your business's taxation year. Common examples of capital assets are computers, office equipment (photocopiers, fax machines), office furniture, buildings, and machinery. As the value provided by these assets is expected to extend past the end of your business taxation year, you cannot take a full deduction for these expenditures in one year. However, as we detail below, you are allowed to deduct a "portion" of the cost of a capital asset for each taxation year it is used in your business. The calculation of the portion that can be deducted on your tax return is called capital cost allowance (CCA).

Capital cost allowance, or CCA, is simply tax lingo for "depreciation" and "amortization." These are terms often used by accountants. Remember this next time you are at a party and want to impress someone with your vast knowledge!

Your business can claim CCA on almost all capital assets purchased (one exception is land). And, of course, the asset must have been acquired for use in your business — not for personal use.

Eligible capital property (ECP) describes assets that do not physically exist. They are referred to as intangible assets and include such items as the purchase of goodwill, a customer or patient list, a marketing quota or government right, and an unlimited franchise, concession, or licence. Technically, you don't claim CCA on ECP, but a special deduction similar to CCA is allowed. The starting point for the deduction is 75 percent of the cost of ECP. The deduction you are allowed is 7 percent of this amount, on a declining basis each year.

Calculating CCA — The declining balance method

For most types of assets, you calculate CCA using the declining balance method of depreciation. The costs of specific types of assets (which is generally the purchase price but can also include freight costs, duty and customs fees, retail sales taxes, and even GST/HST if your business is not a GST/HST registrant) are grouped together to calculate the CCA deduction. And, you guessed it — the government dictates which "class" those specific types of assets go into.

For example, say your business purchased a meeting room table and bunch of chairs. The table and chairs, both being "office furniture," would be treated as one asset, or "pool." CCA is then calculated on the pool balance multiplied by a legislated percentage rate. The remaining "pool balance" is carried to the next year, where again the same percentage is applied to calculate the CCA. Since the pool balance on which the CCA claim is based declines each year, the method is referred to as the declining balance method. This method results in higher CCA deductions in the early years of a capital asset purchase, and lower and lower amounts as the asset ages.

 If your business incurs costs to make rented premises more workable, such costs are referred to as *leasehold improvements*. Leasehold improvements are not depreciated using the declining balance method. Instead, CCA is calculated as the lesser of the following:

1) $$\frac{\text{cost of leasehold improvements}}{5}$$

2) $$\frac{\text{cost of leasehold improvements}}{\text{\# of years in lease + \# years in first renewal period}}$$

 To maximize the speed at which CCA is claimed on your leasehold improvements, negotiate your lease to be a maximum of four years with a renewal period of one year.

CCA is calculated as of the *last* day of your business's taxation year. The CCA calculation is based on the balance of the CCA class at the end of the taxation year. There is no need to do separate CCA calculations for capital assets owned for only part of a taxation year (although the "half-year rule," which we discuss later, does take care of assets purchased during the year). However, if you were not in business for the full year (say you just started up on September 1), you do need to prorate your CCA for your shorter-than-365-day year. In this case you would take your total CCA times 122 days/365 days.

Common CCA classes and rates

For simplicity, the government has assigned CCA class numbers to similar groups of assets (CCA classes).

- ✔ **Buildings:** Class 1: 4 percent

- ✔ **Fences:** Class 6: 10 percent

- ✔ **Boats:** Class 7: 15 percent

- ✔ **Office equipment and furniture:** Class 8: 20 percent (All capital assets eligible for CCA are included in class 8 if they do not fall into any of the other CCA classes.)

- ✔ **Cars, trucks, computer hardware, and systems software acquired before March 23, 2004:** Class 10: 30 percent. (There is a maximum amount that can be used for the capital cost of a car in terms of calculating CCA. We discuss this later in the chapter under "Restriction on the maximum capital cost of a class 10.1 automobile.")

- ✔ **Computer hardware and systems software acquired after March 22, 2004:** Class 45: 45 percent

- ✔ **Computer applications software, uniforms, linens, dies, jigs, moulds, rental videos, and tools under $200:** Class 12: 100 percent

  For purchases after May 2, 2006, the cost limit for tools eligible for the 100 percent CCA rate is increased to $500. Tools, under this new rule, include kitchen utensils and medical and dental instruments, but not computer-related items.

- ✔ **Manufacturing equipment:** Class 43: 30 percent

A CCA example

CCA can best be explained through an example. Let's continue with your business's purchase of a meeting room table and chairs. Remember that the total cost was $1,200. In preparing your tax return for 2006, you know that you cannot deduct the full $1,200 on form T2124 in determining your net income from self-employment. The meeting room table and chairs are good quality (for $1,200? hmm) and probably can be used in your business for several years. In fact, the chairs have a 10-year warranty!

Office furniture is considered a CCA class 8 capital asset with a CCA rate of 20 percent. (You're forced to accept the 20 percent rate whether the chairs are expected to last 5 years, 10 years, or 30 years!)

You would think you could calculate CCA as simply 20 percent of $1,200, or $240. However, there's a catch — it's a special rule called the "half-year" rule. Let's look at what this rule says.

The "half-year" rule dictates that when calculating CCA for the year in which the asset is purchased, only one-half (or 50 percent) of the CCA can be claimed. So, the correct way to calculate the 2006 CCA claim on the office furniture is $1,200 \times 20\% \times 50\% = $120.

Undepreciated capital cost (UCC)

Undepreciated capital cost is the term used to describe the amount of the capital cost at the end of a taxation year to which CCA has not yet been applied. In our CCA class 8 office furniture example, the UCC at December 31, 2006, would be $1,080. It is calculated as follows:

Undepreciated capital cost (UCC) at

January 1, 2006 (assumed)	$nil
Capital cost of additions in 2006	$1,200
Capital cost allowance (CCA) claimed in 2006 (1,200 × 20% × 50%)	($120)
Undepreciated capital cost (UCC) at December 31, 2006	$1,080

In 2007, assuming no further purchases or sales are made, CCA of $216 ($1,080 × 20%) can be claimed.

Sale of capital assets

Let's continue with our CCA class 8 office furniture example to show what happens when an asset used in your business is sold. Say you decided to upgrade the meeting room table and chairs in 2007. Your new table and chairs cost $1,700. The old table and chairs were sold to a used office furniture retailer for $750.

When a capital asset is sold, the UCC is reduced by the lower of the following:

- ✔ The original capital cost of the assets sold (remember, this was $1,200)
- ✔ The sale price — the $750 noted above

When an asset is sold, the half-year rule comes into play once again.

UCC at January 1, 2007 (same as at December 31, 2006)	$1,080	
Add: Additions	$1,700	
Sale of chairs:		
Lesser of:		
Original cost:	$1,200	
Proceeds:	$750	($750)
CCA claim for 2007:		
$1,080 × 20% = $216		
($1,700 – $750) × 20% × 50% =	$95	($311)
Closing UCC (UCC at December 31, 2007)	<u>$1,719</u>	

As illustrated above, if you purchase and dispose of an asset in the same CCA class during the year, you must net the addition and disposal together before applying the half-year rule.

Recapture and terminal loss

So now you know how to handle the CCA calculation when assets are purchased and sold. You can see that as long as assets are purchased for a higher cost than the sale price of previously purchased assets, the UCC will never reduce to nil. However, what if your business sells *all* the assets in a CCA class and does not replace them? Well, two things can happen:

- ✔ **You sell all the assets in a class for *less* than the UCC balance.**

  Let's assume that in 2007 you decide not to upgrade your meeting room table and chairs. You admit to yourself that you don't like meeting clients, so the best way not to meet clients is to get rid of your meeting room furniture. (Perhaps not a good career move, but it works with the example.) Remember, the table and chairs originally cost $1,200. Again, assume you sell the whole set for $750. In this case, the following would happen:

Opening UCC at January 1, 2007	$1,080
(same as UCC at December 31, 2006)	

Sale of chairs:

Lesser of:

Original cost:	$1,200
Proceeds:	$750
Lesser:	($750)
UCC balance after sale	$330

Since you sold all the assets in this class, you shouldn't have any UCC left — there is nothing left to depreciate. However, you have $330 remaining. What this means is that you didn't depreciate the assets fast enough. Therefore, the taxman lets you make this up, by allowing you to claim the full amount remaining as a deduction. After all, you were only using the rate they set — why shouldn't you get the deduction? The $330 is referred to as the *terminal loss* and is fully tax deductible as part of your total CCA claim.

✔ **You sell the assets for *more* than the UCC balance.**

What happens if you sell the table and chairs for $1,800? Sounds good, but there is a downfall. Let's look at the calculation again:

UCC at January 1, 2007	$1,080
(same as UCC at December 31, 2006)	

Sale of chairs:

Lesser of:

Original cost:	$1,200
Proceeds:	$1,800
Lesser:	($1,200)
UCC balance after sale	($120)

See what's happened? Again, you sold everything in the asset pool, so your UCC balance should clear to zero. However, you have a negative UCC balance. This means you've taken too much CCA — the assets did not depreciate as fast as the taxman thought they would. Obviously, the CRA won't let you have too much of a good thing, so it will ask for the extra CCA that you took back (hence the term "recapture") by adding the negative UCC to your income in the year the asset is disposed. Oh, well!

If you sell an asset for more than its original cost, you may also have a capital gain to report. See Chapter 7 for more details.

Restriction on the maximum capital cost of a class 10.1 automobile

The government does not want you driving an expensive car and being able to write off a significant portion in CCA in determining your self-employment income. Therefore, the amount of CCA that can be claimed on an automobile is restricted in certain situations. If you buy a car where the cost exceeds a certain threshold amount, that car cannot go in the regular Class 10 for CCA purposes. Instead, it must go into a special class – namely Class 10.1 – where special rules apply. The threshold amounts are shown in Table 9-2 below. As you can see, if you buy a car in 2006 that costs more than $30,000, you will be allowed to use only $30,000 as your capital cost. The excess can never be written off for tax purposes. The CRA periodically adjusts the maximum amount to take into account rising car prices.

Table 9-2	Maximum Amounts on Which CCA Can Be Claimed on Automobiles	
	Automobiles Purchased in	
	2001–2006	*2000*
Maximum capital cost amount for purposes of claiming CCA on an automobile	$30,000	$26,000

The above limits are before provincial/territorial retail sales tax and GST/HST. If you purchased a car in Ontario, for example, after June 30, 2006, you would pay an 8 percent Ontario sales tax and the 6 percent GST — a total of 14 percent (purchases prior to July 1, 2006, were subject to a 7 percent GST as well as the 8 percent provincial sales tax). The deemed maximum capital cost for claiming CCA on your car purchase in 2006 would be:

- ✔ **For cars leased before July 1, 2006:** $34,500 ($30,000 × 115 percent = $34,500).

- ✔ **For cars leased after June 30, 2006:** $34,200 ($30,000 × 114 percent = $34,200).

Special rules in calculating CCA on class 10.1 automobiles

Keep in mind a few special rules when you're tallying up CCA on your class 10.1 automobile. Have a look to see if any of these circumstances apply to you:

- Calculate CCA on each car on its own. If your business used two cars and they both had an actual capital cost above the limits, your business would have two CCA class 10.1 calculations to make. The purchase or sale of one class 10.1 automobile does not impact the CCA calculation of another CCA class 10.1 automobile.

- Unlike other capital assets, when a class 10.1 automobile is sold, you don't have to calculate recapture or terminal loss. (If you've forgotten, we discussed how recapture and terminal loss was calculated a few pages back.

- Normally when an asset is sold, you are not allowed to claim CCA on that asset. However, for a class 10.1 asset, a special rule allows you to claim one-half of the CCA you would have otherwise been allowed to deduct had you continued to own the asset.

Lines 137 and 164: Reporting Professional Income

The term *professional income* refers to the net income earned by a professional. So who's a professional? The CRA does not provide an exact definition. However, it is fairly safe to say a professional is a person who earns fees from an occupation for which he or she had to go to school for a long time before being "certified," "licensed," or somehow approved to do what he or she does. If you are a professional, you make most of your money from providing services rather than selling goods. The CRA offers these examples of professionals: accountants, dentists, lawyers, medical doctors, chiropractors, and veterinarians.

Essentially, professionals calculate their net income from their profession the same way as most self-employed individuals calculate their business income. The comments we have made in this chapter so far with respect to calculating business income apply equally to those who report professional income on their tax return.

There are two main differences in reporting professional income as opposed to business income:

- ✔ Use form T2032, "Statement of Professional Activities," in place of form T2124.
- ✔ Professionals may need to deal with work-in-progress (WIP), which we explain below.

Form T2032, "Statement of Professional Activities"

Form T2032 is similar in design to the T2124 ("Statement of Business Activities"). In fact, the numeric line references on T2032 are identical to those on T2124. It is expected that a professional does not sell goods, so the T2032 has no section to compute the cost of goods sold.

The income section of the T2032 includes lines to allow you to correctly account for work-in-progress (WIP).

Work-in-progress (WIP)

A unique characteristic of a professional is his or her ability to claim an amount for *work-in-progress (WIP)*. WIP represents a professional's unbilled time. Say what? A professional's fees are usually based on time. The value of WIP is based on a professional's fees that have been earned but not yet billed.

We'll walk you through this one by looking at the case of Richard — Rick, for short — who is a lawyer specializing in family law in Windsor, Ontario. Rick schedules an appointment on December 31, 2006, to meet with Caroline.

Before they meet, Rick explains to Caroline that the meeting will be an hour in length and that his rate is $200 per hour. Coincidentally, the year-end for Rick's practice is December 31. At the end of the meeting, Caroline offers to pay the $200. Rick suggests she wait for a bill that he will get to her in mid-January 2007. Caroline agrees — she likes the idea of keeping her $200 a little longer. (A lawyer not taking money? Whassup? The reason will become obvious in a tip noted soon!) After the meeting Rick records the one hour of time in his bookkeeping system. In entering the time, he records $200 of work-in-progress and $200 of fee revenue earned.

Because Rick has only recorded the time but has not billed it, the amount is not yet receivable from Caroline. It will become receivable once the bill is issued to her in mid-January 2007.

Let's assume that for his year ended December 31, 2006, Rick has billed all of his clients except Caroline. (Yes, this is unrealistic, but bear with us as we make a point!) Rick's total fees billed in 2006 are $200,000. On line A of schedule T2032, he reports revenue of $200,200. This is because Rick has earned the $200,000 he has billed to his other clients *plus* the $200 he has yet to bill Caroline. Remember, under the accrual method of accounting you report revenue on an "as earned" basis.

When a professional has significant work-in-progress, he or she may end up paying a great deal of tax on income for which a bill has not been rendered. The tax rules recognize this problem and permit certain professionals to deduct year-end WIP in calculating their gross income subject to tax in the year. The WIP that was deducted in the prior year must be added back in calculating gross income for the current year.

Let's continue with Rick. Assume that back on December 31, 2005, Rick's previous tax year-end, he had $50 in WIP.

Rick would calculate his 2006 gross income subject to tax in the following way:

Professional fees — includes WIP — at December 31, 2006 (line A on form T2032)	$200,200
Minus WIP at December 31, 2006	($200)
	$200,000
Plus WIP at beginning of taxation year (WIP at January 1, 2006, would equal WIP at December 31, 2005)	$50
Gross income (line 8299 on form T2032)	$200,050

So, a professional deducts WIP from gross income at the end of a taxation year to calculate his or her net income from self-employment. If the professional delays billing clients for services rendered in one year until the next year, he or she will defer the tax payable on those services for one year. This is an especially good tax planning idea when tax rates are dropping from one year to the next. The tax is deferred, plus it is subject to a lower rate! However, the longer you wait to bill, the longer you wait for the cash. Make sure your business's cash flow is okay before considering such a tax deferral strategy.

Lines 139 and 166: Commission Income

If you earn self-employed commission income, you will detail all of your income and expenses on the T2124, "Statement of Business Activities," just like for any other business. The good news is that if you've already read the section on business income, you're now an expert! There are no additional special rules for commission income.

Just because you earn commission income does not mean that you have to report it as self-employment income. Many commissioned salespeople are actually employees. Not sure of your status? If you've received a T4 slip outlining your commissions, you're an employee. Although you'll find you have more tax deductions if you are self-employed, commissioned employees are also allowed to deduct some of their expenditures for tax purposes. We discuss some of the more common deductions available to commissioned employees in Chapter 10.

Lines 141 and 168: Farming Income

Lines 141 and 168 are where a farmer reports gross and net income figures. If you're operating a farm business — which can include activities such as soil tilling, raising livestock, or even beekeeping — Form T2042, "Statement of Farming Activities," is for you!

Method of accounting

If you are a farmer, you can use the cash method of accounting rather than the accrual method to calculate the net income of your farm business. If you used the accrual method in a prior taxation year, you can switch to the cash method. However, to

switch from the cash method to the accrual method you need
permission from the CRA.

Form T2042, "Statement of Farming Activities"

Form T2042 serves the same purpose as T2124, "Statement of
Business Activities." The form simply acts as a schedule to summarize the income and expenses of operating a farm. We'll detail
some of the unique features of T2042 below.

The Mandatory Inventory Adjustment (MIA — Line 9942)

The MIA applies only to those in farming who record their income
and expenses in the cash method of accounting.

Why is there an inventory adjustment? The impact of the inventory
adjustment rules is to reduce the amount of net loss a farm business
can have. (*Warning:* Do not mix up the inventory adjustment rules
with "restricted farm losses." We discuss restricted farm losses
later.) Why do the rules work to minimize a farm loss? Like any self-
employment loss, a farm loss can be used to offset other sources of
income you may have — interest, dividends, capital gains, pension,
or perhaps employment income or other sources of self-employment
income. A large farm loss could significantly reduce your taxable
income — which, of course, reduces the tax you pay. You can see
why there would be rules to prevent this! In using the cash method of
accounting, inventory is ignored. When preparing a T2042 using the
cash method of accounting, you deduct the cost of all items purchased for resale — even if they remain unsold at the end of the year.

Say you purchase a number of calves during the year as part of your
beef cattle farm operation. You may keep these for a year or a year
and a half before they are sold. If you are operating a dairy farm,
you may hold on to your cattle for a number of years before they
are sold. Under the cash method, the amounts paid are deducted
fully in the year purchased. Where significant purchases are made
in a year, the farm loss could be, well, significant! (And that's no
bull . . . okay, sorry.)

The MIA rules work to minimize the amount of loss that can be
claimed when, at the end of the year, products purchased for
resale have not yet been sold.

An MIA must be made on your 2006 T2042 if the following exist:

- There is a net loss reported on line 9899 of the T2042.
- At the end of your 2006 taxation year, you had inventory on hand.

The MIA is calculated as the lesser of the following:

- The net loss reported on line 9899 of the T2042
- The market value of the inventory at the end of the taxation year.

You can see that where the farm inventory is at least equal to the loss on line 9899, the MIA will wipe out the farm loss.

Optional Inventory Adjustment (OIA — Line 9941)

Like the MIA, the OIA is an addition you make to your line 9899 net income or loss for 2006. The amount would be deducted on your 2007 tax return.

The maximum amount of the 2006 OIA addition is equal to the market value of inventory at the end of the taxation year less the Mandatory Inventory Adjustment (MIA).

Why would someone decrease his or her farm loss by making an OIA? Good question! Remember, an OIA added to net income or loss in the year is a deduction in the subsequent year. If the expectation is that the net income of the farm will be higher next year, a deduction may prove more valuable next year because the deduction will be worth more in tax savings when it can shelter farm income subject to tax at a higher marginal rate.

What if your farming business has a loss?

A unique rule regarding self-employment income generated from farming is the treatment of losses. If your farm operated at a loss for 2006, the net loss would appear on line 9946 of T2042. This may not be the amount you carry to line 141 on page 2 of your tax return. Your farming loss may fall into one of these three categories:

- Fully deductible
- Partly deductible
- Non-deductible

As with other self-employment income activities, for your net farm loss to be deductible you must operate your farm as a business. The CRA considers you to be in the business of farming if there is no personal element to your farming activities and you are running the farm as a commercial endeavour.

If you are operating your farm as a business, and farming is your chief source of income in a year, your loss would be fully deductible.

Part-time farmer — The "restricted farm loss" rules

The CRA considers farming to not be your chief source of income when you do not rely on farming alone for your livelihood. If you have other sources of income, such as employment income or other sources of self-employment income, farming would not be considered your main source of income.

When you operate your farm as a business but farming is not your chief source of income in the year, the loss you claim will be "restricted." In other words, the maximum loss you can claim on your tax return will be less than your actual loss — your actual loss will be partly deductible. Any denied loss is called a "restricted farm loss."

Whether your farm loss is fully or partly deductible is a question to answer each year. In some years farming may be your chief source of income, and in some years it may not.

The maximum loss that you can claim if farming is not your chief source of income is calculated as follows:

100% of the first $2,500 of the loss + 50% of the remaining loss

The maximum loss that can be claimed is $8,750. If you are mathematically inclined you can calculate that to be able to deduct $8,750 you would need to have at least a $15,000 actual farm loss. Any farm loss more than the farm loss you can claim is called a *restricted farm loss.*

A restricted farm loss can be used to reduce any net farm income you may have reported in the three prior years — 2005, 2004, and 2003. And thanks to the 2006 federal budget, restricted farm losses incurred in 2006 and after can be carried forward for up to 20 years.

To carry a loss back (referred to as a *loss carryback*) to any or all of these years, you must complete form T1A, "Request for Loss Carryback," and file it with your 2006 tax return.

When your farm loss is not deductible at all

As noted above, for your farm to be considered a business it must not be a personal endeavour and must be undertaken in pursuit of a profit. When the farm is not being run as a commercial endeavour, and losses are being incurred, the expenses are considered personal expenses and are not deductible at all. No carryback or carryforward provisions are available. Generally, "farmers" in this category include those who do not look to farming as their chief source of income and consider farming to be only a hobby.

To determine whether farming is your chief source of income the CRA will look to a number of factors, including time spent, capital committed, and profitability (both actual and expected).

Lines 143 and 170: Fishing Income

In this final section of the chapter we look at the tax rules that apply to those earning self-employment income from fishing.

What is fishing income?

What does the CRA consider fishing income? Let's take a close look. This category includes the following:

- ✔ Amounts received from the sale of fish, lobster, scallops, and so on;
- ✔ Amounts received from other marine products: Irish moss, herring scales, herring roe, seal meat and flippers, seaweed, kelp, roe on kelp, and so on.

If your self-employment income is earned from fishing activities, you report your income in the same fashion as do other self-employed individuals — with a few differences. This section highlights some of these differences. As with farming, you can use the cash method of accounting to calculate the net income of your fishing business.

T2121, "Statement of Fishing Activities"

This form is used to report the income and expenses of your fishing business. It is similar to T2124, "Statement of Business Activities."

Expenses

Enter details of expenses on page 2 of the T2121. The expense categories provided are customized a little to reflect items of a fishy nature (okay, we had to say that). For example, the expense categories include "bait, ice, salt, crew shares, gear, and nets and traps."

Food

The cost of food provided to your crew when you fish offshore is deductible. Food provided on-shore is deductible provided you considered the food a taxable benefit to your employees.

If a benefit is considered taxable, you must include the value in the employee's total employment income reported on his or her T4 slip. You can still claim a deduction when you do not consider the food a taxable benefit, provided your boat is at sea for 36 hours.

Nets and traps

Nets and traps are considered to include lines, hooks, buoys, and anchors. Line 9137 on the T2121 is where your fishing business can claim a deduction for nets and traps. However, the full cost of the nets and traps acquired in the year cannot be deducted. The amount that can be deducted is determined under one of two methods:

- ✔ **CCA method:** Your business treats its nets and traps as a capital asset and claims capital cost allowance (CCA). Nets and traps are CCA class 8 capital assets. The CCA rate for class 8 is 20 percent. We discuss CCA earlier in the chapter.

- ✔ **Inventory method:** Nets and traps are considered inventory. At the end of each taxation year, the value of all the nets and traps is determined. If the value is less than the inventoried cost, a deduction is claimed on line 9137 for the loss in value.

Chapter 10

Tips for Deductions to Calculate Net Income

- -

In This Chapter

▶ Understanding what "net income" is and its importance

▶ Making the most out of RRSPs

▶ Writing off child-care expenses

▶ Benefiting from your moving costs

▶ Ensuring you are up to date on the deduction for support payments

▶ Knowing when your legal expenses are tax deductible

▶ Deducting your employment expenses

▶ Getting a rebate of GST/HST you've paid

- -

*S*o what, exactly, is net income — aside from line 236 on your tax return? It is the amount you arrive at when you subtract from your total income (line 150) the deductions permitted on lines 207 to 235. You would think that this is the amount of income on which you should pay tax. Well, no. The amount you pay tax on is your taxable income from line 260. We discuss the calculation of taxable income in Chapter 11. (The good news: taxable income can never exceed net income!)

Why is calculating your net income so important? Even though we don't pay tax based on net income, it is an essential calculation. Take a look — this one calculation influences these amounts:

✔ Provincial or territorial tax credits you can take advantage of (Chapter 14, line 479)

✔ GST/HST credit you are entitled to (Chapter 13, line 457)

✔ Medical expenses you can claim (Chapter 12, lines 330 and 331)

✔ Refundable medical expenses supplement you can claim (Chapter 13, line 452)

✔ Charitable donations you can claim (Chapter 12, line 349)

✔ Social benefits you must repay (Chapter 5, Old Age Security; Chapter 8, Employment Insurance benefits)

✔ Spousal credit your spouse or common-law partner can claim in respect of you (Chapter 12, line 303)

✔ Eligible dependant credit another person may be able to claim for supporting you (Chapter 12, line 305)

✔ Disability amount available for transfer from you to another person (Chapter 12, line 318)

The lower your net income, the better off you are in terms of minimizing your tax liability and taking advantage of some of the above-noted tax credits! Don't miss taking any tax deductions you are entitled to!

Let's walk through the tax deductions available in calculating your net income, line by line.

Line 206: Pension Adjustment

Okay, so maybe the pension adjustment isn't the best place to start, but 206 is the first line in this section of your tax return. You see, this line really doesn't provide a tax deduction. In fact, line 206 is a *disclosure line* only. (A disclosure line on a tax return is where there is a requirement to note a figure, but that figure will not have an impact on the calculation of your tax liability or refund.) So what is the point of disclosing your pension adjustment here? Well, your pension adjustment (which shows up on your T4 slip) reduces your 2007 RRSP contribution limit — the amount that you can contribute to an RRSP in 2007 and get a full tax deduction.

Generally, the *pension adjustment* (PA) is the increase in value of your retirement benefits under a *Registered Pension Plan* (RPP) or *Deferred Profit-Sharing Plan* (DPSP). RPPs and DPSPs are plans set up by employers to assist employees in saving for retirement. As the value of your RPP/DPSP increases, the amount you can contribute to your RRSP decreases. The PA is a component used in the formula to calculate your RRSP deduction limit. The pension adjustment reported on your 2006 T4 will reduce your 2007 RRSP deduction limit on a dollar-for-dollar basis.

When you receive your tax assessment from the CRA after filing your 2006 tax return, you will see that the 2006 PA amount you disclosed when filing your tax return is included in the formula to calculate your 2007 RRSP deduction limit.

A *pension adjustment reversal* (PAR) often arises when you leave an employer where you were a member of the company pension plan. A PAR indicates that the pension adjustments (PAs) reported on your T4s over the years were too high — this means that your pension adjustments were overstated, so your RRSP deduction limits were understated. The PAR simply corrects the understatement in your RRSP deduction limit. In fact, a PAR indicates your RRSP deduction limit is being increased — this is good news!

Your employer must send you a T10 slip to report your PAR to you within 60 days after the end of the calendar year quarter in which you left your job. If you left your job in the final quarter, you should receive your T10 slip by January 30.

Line 207: Registered Pension Plan (RPP) Deduction

Enter on line 207 the amount that *you* paid into your RPP during 2006. The amount you paid into your RPP will usually be noted in box 20 of your T4 slip from your employer. It may also be reported in box 32 of T4A slips you received or on receipts provided by your union or the pension plan itself.

The full amount noted on the tax information slips is usually tax deductible. This may not be the case under the following circumstances:

- ✔ The amount is greater than $19,000
- ✔ Your T4 or T4A slip indicates a past-service amount for services provided before 1990

Contributions to your pension plan for past services are considered "past-service contributions," meaning the contributions were made for work you did in prior years. The contributions, made by you, are generally made to upgrade the pension benefits you'll be entitled to in the future. Past-service contributions are often made in a lump sum. You may hear people refer to past-service contributions as "buying back service," or buying increased pension benefits — paying some money now for an increased pension down the road.

Ask your pension plan administrator if you are entitled to buy back any service. Based on your age, your years to retirement, length of service, and the dollars involved, it can be beneficial in terms of your future pension entitlement to buy back service!

Contributions for current service and past service for 1990 and later years

Your total contributions for current service and past service for 1990 and later years can usually be found in box 20 of the T4 slips you received from your employer. The full amount is to be included on line 207 of your tax return.

Past-service contributions for years before 1990

If your current and past-service contributions for 1990 and later years exceed $3,500, you will find that none of your past-service contribution for years before 1990 is deductible on your current-year tax return. However, all is not lost! Those contributions will be eligible for deduction in 2007 and subsequent years.

Line 208: Registered Retirement Savings Plan (RRSP) Deduction

Next to the ability to sell your house tax-free due to the principal residence exemption (see Chapter 7), the RRSP is Canada's best tax shelter. Yes, we said tax shelter. Many people believe a tax shelter is some very creative (perhaps sleazy) tax planning idea available only to the wealthy. Not true! Almost every taxpayer who has a job or is self-employed can take advantage of RRSPs.

What is an RRSP?

To easily understand what a registered retirement savings plan (RRSP) is, think of it as your own personal pension plan that has been CRA-approved ("registered"). An RRSP is an arrangement that allows you to save for your retirement on a tax-friendly basis when you've earned certain types of income but haven't necessarily been able to contribute to an employer's pension plan.

Tax savings provided by RRSPs

The government wants you to save for your retirement. To encourage this, an RRSP offers two main tax advantages:

- ✔ A tax deduction for contributions made to an RRSP
- ✔ Tax-free growth while the funds remain in the RRSP

With an RRSP, no tax is payable until you make a withdrawal from your plan. (We talk more about RRSP withdrawals in Chapter 8.) You hope that the tax payable on RRSP withdrawals will be less than the tax saved when you took the deduction for making an RRSP contribution. This will occur if you will be in a lower tax bracket during your retirement years than the tax bracket you were in when you made your RRSP contributions.

A better idea is to have the withdrawal taxed in your spouse's hands if he or she will be in a lower tax bracket than you are at the time of the withdrawal. This is especially advantageous if you already have significant retirement income (say, pension income from an RPP) and your spouse has little. We know this sounds too good to be true, but you can do it by making spousal RRSP contributions. Spousal RRSP contributions are discussed later in this chapter.

Setting up an RRSP

Are you reading this after December 31, 2006? Don't worry — it's not too late to set up an RRSP and get a tax deduction for 2006! Contributions made to an RRSP on or before March 1, 2007, qualify for a tax deduction on your 2006 tax return. (Neat, eh?)

You can set up an RRSP in many places: a bank, a trust company, or through your investment planner. It is as simple as filling out a form and handing over the money. After you contribute to the RRSP, you will be provided with an "official RRSP receipt." This is what you will use to support the RRSP deduction that you claim on your 2006 tax return.

Self-directed RRSPs

Banks and trust companies commonly offer deposit-based RRSPs. The money you contribute is usually invested in a number of investment vehicles, although the choice may be limited. If you would prefer more diversity and flexibility in your RRSP investing, you should consider a "self-directed RRSP." Don't worry — "self-directed" does not mean that you are on your own. You can work with your investment adviser to decide which investments are appropriate for your RRSP given your investment goals and risk-tolerance levels. For example, you may choose a variety of mutual funds, stocks, bonds, other specialty investments, or even cash to hold in your RRSP.

There is an annual cost to maintain a self-directed RRSP, so in order to justify this cost you should generally wait until your RRSP assets reach $20,000 before setting up this type of plan.

RRSP contributions in kind

Wanna set up an RRSP or contribute to an existing RRSP, but find yourself short on funds? Well, provided you already own an investment that is eligible for an RRSP (we provide a list below), why not contribute the investment itself to your RRSP? This is called a *contribution in kind.* But be careful. If you contribute an investment that has gone up in value from the time you acquired it, a capital gain (see Chapter 7) will be triggered that will be taxed on your 2006 return. If the investment has gone down in value, you would think you would be entitled to a capital loss. No such luck. Why not? Because the taxman says so.

If you are thinking about contributing investments that have declined in value, you should sell the investment, claim the loss, and then donate the cash. This way, you won't lose out on claiming the capital loss. Don't repurchase that same investment back in the RRSP, though. This will mean you still won't be allowed to claim your capital loss. Instead, use the cash to repurchase something similar (but not the identical investment) — or, if you'd prefer, something totally different — inside your RRSP.

What investments are "RRSP eligible"?

An RRSP is not an investment in itself; the money you put into it must be used to purchase investments. The following is a list of investments that you may hold inside your RRSP:

- ✔ Cash, guaranteed investment certificates, term deposits, Treasury bills
- ✔ Canada Savings Bonds, Canada RRSP bonds, and government bonds
- ✔ Publicly traded shares and bonds, warrants, options, and Canadian limited partnerships
- ✔ Certain private corporation shares, as long as you and your family own less than 10 percent
- ✔ Mutual funds, segregated funds, and labour-sponsored funds
- ✔ Certain mortgages, including a mortgage on your own home
- ✔ Investment-grade gold and silver bullion coins and bars (great news for all you pirates out there!)

Prior to 2005, you were permitted to hold a maximum of 30 percent in foreign investments in your RRSPs and other tax-deferred retirement plans, or face a penalty. The remainder was required to be Canadian content. This was known as the foreign property or foreign content rule. Foreign property investments included foreign company shares, and mutual funds investing primarily in foreign companies. To increase the investment choices for Canadians within their retirement plans, this rule was eliminated for 2005 and subsequent tax years. Since you now have more flexibility in choosing foreign investments for your RRSP, it's a good time to take a close look at your investment choices, perhaps with the help of a financial adviser, to ensure your retirement funds are well diversified.

If your RRSP holds an ineligible investment, it will be subject to a tax of 1 percent per month on the value of the ineligible investment.

How much can you contribute to your RRSP?

By now you might be convinced that an RRSP would be a great way for you to save for your retirement and to gain some tax benefits. So, why not sell the farm, so to speak, and put all your net worth into the RRSP? Well, slow down, Nelly. Not just anyone can set up an RRSP, and there are limits to how much you can contribute.

Generally, any person who has "earned income" in Canada can contribute to an RRSP. The amount that you are allowed to contribute is based on a formula involving three numbers:

- 18 percent of your prior year's "earned income," to a dollar limit maximum set by the Department of Finance (the maximum for 2006 is $18,000);

- Less the pension adjustment, PA (discussed above at line 206); and

- Plus the pension adjustment reversal, PAR (also discussed above at line 206).

What is earned income and how is it calculated?

The main consideration in determining your RRSP deduction limit is 18 percent of your prior year's "earned income." For purposes of determining your RRSP deduction limit, earned income consists of the following:

- Your salary, including taxable benefits (box 14 of your T4);

- Self-employed business income;

- Rental income and royalty income;

- Taxable spouse and child-support payments received;

- Amounts from supplementary unemployment benefit plans;

- Research grants; and

- CPP and QPP disability pension (see Chapter 5).

To compute earned income, deduct the following:

- Union or professional dues deducted on your tax return (line 212);

- Employment expenses deducted on your tax return (line 229);

✔ Losses from self-employment (see Chapter 9);

✔ Losses from rental operations (see Chapter 8); and

✔ Support payments deducted on your tax return (line 220).

Limit set by the Department of Finance

As mentioned above, the maximum amount that can be contributed to an RRSP in a given year is limited by earned income and amounts set by the government.

The maximum amount you may contribute to your RRSP will increase in future years (although you are still limited to 18 percent of your earned income). The limit for 2006 is $18,000. The limits are scheduled to rise as follows:

2007	$19,000
2008	$20,000
2009	$21,000
2010	$22,000
2011	indexed to inflation

Finding out your 2006 RRSP contribution limit

There are four ways to find out your 2006 RRSP contribution limit:

✔ **Look at your 2005 Notice of Assessment:** You would have received your assessment from the CRA after filing your 2005 return. Your 2006 RRSP contribution limit is highlighted on the assessment. Any unused RRSP deduction room from prior years is added in to compute your contribution limit. Although you can carry forward all your unused RRSP contribution room, don't wait to make your RRSP contribution. By contributing today, you'll reap the benefits of an immediate tax saving from your RRSP deduction and tax-free growth while your money is inside your RRSP.

✔ **Call the TIPS (Tax Information Phone Service) toll-free number** (1-800-267-6999) and ask what your limit is.

✔ **Calculate it yourself.**

✔ **Go to My Account on the CRA Website** (www.cra-arc.gc.ca).

Overcontributions to your RRSP

Generally, the amount you contribute to your RRSP will be equal to the RRSP deduction you will take on line 208 of your return. However, the total amount you have contributed to your RRSP may exceed the amount you claim as a deduction if you do one of the following:

✔ **You accidentally overcontribute to your RRSP:** You are permitted to overcontribute to your RRSP. However, the overcontribution is not tax deductible in the year it is made. And if your overcontribution exceeds $2,000, you will find yourself in a penalty situation if you don't withdraw the excess contribution. The penalty is 1 percent per month of the overcontribution in excess of $2,000 — that amounts to 12 percent per year!

Many people will overcontribute by exactly $2,000, since there will be no penalty and the funds can earn income inside the RRSP tax-free. Moreover, the $2,000 can be deducted on a subsequent year's tax return where you may not have contributed up to your maximum.

✔ **You don't deduct some or all of the RRSP contribution you have made:** Why would you not take a tax deduction when it is available? Well, you may plan on being in a higher tax bracket in the future. Even though you make an RRSP contribution during the year, you don't need to take the deduction that same year. You can save the deduction for a tax year when the deduction is more valuable.

Spousal RRSPs

When you make your RRSP contribution, you have the option of putting the contribution in your own RRSP or a spousal RRSP, or a combination thereof. A spousal RRSP is an RRSP to which you contribute the funds, although your spouse is the one who receives the funds when withdrawn. This means your spouse — not you — makes withdrawals from the plan and pays tax on those withdrawals.

Ideally, both you and your spouse should have equal incomes in retirement. You should make a spousal contribution if your spouse will be in a lower tax bracket than you when the money is eventually withdrawn. This way, you get the reduction at a high tax rate, and your spouse pays the tax at a lower one.

But beware: If your spouse makes a withdrawal from a spousal plan in the year or within two calendar years of when you last made a spousal RRSP contribution, you — not your spouse — will be subject to the tax on the amount of the withdrawal that relates to contributions you made during this three-year period.

You are not entitled to additional RRSP contribution room in order to make a spousal contribution. The total contributions to your own plan, plus your spouse's, cannot be greater than your total RRSP contribution limit. (Your spouse's contribution limit does *not* impact how much you can contribute to a spousal RRSP.)

The RRSP Home Buyers' Plan (HBP)

Normally, withdrawals from your RRSP are fully taxable to you in the year of withdrawal. We talk about this in Chapter 8. However, if you wish, you can withdraw up to $20,000 from your RRSP tax-free for buying a home, as long as you or your spouse hasn't owned a home that you occupied as your principal place of residence in the past four years. Your spouse can make use of the HBP too, leaving a potential for $40,000 to go toward the home purchase, provided your spouse also hasn't owned a home in the past four years and you are purchasing the home jointly.

The withdrawal is treated as a loan from your RRSP, to be repaid over a period of no more than 15 years. The first repayment, a minimum of one-fifteenth of your HBP withdrawal, must be paid back in the second calendar year following the year in which you made the withdrawal. If you took out a $20,000 HBP loan in November 2004, for example, you must repay at least $1,333 (one-fifteenth of $20,000) before the end of 2006. If you do not make the repayment, the $1,333 is included in your income. Yikes!

It's easy to make an HBP repayment. You simply make a contribution to your RRSP. On schedule 7 of your tax return, you note the total of your RRSP contributions and then allocate a portion of the contributions to the annual HBP repayment. (That amount doesn't qualify for an RRSP deduction because it is simply a repayment of an amount borrowed from your RRSP.)

If you contribute to your RRSP and then withdraw the funds within 90 days for the HBP, you won't be able to claim a deduction for that contribution. Always allow your contributions to sit for 91 days or more before making a withdrawal under the HBP.

There is no restriction on speeding up your HBP repayment. It makes good financial sense to repay the withdrawals as soon as you can, because the sooner the funds go back into your RRSP, the greater the tax-free growth in value!

RRSPs and the Lifelong Learning Plan (LLP)

The LLP works in a similar way to the HBP. Funds can be withdrawn on a tax-free basis to fund full-time education or training for you or your spouse. The maximum withdrawal is $10,000 per year, or up to $20,000 over a four-year period. You need to repay the funds to your RRSP over a period of no more than ten years. The minimum repayment is one-tenth of the LLP withdrawal. The first repayment is due on the earlier of the following:

 ✔ The second year after the last year you (or your spouse) were able to claim the "education amount" on line 323 of the tax return (Chapter 12).

 ✔ The fifth year after your first withdrawal under the LLP.

You make your LLP repayments in the same fashion as you would make the HBP repayments noted above. You simply contribute to your RRSP, and on schedule 7 designate what portion of your RRSP contribution is for your LLP repayment.

Transferring a severance or retiring allowance into your RRSP

If you are going to receive a severance or retiring allowance from an employer you worked for since before 1996, you may be able to put all or a portion of the payment directly into your RRSP (see Chapter 8). (Sorry, it can't go into a spousal RRSP.) This is referred to as a "transfer," and is attractive for two reasons:

 ✔ No income tax needs to be withheld on the portion of the payment being transferred directly into your RRSP. A direct transfer means the cheque goes from your employer to your RRSP — you don't even get to touch the money!

> ✔ The portion transferred to your RRSP is in addition to your regular RRSP contribution limit. You can still contribute up to your RRSP contribution limit, in addition to the portion of the severance transferred to your RRSP.

It's not critical that you roll your retiring allowance directly into your RRSP — this transfer can be made later. But be sure to make the contribution within 60 days following the end of the year in which you received your payment. If you don't contribute before this time, this special contribution room is lost forever!

If any portion of your retiring allowance or severance cannot be transferred directly to your RRSP, consider using it to make a regular RRSP contribution (or a spousal contribution). In fact, you can ask your employer to directly transfer your ineligible retiring allowance into your RRSP and no tax has to be taken off the payment. If you are leaving an employer where you were part of a regular RPP, you might find you actually have more unused room than ever before if you have a PAR (we talk about PARs earlier in this chapter).

Line 209: Saskatchewan Pension Plan (SPP) Deduction

If you have made contributions to the SPP, you can deduct the least of the following amounts on your 2006 tax return:

> ✔ Amounts contributed to the SPP for yourself or your spouse from January 1, 2006, to March 1, 2007, excluding any contributions deducted on your 2005 tax return.
>
> ✔ Your 2005 RRSP deduction limit less the RRSP deduction you claimed on line 208, excluding any amounts transferred to your RRSP (that is, a portion of a severance or retirement allowance received that was transferred to your RRSP).
>
> ✔ $600.

Line 212: Annual Union, Professional, or Like Dues

Since you are taxed on pretty much all your income, it's logical that costs incurred to earn the income are deductible. It is logical — but no one ever said the *Income Tax Act* was logical. One of the deductions permitted is the cost of belonging to a union or to a professional body, or the cost of carrying professional or malpractice insurance. Union dues paid are noted in box 44 of your T4. Fees paid to professional organizations are usually receipted. If your employer pays the fees for your professional memberships or insurance, the employer gets the tax deduction — you don't, even if the receipt is in your name.

If you paid GST or HST on your union or professional dues, you may be able to have the GST refunded to you. Refer to the section near the end of Chapter 13 on the "Goods and Services Tax (GST)/Harmonized Sales Tax (HST) Rebate."

Line 214: Child-Care Expenses

Our government recognizes that many of us incur child-care expenses in order to be able to work. Our government also acknowledges that you may incur child-care expenses in order to be able to go to school to train for a job.

How much is deductible?

Here are the maximum child-care expenses that can be claimed per eligible child in 2006:

Disabled child — regardless of age	$10,000
Child under age 7 on December 31, 2006	$7,000
Child aged 7 to 16 on December 31, 2006	$4,000

However, the maximum deductible is also restricted to two-thirds of your "earned income." Don't get the definition of "earned income" for purposes of the child-care deduction mixed up with the definition of "earned income" for your RRSP deduction. For purposes of the child-care expense deduction, "earned income" consists of:

- Employment income, including tips and gratuities
- Self-employment income
- Research grants
- CPP and QPP disability benefits
- Government payments under a plan to encourage employment

To claim a deduction for a child, the child must be your child, your spouse's child, or a child dependent on you or your spouse; and the child must have a net income in 2006 of $8,839 or less.

Eligible child-care expenses include payments to the following:

- ✔ Individuals providing child-care services. Payments to the child's mother, father, or a related person under 18 are not eligible. Individuals providing child care must provide a receipt with their social insurance number noted. Other child-care providers simply need to provide you with a receipt.

- ✔ Daycare, child-care centres, and day nursery schools

- ✔ Schools where part of the fee is for child care (such as before- and after-school care)

- ✔ "Day" camps and "overnight" camps

Where payments are made to facilities providing overnight lodging and boarding, such as overnight sports schools, boarding schools, or camps, the eligible deductible amount is restricted to:

- ✔ $175 per week per disabled child of any age

- ✔ $175 per week per child under age 7 on December 31, 2006

- ✔ $100 per week per child aged 7 to 16 on December 31, 2006

Form T778: Claiming a deduction for child-care expenses

You will need to complete form T778, "Child Care Expenses Deduction for 2006."

Who gets to claim the deduction?

If a child lives with both parents, the parent with the lower income claims the child-care expense deduction. However, as with everything, there are exceptions to this general rule.

Where one of two supporting persons has no net income, the deduction for child-care expenses will be "wasted." We often see this when someone is self-employed but has so many business expenses in the year that there is no net income. Therefore, where possible, try to ensure that the supporting person with the lower income has "earned income." For example, if you are self-employed, you might want to forgo some of your discretionary tax deductions such as CCA to create more income from which to deduct your child-care expenses. As noted above, the deduction for child-care expenses cannot exceed two-thirds of earned income. So, for a maximum claim, the earned income of the lower-net-income supporting person needs to be three-halves (or 150 percent) of the eligible child-care costs incurred.

Are you the only supporting person? If so, you make the claim for the child-care expenses deduction.

Can the supporting person with the higher net income ever deduct child-care expenses? Yes, if the supporting person with the lower net income was in one of these situations:

- ✔ In school. (The school can be a secondary school, college, university, or an "educational institution" certified by Human Resources and Skills Development Canada [HRSDC] for courses that develop or improve occupational skills.)

- ✔ Not able to take care of children because of a mental or physical disability.

- ✔ In jail for at least two weeks in 2006.

Supporting persons living apart

Where supporting persons were living apart for all of 2006 by virtue of a marriage breakdown (whether a legal or common-law relationship), each is entitled to a deduction for child-care expenses. The aggregate claimed by the supporting persons cannot exceed the overall limits noted above.

If you separated from your spouse in 2006 and you are the higher-net-income supporting person, you can make a claim if you and your spouse were living apart on December 31, 2006. A claim will be allowed to you if you and your spouse were separated for at least 90 days beginning sometime in 2006 and the child-care expenses claimed by you were actually paid by you. The claim period is restricted to the period of separation.

Line 215: Disability Supports Deduction

If you suffer from a severe and prolonged mental or physical impairment you are able to deduct certain amounts paid to an attendant, provided that attendant is needed to enable you to go to work or school. In addition, you are also able to deduct certain disability supports expenses you incur for those same purposes. You need to complete form T929 to claim these deductions.

Amounts reimbursed by a non-taxable payment, such as insurance, are not eligible for the disability supports deduction. You also can't claim any expenses that you've claimed a medical expense credit for already. (See Chapter 12, lines 330 and 331 — no double-dipping!)

To be eligible to claim this deduction, you must have a severe and prolonged impairment that restricts your activities of daily living and is expected to last for at least 12 months. As with the disability credit amount (Chapter 12, line 316), your doctor needs to complete and sign form T2201, "Disability Tax Certificate," and you must file it with your tax return. If you've already submitted this form to claim the disability tax credit, there's no need to file it again.

What types of expenses qualify?

The disability supports deduction comprises two types of expenses. The first is attendant care expenses. Qualifying amounts include amounts paid to an attendant to enable you to perform the duties of employment, to carry on a business, to carry out research for which you receive a grant, or to go to school. The attendant must be over the age of 18, and cannot be your spouse or common-law partner.

You may also deduct the cost of certain disability support items you've incurred to allow you to work or go to school. The types of deductions that will qualify are specific and include the following:

- Sign language interpretation services and real-time captioning services if you have a speech or hearing impairment
- Teletypewriters to enable those who are deaf or mute to make and receive phone calls

- ✔ Devices that help the blind to operate a computer, such as a Braille printer

- ✔ Optical scanners or similar devices that enable blind individuals to read print

- ✔ Electronic speech synthesizers that enable mute individuals to communicate using a portable keyboard

- ✔ Other services or devices if certified by a medical practitioner, including talking textbooks and tutoring or note-taking services.

- ✔ Job coaches, deaf-blind interveners, and Braille note-takers

Is the disability support required for you to go to work?

Of course, there's a limit to the amount you can deduct. If the disability support is required to enable you to go to work, the limit is the lesser of the following:

- ✔ Your "earned income" for the year

- ✔ The qualifying amounts you paid for the disability support during the year.

As it pertains to the disability supports deduction, here's yet another definition of "earned income" (you'd think the CRA could come up with a new name). In this case, it's the sum of the following:

- ✔ Net income from a business

- ✔ Gross employment income

- ✔ Net research grants

- ✔ Training allowances paid under the *National Training Act*

Is the disability support required for you to go to school?

If the disability support is required to enable you to attend a designated educational institution or secondary school, the limit is the least of the following:

- ✔ Your income from other sources (up to a maximum of $15,000)

- ✔ $375 times the number of weeks of attendance at the institution or school

- ✔ The qualifying amounts paid to the attendant during the year

Line 217: Business Investment Loss (BIL)

In Chapter 7, we discuss capital gains and capital losses. A capital loss occurs when you sell an investment for less than you paid for it. A capital loss can be used only to shelter or offset capital gains from tax — it cannot be used to shelter other types of income (say, employment income, pension income, interest, or dividends) from tax.

A business investment loss (BIL) is a special type of capital loss. A business investment loss, or a portion of that loss, can be deducted in the year incurred, to shelter any type of income — not just capital gains — from tax.

A BIL occurs when you sell your shares or debt in a small business corporation at a loss. (Refer to Chapter 11 for a discussion of small business corporation shares.) A BIL will also arise if you were deemed to dispose of the shares or debt when the corporation became bankrupt, insolvent, or no longer carries on business and the fair market value of the shares is nil.

Calculating the deductible portion of the BIL

Report your true loss on line 228 on your return. This is the difference between your proceeds of disposition (which may be nil!) and the tax cost of the investment (which is normally what you paid for the investment). However, as with capital losses, only 50 percent of a BIL is tax deductible. This is logical since only 50 percent of the gain on the sale of an investment is taxable. The deductible portion of a BIL is referred to as an allowable business investment loss (ABIL).

If you have used any portion of your capital gains deduction (see Chapter 11), this will reduce the amount of the BIL that you can deduct. Once any necessary reductions in the amount of the loss are calculated, the remaining loss to be deducted on your current year's tax return is reported on line 217.

Let's look at an example. In 1999, Abdul lent $100,000 to assist a small business corporation in starting up a new Internet business. Unfortunately, in July 2006, the corporation went bankrupt, leaving Abdul with nothing. Back in 1992, Abdul had claimed a capital gains deduction to shelter a $10,000 capital gain he had incurred.

Abdul will report a BIL of $100,000 on line 228. However, his actual BIL eligible for a deduction is reduced by the 1992 capital gain that was sheltered from tax by the capital gains deduction. Therefore, his BIL eligible for deduction is $90,000 ($100,000 – $10,000). He can claim one-half of this amount, or $45,000, as his ABIL on line 217. The $5,000 ($10,000 × 50%) that could not be claimed as an ABIL is treated as a regular capital loss.

Line 219: Moving Expenses

If you moved at least 40 kilometres in 2006 to start a job (even if just a summer job), start a business, or for full-time post-secondary education, you may be eligible to deduct at least a portion of your moving expenses.

The eligible moving expenses may be deducted only from your employment or self-employment income earned at the new location. If your 2006 eligible moving expenses exceeded your 2006 income at the new location, the excess can be carried forward for deduction on your 2007 tax return.

What moving expenses are eligible?

Most moving expenses are eligible for a tax deduction. Specifically, they are as follows:

- ✓ Travelling expenses, including automobile expenses for you and your family
- ✓ Meals and accommodation on the way to the new residence
- ✓ Costs of moving your stuff (moving van, storage, insurance, and so on)
- ✓ Costs for up to 15 days for you and your family for meals and temporary stay
- ✓ Costs of cancelling your lease on the old residence
- ✓ Costs of selling your old residence (advertising, legal fees, real estate commission, and mortgage prepayment penalty if applicable)
- ✓ Costs of maintaining your old residence when vacant (including mortgage interest and property taxes) to a maximum of $5,000
- ✓ Legal fees and land transfer fees paid in acquiring the new residence, provided you sold the prior residence as a result of the move

✔ Fees for utility disconnection and hook-ups

✔ Incidental costs related to the move (for example, costs of changing your address, costs of acquiring new auto and driver's licences)

With respect to automobile and meal costs incurred while moving, the CRA permits you to either claim the actual costs or to use a flat rate. The CRA refers to the flat rate system as the "simplified method" — appropriately named, we would say. Where you use the flat rate, you don't need to retain receipts.

The flat rate for automobile travel varies by province or territory. If you don't use the flat rate, you need to track all the costs of operating the car for a year (gas, maintenance, insurance, interest on car loans, depreciation, and so on). You then need to prorate the total of these costs by taking the number of kilometres driven for the move over the total number of kilometres driven for the complete year. (Ugh — that's a lot of math.)

The flat rates for automobile and meal costs change every year and are posted on the CRA's Web site at `www.cra-arc.gc.ca/tax/individuals/topics/income-tax/return/completing/deductions/lines248-260/255/rates-e.html`

Employer-paid or reimbursed moving expenses

You can deduct moving expenses only to the extent that the expenses were incurred by you. You cannot deduct expenses that were paid for by your employer, or that you incurred and were later reimbursed for by your employer. On the other hand, if your employer provided you with an allowance, this amount must be included in your income. Make sure you then claim any eligible moving expenses as a deduction.

When possible, always get your new employer to reimburse you for your moving expenses. This is advantageous for a number of reasons:

✔ You will not be out any money. Even in the top tax bracket, a tax deduction is worth less than 50 cents on the dollar. This means that for each dollar you deduct, you save less than 50 cents in tax. Isn't it better to have your employer give you back the full dollar? (The employer can claim a deduction for amounts reimbursed to you.)

> ✓ Some moving costs are *not* tax deductible. You definitely want to be reimbursed for these.
>
> ✓ You avoid the hassle of detailing all your moving expenses on your tax return, plus you are far less likely to have the CRA question your return.
>
> ✓ You do not need to wait for a tax refund to get your money back.

The CRA has stated that your employer can provide you with a non-accountable allowance of up to $650 as a reimbursement of moving expenses. The allowance will not be considered income provided you certify in writing that you incurred moving expenses of an amount at least equal to the allowance you received.

Coming to or leaving Canada?

In most situations, moving expenses are not deductible if you are moving to or from Canada. (In this situation, you definitely want to have your employer reimburse your moving expenses!) However, if you leave Canada to study full time, your moving expenses may be deductible. They would be deductible against income from scholarships, fellowships, research grants, and similar awards that are reported on your Canadian tax return. This assumes that even though you are studying outside Canada, you continue to be a Canadian resident for tax purposes. If you are a full-time student and you came to Canada, you can deduct your moving expenses against these same types of income earned in Canada.

How do you claim moving expenses on your tax return?

To claim moving expenses, complete form T1M, "Moving Expenses Deduction." On this form you report where you moved from and to, why you moved, and the specific details and dollar amounts of your moving costs. Oddly, you are not required to file either the T1M or any moving receipts with your tax return. However, you are required to keep these on hand in case of a CRA query. And trust us, queries happen quite often.

Lines 220 and 230: Support Payments Made

Support is the word that replaced "alimony" and "maintenance" payments a few years back. Support refers both to payments made for spousal support and to those made for child support. It is important to differentiate between spousal and child support because each has its own criteria regarding permissible tax deductions.

Line 230 is simply for disclosure. Here you insert the amount of spouse and child support paid. As detailed below, all support payments may not be tax deductible. Enter the deductible portion on line 220.

 Whether you receive the support for yourself or for your children, you should refer to Chapter 8, line 128, to determine what is taxable or not taxable in your hands. You will see that the deduction/income inclusion criteria mirror each other. Where one taxpayer has a deduction, one will have an income inclusion. If no deduction is available, there is no income inclusion. If you are paying a lawyer to help you collect support, the fees are likely tax deductible!

 Though it can be emotionally draining to go through the process of finalizing the agreement, our experience in dealing with many separated and divorced individuals is that the agreement is vital in maintaining some sanity and in ensuring your financial protection. You should contact a lawyer specializing in family law as soon as possible to protect your rights to support, your assets, and your children.

Spousal support

Payments to an ex-spouse — including an "estranged" (separated) spouse — are in most cases tax deductible. To support the deduction, you must have a written agreement or court order signed by both you and your ex-spouse that specifically stipulates the amounts to be paid. If there is no agreement or court order, the amounts paid are not tax deductible. However, an agreement can provide for at least some of the pre-agreement spousal support payments to be tax deductible, as we explain below.

 The support payments must be periodic; that is, monthly. Lump-sum payments do not qualify for a tax deduction.

Any payments you made prior to the date of a court order or a written agreement *can* be considered to have been paid under an order or agreement, and therefore are tax deductible. However, the order or agreement must stipulate that any prior payments made are considered to have been paid (and therefore are potentially deductible) pursuant to the agreement. Only payments made in the year that the order or agreement is finalized, and the preceding year, qualify for the retroactive treatment. Get the separation agreement drawn up promptly!

Note: If you are on the receiving end of spousal or child support payments see Chapter 8 for more details on their tax treatment.

Child support

Child support rules took a dramatic shift on May 1, 1997. There are now three sets of rules, and you need to determine which ones apply to you. Your child support payments may or may not be tax deductible. The three sets of rules are detailed below.

Child support order or agreement made before May 1, 1997

If you are making payments under an order or agreement made before May 1, 1997, your payments are tax deductible. (Your ex-spouse will include the amounts in his or her income.)

Child support order or agreement made on May 1, 1997 or later

Your payments under a May 1, 1997, or later agreement or order are not tax deductible. (They are not taxable in the hands of your ex-spouse.)

Modification of a pre–May 1, 1997 child support order or agreement

If you are making tax-deductible payments under a pre–May 1, 1997 order or agreement, you may find that your payments suddenly cease to be tax deductible under one of the following circumstances:

- ✔ The order or agreement is amended to increase or decrease child support payments (and, therefore, considered a new agreement and subject to the new rules).

- ✔ You and your ex-spouse elect to have the newer rules apply to your old agreement.

Line 221: Carrying Charges and Interest Expenses

Certain expenses you incur to earn investment income are tax deductible. Briefly, these are:

- ✔ Investment counsel and management fees (only the portion of these fees related to services for your non-RRSP investments are deductible)

- ✔ Safekeeping, custodial, and safety deposit box fees

- ✔ Tax return preparation fees, if you have income from a business or a property

- ✔ Interest on money borrowed to earn investment income, such as interest and dividends — but not capital gains

Brokerage commissions are not tax deductible as a carrying charge because they form part of the tax cost on the purchase of an investment or reduce the proceeds on the sale. See Chapter 7 for more information on the calculation of capital gains and losses.

Detail eligible carrying costs and interest in Part IV of schedule 4 of your tax return, "Summary, Carrying Charges and Interest Expenses." Then enter the total on line 221.

More on interest that can be deducted

Interest costs are deductible if you've borrowed money to invest in a business or *earn income from property*. Income from property includes interest, dividends, rents, and royalties.

Capital gains are not considered to be income from property. Therefore, if you're earning only capital gains and do not have the potential to earn income from property, the taxman may deny your deduction. Keep in mind that if you're investing in stocks or equity mutual funds, there's usually the potential to earn dividends. This will normally be enough to keep your interest deductible.

Interest can continue to be tax deductible even if you have sold the investment, provided the entire sale proceeds are used to pay down the loan or to purchase another investment.

At the time of writing, a set of draft rules in the *Income Tax Act* threatens to deny interest deductions and other investment expenses when there is no reasonable expectation of cumulative profits (excluding capital gains) from the investment in question. Plainly stated, your deductions may be denied if you are not expecting to earn enough interest and dividends from your investment over the expected holding period to cover your interest costs over that same period. These rules were slated to apply starting in 2005; however, further refinements are expected. If you are interested in borrowing to invest, you might want to speak to a tax professional first to see where these rules stand, and to help choose investments that will ensure you get a tax deduction. And you can be sure we'll fill you in on all the details when we can!

If you live in Quebec, you have additional rules to worry about. Specifically, for Quebec tax purposes, you can deduct interest (and other investment expenses) only to the extent you've reported investment income in the year. Investment income for these purposes includes taxable capital gains. Any interest that is not deductible can be carried forward to offset investment income you have in future years.

Line 224: Exploration and Development Expenses

Did you invest in an oil and gas or mining venture in 2006 or in a prior year? The type of investment may have been called a "limited partnership," a "flow-through share" investment, or simply a "tax shelter." Whatever the term, if you did invest you are probably entitled to some special tax deductions. One of the attractive features promoted in the selling of oil, gas, and mining investments is the tax write-offs (slang for "deductions") available.

If you are contemplating an investment in an oil, gas, or mining venture, be sure you completely understand the risks associated with the investment. A general rule is that the greater the tax saving, the riskier the investment. Be sure that such an investment falls within your risk-tolerance comfort zone. You should invest based on the quality of the investment — not the tax saving provided by the investment.

Why are these tax deductions made available? Well, in Chapter 1 we noted that our *Income Tax Act* serves two purposes: to provide cash necessary for the government to operate, and as a tool for many government initiatives. The government thinks it is a good idea to encourage oil, gas, and metal exploration in Canada, so the

Act contains provisions to encourage these activities. The Act provides oil, gas, and mining companies with significant write-offs for the following:

- ✔ Canadian exploration expenses (CEE) — 100 percent deduction
- ✔ Canadian development expenses (CDE) — 30 percent deduction
- ✔ Canadian oil and gas property expenses (COGPE) — 10 percent deduction

Since many exploration companies do not have sufficient money to go out and explore for oil, gas, and metals, the Act permits these companies to turn to you for the funds. You are the one actually funding the exploration and development, so you get the attractive tax deductions. This is referred to as the expenses being "renounced" to you. Since exploration is the government's main initiative, and the exploration phase has the greatest chance of failure, the write-offs are greatest when funds are expended on exploration.

How to claim exploration and development expenses

The promoter of the oil, gas, or mining venture will provide you with all the information you need. Depending on the structure of the investment, you will receive a T101, T102, or T5013 slip. Instructions are provided on the back of these forms to assist in calculating your deduction.

You do not have to take the maximum deduction. Any amount not claimed will carry over to the following year for a potential deduction using the same percentage figures. Why would you not want to take a deduction? Perhaps you expect to be in a higher tax bracket next year, so the deduction will be worth more in tax savings if you wait.

Line 229: Other Employment Expenses

You may be one of many employees who are required to fund the costs of carrying out your employment duties. These costs can vary from taking prospective customers out to lunch to using your own car for sales calls to perhaps using space in your home or apartment for work purposes. If your employer doesn't directly reimburse you for these costs (usually via an expense report), one of two things likely happens:

✔ Your employer pays you an allowance to cover your expenses but the allowance is included in your T4 employment income. In other words, you pay tax on the allowance.

✔ Your employer does not pay you an allowance. You are simply required to pay your own expenses.

If you fall into one of these categories, you should be able to claim a deduction for at least some, if not all, of the expenses you incur to do your job.

If you do not fall into one of these categories, don't be overly jealous of those who do. Though it is nice to be able to deduct employment expenses, there are limits on what you can claim, and it would be better if your employer simply reimbursed the costs. The reimbursement would not be a taxable benefit to you. With a reimbursement, you would not be out any money. Your employer would return to you every dollar you spent in doing your job. In deducting employment expenses, the best you can do is receive about a 46-cent refund for every dollar deducted — and this assumes you are in the top tax bracket, which means your taxable income after all deductions (including the deduction for employment expenses) exceeds $118,285.

Who is eligible to deduct employment expenses?

To deduct the expenses you incur to carry out your employment duties, the following must apply to you:

✔ You must be **required** to pay expenses to earn your employment income (in the CRA's words, you must be required to incur the expenses under the terms of your employment contract, whether or not you have a written contract).

✔ Your employer must provide you with a form detailing the expenses you are required to incur. The form is T2200, "Declarations of Conditions of Employment." It is completed and signed by your employer — not you.

Form T777, "Statement of Employment Expenses"

The CRA publishes form T777 to assist you in gathering and summarizing your employment expenses. This is the form used by the majority of employees. The total of your eligible employment expenses from the T777 is carried over to line 229 on your tax return.

A second employee expense form, TL2, "Claim for Meals and Lodging Expenses," is used by employees involved in air, rail, bus, and trucking industries. Another form that can come into play is form GST370, "Employee and Partner GST/HST Rebate Application." Most employees like this form because it works only one way: It assists you in calculating the amount of GST/HST you can recover from the government! (We talk more about GST/HST rebates later in this chapter.)

 The employment expenses you deduct are to include the GST, HST, and provincial and territorial sales taxes you paid. Do not separate the GST/HST or provincial/territorial sales taxes from the non-tax portion of your expenses. If you lived in Alberta (no provincial sales tax) and purchased $100 of deductible supplies to do your job, you would actually pay $106 when the GST is added. It is the $106 that is included in your employment expenses on the T777.

 If you are eligible to claim a deduction for employment expenses, record keeping is **vital** for a number of reasons. One, you don't want to miss out on claiming a legitimate expense. If you do, you overstate your tax liability! Two, the CRA can request employees to provide support for the expenses claimed on their tax return. The CRA is usually happy to accept the deduction for employment expenses, provided the support (receipts, invoices, ticket stubs, kilometre log, and so on) is organized and available for inspection should it be requested. Third, you simplify your tax return preparation. Don't even think of bringing a shopping bag (or the infamous shoebox) full of receipts and stuff to an accountant in late April and expect to be pleasantly welcomed!

What's deductible and what's not?

Let's look at an example. Fiona took an industrial sales job with Warton Products Inc. of Stratford, Ontario, on February 1, 2006.

Her conditions of employment were that she was to be paid on a commission basis and that she was required to do the following:

- ✔ Pay for her own office supplies (paper, toner, postage, and so on)
- ✔ Pay the salary of her part-time assistant, Katy
- ✔ Provide a home office for her and Katy. Fiona was not provided with a workspace at Warton
- ✔ Provide her own car because the job involved significant travel in southern Ontario

During 2006, Fiona made commissions of $90,000. She paid GST on her expenses when applicable. All her expenses were incurred in Ontario, so she did not pay any HST in 2006.

Table 10-1 compares the expenses that can be deducted by an employee earning a salary and those that can be deducted by an employee being paid on a commission basis.

Table 10-1 Can It Be Deducted?		
Expense	Earning Salary	Earning Commissions
Legal fees to collect wages, salary, or commissions owed	Yes	Yes
Accounting fees for tax return preparation	No[1]	Yes
Advertising and promotion	No	Yes
Entertainment for customers	No	Yes[2]
Food and beverage[3]	Yes[2]	Yes[2]
Lodging and travel	Yes[4]	Yes
Parking[5]	Yes	Yes
Automobile expense	Yes	Yes
Office supplies[6]	Yes	Yes
Uniforms	Yes	Yes
Clothing, dry cleaning, makeup and hairstyling	No	No
Computer or fax purchase	No	No
Computer or fax lease	No	Yes

Expense	Earning Salary	Earning Commissions
Cell phone purchase	No	No
Cell phone lease	No	Yes
Cell phone airtime[7]	Yes	Yes
Long-distance calls[7]	Yes	Yes
Internet[8]	Yes	Yes
Licences[9]	No	Yes
Salaries to assistants[10]	Yes	Yes
Office rent[10]	Yes	Yes
Home office[10]	Yes	Yes

Notes

1. An alternative filing opportunity is to claim the accounting fee as a carrying charge on schedule 4. Refer to comments regarding line 221 earlier in this chapter. It deals with the deduction available for carrying charges and interest expenses.

2. Only 50 percent of entertainment, food, and beverage expenses can be deducted. This restriction also applies to gift certificates for these items.

3. Food, beverage, and lodging are deductible only if your employer requires you to be away from the municipality or metropolitan area where your employer is located for at least 12 hours.

4. You can deduct travel expenses if you were normally required to work away from your employer's business or in different places, and you did not receive a non-taxable allowance to cover travelling expenses.

5. The CRA's position is that parking costs at your employer's office are not deductible because they are considered a personal expense. However, if you need to go to the office before or after seeing a customer, or to work at a different location, we would argue that the parking in these circumstances should be deductible.

6. Supplies must be used directly in your work and for nothing else. The CRA takes the position that these supplies include "pens, pencils, paper clips, stationery, stamps, street maps, and directories." They do not include items such as briefcases or calculators. Tools are not deductible unless you are a tradesperson. We discuss tools later in this chapter.

7. Restricted to work-related cost of calls and airtime.

8. The CRA's guide "Employment Expenses" is silent on Internet charges. We would expect the CRA to permit at least a portion of Internet fees if the Internet is needed to do your job. (Hey, you need an e-mail address, don't ya?)

9. Annual licence fees are deductible if needed to carry out work (for example, real estate and insurance licences).

10. Your employer must specifically indicate on form T2200 that you are required to incur these costs.

Assuming Fiona spent $5,300 on office supplies and $4,000 for Katy's salary, she would be entitled to a full deduction of $9,300. This is a hint of what comes later. The amount spent on supplies includes 6 percent GST.

Automobile expenses

If you pay your own automobile expenses and are required to use your car to carry out your employment duties, you can deduct a portion of your costs in completing your income tax return. As noted above, your employer would indicate on form T2200 that you need to supply your own car and incur expenses to keep it on the road. Here are some types of automobile expenses that can be deducted:

- ✔ Fuel
- ✔ Repairs and maintenance
- ✔ Insurance
- ✔ Licence and registration fees
- ✔ Leasing costs
- ✔ Interest incurred on a loan to purchase a car
- ✔ Capital cost allowance (CCA or tax depreciation)

It is only the "employment use" portion of automobile expenses that is included in your deductible employment expenses. The CRA states that driving only to and from work is personal use — not employment use. However, if you need to go out in your car in the middle of the day (say, to see a potential customer), or perhaps on your way to or from work, the whole trip can be considered employment use.

Recall that Fiona started working at Warton on February 1, 2006. She was required to provide her own car. Fiona used her Honda Civic, which she had leased a few years back. Her lease costs for the period were $3,300 ($300 per month for 11 months). From February to December 2006, Fiona drove the Civic a total of 20,000 kilometres — 15,000 were work-related.

Fiona, being ever fearful of a CRA query, kept a log in her glove compartment that detailed her work trips and kilometres driven. She updated the log daily. Based on the kilometres, you can see that Fiona used her car 75 percent of the time for work and 25 percent for personal use. Fiona can deduct 75 percent of her automobile expenses in calculating her deductible employment expenses.

Do you really need to keep a log of your kilometres driven for employment use? Yes! If you are asked by the CRA to support your automobile expenses, they will ask to see your log of kilometres. So get in the habit of keeping the log in the car. Every time you get in the car, you should make an entry of where you are going, and later where you have been and the kilometres travelled. You will thank us if the CRA comes knocking!

Let's calculate Fiona's automobile expenses:

Expenses	Dollar Value
Fuel	$2,000
Maintenance and repairs	$1,500
Insurance	$1,100
Licence and registration	$125
Lease	$3,300
Other — car washes	$100
Total expenses	$8,125
Employment use portion	75 percent
Allowable amount of automobile expenses that Fiona can deduct on her tax return	$6,094

Capital cost allowance (CCA) when an automobile is owned rather than leased

In the above example, Fiona leased the car she used to carry out her employment duties. What would the impact be if Fiona owned the car? Before heading back to our example, let's look at something called *capital cost allowance* — CCA for short. It is the tax term for depreciation.

Because your car is expected to last more than a year, its cost cannot be completely deducted in computing your employment expenses. However, a percentage of the car's capital cost allowance can. The first step in determining the CCA you can deduct is to decide whether your automobile is "class 10" or "class 10.1" for CCA purposes. Both CCA classes 10 and 10.1 calculate the maximum CCA that can be claimed at a rate of 30 percent calculated on the declining-balance method of depreciation which involves applying the depreciation rate against the non-depreciated balance. Instead of spreading the cost of the asset evenly over its life, this system expenses the asset at a constant rate, which results in declining depreciation charges each successive period.

Note: Use class 10.1 if your car cost $30,000 or more (before PST and GST or HST) and class 10 if it cost less than $30,000.

In the year you purchase an automobile, the "half-year" rule applies – meaning you can only take 50% of the CCA you would otherwise be entitled to. This results in a CCA calculation at 15 percent (30 percent × ½ = 15 percent). The determination of whether your car is considered a "class 10" or a "class 10.1" automobile is important, as the CCA on class 10.1 automobiles is restricted to a maximum amount. The restrictions on CCA and other automobile expenses are discussed shortly.

Assume that rather than leasing her Honda Civic, Fiona purchased the Civic in 2006 for $23,000, taxes included. (By the way, this car qualifies as class 10 — therefore, no restrictions apply in calculating CCA.) Let's take a look at how Fiona would calculate CCA for 2006 and 2007.

Before calculating CCA, Fiona would calculate her employee expense deduction for the operating expenses of her car in the same way as above. She would add up the amounts she spent for fuel, repairs, licensing, insurance, and so on. (Of course there would be no leasing costs, as we are assuming here that she owns the car!) She would then multiply the total amount of expenses by the employment-use portion. As in the preceding example, 75 percent was used for the 2006 year. We'll assume the appropriate employment usage figure was also 75 percent for 2007.

Table 10-2 summarizes how Fiona would calculate CCA for 2006 and 2007.

Table 10-2 Fiona's Capital Cost Allowance (CCA) Schedule for 2006 and 2007

Year: 2006		
Undepreciated capital cost (UCC) at January 1, 2006	$0	
Acquisitions in year	$23,000	
Subtract – one-half[1]	($11,500)	
Base for 2006 CCA calculation	$11,500	
CCA at 30 percent[2]	($3,450)	
Add back one-half subtracted above	$11,500	
UCC at December 31, 2006	$19,550	
Year: 2007		
UCC at January 1, 2007 (as above)		$19,550
CCA at 30 percent[2]		($5,865)
UCC at December 31, 2007		$13,685

Notes

1. This part of the calculation results in only half of the capital cost of the acquisitions in 2006 being depreciated. While the CCA rate is 30 percent, the subtracted amount results in the CCA being only 15 percent — half of 30 percent. This calculation is referred to as the "half-year" rule.

2. Remember that Fiona used her car only 75 percent of the time to carry out her employment duties. Therefore, her tax deduction is 75 percent of the CCA calculated. In 2006 — $3,450 × 75% = $2,587.50. In 2007 — $5,965 × 75% = $4,398.75.

 Claiming CCA, whether for an automobile or any asset on which CCA can be claimed, is optional. A taxpayer (whether employed or self-employed, or perhaps a corporation) may decide to claim less than the maximum CCA, or no CCA at all! Although at first it may seem odd that a taxpayer would not take maximum advantage of a tax deduction available, there are some logical reasons for this. For example, perhaps the taxpayer will be in a higher tax bracket next year. This will result in a greater tax reduction than if the CCA is taken this year.

Restrictions on certain automobile expenses

If you are entitled to deduct a portion of your automobile as employment expenses, you deduct only the "business use" portion of the expenses you actually paid. This is true for most of your expenses. The amount you pay is the starting point in determining what you can deduct. However, there are three exceptions to this:

- ✔ Automobile leasing costs (see Table 9-1 in Chapter 9)

- ✔ Interest on car loans (see Table 9-1 in Chapter 9)

- ✔ Capital cost on which CCA will begin to be calculated (see Table 9-2 in Chapter 9)

When these exceptions apply, you will find that the amounts you use to begin calculating your deductible automobile expenses are less than you actually paid. And remember, these maximums apply *before* you prorate your automobile expenses between employment use and business use.

Let's look at Oscar's situation. Oscar is a salesman. On January 1, 2006, he leased a Mercedes. His monthly lease cost is $850. Oscar uses his car 60 percent for work. He expects that his monthly effective tax deduction will be $510 ($850 × 60 percent), or $6,120 per year. He is not worried about the lease cost restriction because he understands the maximum cost for leases commenced in 2006 is $800 (see Table 9-1). Oscar is wrong! The effective tax deduction he will have is the $800 per month maximum multiplied by his 60-percent employment use, which results in a tax deduction equal to $480 per month, or $5,760 for all of 2006.

Home office expenses

If your employer requires you to provide space in your home or apartment to carry out your employment duties, your employer must indicate this on form T2200 and provide it to you. If you do maintain a home office, you can deduct a portion of the expenses related to maintaining the workspace. This includes a portion of the expenses that you incur anyway, such as monthly utilities and rent.

For the costs to be deductible, you must ensure your workspace meets one of two tests — you don't have to meet both! Under the first test, the workspace must be the primary place where your employment duties are carried out. A sales representative employed by a company may work from home and rarely "go to the office." A part-time night school teacher may not have an office at a school and must plan lessons and mark exams at home.

If the first test is not met, all is not lost. You may still qualify to deduct home office expenses if your workspace is used exclusively to carry out your employment duties and you use the space on a "regular and continuous" basis for meeting customers or clients or others associated with carrying out your duties. Infrequent meetings or frequent meetings at irregular intervals won't cut it.

Deductible home office expenses

As Table 10-3 details, an employee paid on a commission basis is able to deduct more home office expenses than an employee paid by salary.

Table 10-3	Home Office Expenses Deductions	
	Earning Salary	*Earning Commissions*
Electricity, heat, and water	Yes	Yes
Maintenance	Yes	Yes
Rent	Yes	Yes
Property tax	No	Yes
Home insurance	No	Yes
Mortgage interest	No	No
Mortgage principal	No	No

Expenses such as telephone and Internet charges are not mentioned here. Though you may think of these as a home office expense, they can be deducted as "supplies" in completing form T777. The CRA's position is that long-distance charges for calls made to carry out your employment duties can be deducted, but that the monthly charges for your residential phone line cannot — not even a portion of them. However, if you have a separate phone line for your employment, the full costs associated with this phone can be deducted.

Transport employees

If you are employed in the transport industry (air, rail and bus travel, and trucking), you and your employer are required to complete form TL2, "Claim for Meals and Lodging Expenses." The total of the amount deductible is to be included on line 229 of your tax return. Like non–transport industry employees, you may be eligible for a GST/HST rebate.

Musicians' instruments

In addition to the costs noted above for employees, if you're a musician you may be entitled to deduct capital cost allowance on your instrument (Class 8 — 20 percent declining basis) as well as any amounts paid for the maintenance, rental, and insurance of the instrument. To claim these amounts, you must be required, as a term of your employment, to provide your own musical instrument.

Artists' expenses

If you're an employed artist, you'll enjoy some deductions in addition to the "regular" employee expenses. The CRA considers you an artist if you do any of the following:

- ✔ Create (but don't reproduce) paintings, prints, etchings, drawings, sculptures, or similar works of art

- ✔ Compose dramatic, musical, or literary works

- ✔ Perform dramatic or musical work, as an actor, singer, or musician

- ✔ Belong to a professional artists' association that is certified by the Minister of Canadian Heritage

An artist who earns income from any of the above activities may deduct related expenses incurred to earn this income. Again, these "related" expenses are in addition to the regular employment expenses deductible by all types of employees who are required to incur these expenses as part of their job.

Tradespersons' tool expenses

Tradespersons who acquire eligible tools after May 1, 2006, for employment can deduct the cost exceeding $1,000 each year up to a maximum of $500 dollars per year.

Mechanics' apprentices

A mechanic's apprentice can deduct a portion of the cost of tools acquired in a year on his or her personal tax return. Those of you with a "vehicle mechanic in training" in the family will know what a significant investment these tools are in relation to income, and will likely want to join us in saying, "Yay!"

Unfortunately, a deduction for the full cost of the tools is not allowed. The allowable deduction amount is the total cost of new tools acquired in a taxation year, less the greater of $1,000 or 5 percent of the individual's apprenticeship income for the year.

Any part of the eligible deduction that is not taken in the year in which the tools are purchased can be carried forward and deducted in subsequent taxation years. You can also claim a GST/HST tax credit for the sales taxes paid on the deductible portion of the tools.

Goods and Services Tax (GST)/Harmonized Sales Tax (HST) rebate

The *Goods and Services Tax* (GST) and *Harmonized Sales Tax* (HST) are consumer taxes. This means that if you incur GST or HST in carrying out your employment duties, you are really incurring it on behalf of your employer's business — not as a consumer. Therefore, the GST or HST should be refunded or rebated to you because it was not incurred for a consumer purchase.

The GST rate decreased from 7 percent to 6 percent effective July 1, 2006. As a result, for 2006 you may have some expenses with 7 percent GST and some with 6 percent GST.

Say you purchase a gift to give to one of your best customers. The actual price of the gift was $100, but you paid $106 when GST was added. (For simplicity, we've assumed you bought this gift in a non-HST province and we've ignored retail sales tax.)

The $6 paid was not in respect of a consumer purchase. Therefore, the $6 should be refunded or rebated to you. This is referred to as a GST rebate. It is calculated using form GST 370, "Employee and Partner GST/HST Rebate Application." Note the $6 on line 457 of your tax return, and it will either decrease the income tax you owe or increase your tax refund!

What if the gift was for your mother? Well, there is no employment aspect to this purchase, so the $6 is not refundable — it becomes a true cost to you because you are acting as a consumer in making this gift purchase. The $6 is not going to be returned to you . . . but your mom will appreciate the gift.

Assessing your eligibility for the GST/HST rebate

If you have to pay your own expenses to carry out your employment duties, you are probably able to claim a rebate for the GST and HST included in your expenses. You are not eligible to claim the GST/HST if either of the following applies to your situation:

✔ Your employer is not a GST/HST registrant

✔ Your employer carries on a GST/HST-exempt activity, which includes one of the following:

- Health care (for example, a medical or dental practice)

- Financial services (for example, banking, insurance, and investing)

Expenses that qualify for the GST/HST rebate

Expenses you paid GST/HST on and deducted on form T777, plus the GST/HST component of the union or professional dues deducted on line 212 of your tax return qualify for the GST/HST rebate.

Expenses that do not qualify for the GST/HST rebate

You probably did not pay GST/HST on all your expenses because some did not attract GST/HST.

✔ Expenses where no GST/HST was incurred.

- You may have paid for goods or services that are GST exempt, such as some membership fees and dues, insurance, licences, and salaries to assistants.

- You may have incurred employment expenses where no GST/HST was paid because the vendor of the goods or provider of the service was not registered for GST and, therefore, did not charge GST.

✔ Personal-use portion of employment expenses. You cannot claim a GST/HST rebate in connection with GST/HST paid on the personal portion of your automobile and home office expenses.

How to calculate and claim your GST/HST rebate

The rebate you are entitled to is calculated on form GST370, "Employee and Partner GST/HST Rebate Application."

Earlier in this chapter we saw that Fiona was able to deduct the following employment expenses:

Office supplies	$ 5,300
Salary to Katy, Fiona's assistant	$4,000
Automobile expenses (assuming her car was leased)	$6,094

Home office expenses	<u>$465</u>
Total employment expenses	<u>$ 15,859</u>

Fiona would use form GST370 to calculate her 2006 GST/HST rebate. As Fiona incurred GST only (no HST), she will use only the GST portion of the form.

GST rebate on eligible expenses

Total employment expenses per T777		$ 15,859
Less non-eligible expenses (expenses on which no GST was paid)		
Salary to Katy		$4,000
Employment-use portion claimed of:		
Car insurance	$1,000 × 75% business usage	$750
Car licence and registration	$125 × 75% business usage	$94
Water	$100 × 10% business usage	$10
House insurance	$300 × 10% business usage	$30
Property tax	$2,000 × 10% business usage	$200
Total expenses eligible for the GST rebate		$10,775
Multiply-by factor to "back out" 6% from total		6/106
GST employee rebate (to line 457 on tax return)		$610

Fiona will put the $610 on line 457 of her tax return. It will serve to reduce the total tax owing on her tax return or increase the refund owing to her.

Now you say, *HOLD IT!* You've just realized that Fiona received two benefits:

- ✔ She got a tax saving from being able to deduct the GST component of her employment expenses.

- ✔ She received back the GST she paid.

Isn't this double-dipping on a tax/GST break? Congratulations on being so observant. Fiona has indeed received a double benefit. In fact, the government purposely designed the system this way! (Who else could?) However, when Fiona does her 2007 tax return, the double benefit will be taken away. The prior-year GST/HST rebate must be included in your current year's taxable income. So, effectively, the GST/HST portion of employment expenses deducted on a tax return in one year are added back to income in the immediately subsequent year's tax return. In year one you have the benefit of deducting the GST/HST portion of the employment expenses. In year two the amount is added back to income.

So, if we get back to Fiona's situation we will see that she'll include the $610 on line 104 of her 2007 tax return. It will be fully subject to tax in 2007. After two years and two tax returns, the only double-dipping Fiona will do is at Dairy Queen.

Provincial and territorial sales taxes

There is no rebate for provincial and territorial sales taxes. They simply remain part of the costs you incurred in carrying out your employment responsibilities.

Line 231: Clergy Residence Deduction

An employed clergyperson may be able to claim a deduction in computing his or her net income in respect to his or her residence. A deduction is permitted when an individual is

- ✔ In charge of or ministering to a parish, congregation, or diocese, or

- ✔ Engaged exclusively in full-time administrative service by appointment of a religious order or religious denomination.

If a member of the clergy has free accommodation, the value of this benefit is included in his or her income. It is usually reported on a T4. The amount is included in the total employment income noted in box 14 and highlighted separately in box 30. The deduction available is equal to this benefit. Hence the cleric is subject to tax only on the salary component of his or her employment income.

If free accommodation is not provided, a claim can be made for the amount paid as rent or the fair rental value of the accommodation owned by the clergyperson. The deduction cannot exceed the employment income earned as a clergyperson. If the clergyperson receives a housing allowance from an employer, the allowance is included in income. However, the income inclusion can be offset with the cleric's residence deduction.

To claim these deductions, complete form T1229, "Clergy Residence Deduction."

Line 232: Other Deductions

You can deduct a variety of expenses on line 232 if they apply to you. These include certain legal fees; repayments of OAS, CPP, and EI; withdrawals of RRSP overcontributions; and unclaimed foreign tax credits.

Legal fees

Tax-deductible legal fees include:

- ✔ Legal fees paid to object to or appeal an income tax assessment.
- ✔ Legal fees paid to collect a severance or retirement allowance or a pension benefit. You can claim fees only up to the amount of the payment received in the year — minus any amount transferred to your RRSP. If you cannot claim all your legal fees in the year paid, they may be able to be claimed over the next seven years.
- ✔ Certain legal fees paid in respect to marital breakdown and spousal and child support.

The tax authorities have relaxed their stance on the deductibility of legal fees incurred to obtain spousal support. Previously these fees were not deductible, but they are now. You have always been permitted a deduction for legal fees to collect child support, and now this has been expanded to allow a deduction for legal fees incurred to *increase* child support as well.

Ensure your lawyer details the bill such that fees for tax deductible services are highlighted!

Repayments of OAS, CPP, QPP, and EI benefits

Sometimes the government sends you too much money. If you have been paid benefits in excess of what you are considered to be entitled to, Social Development Canada (SDC) or Human Resources and Skills Development Canada (HRSDC) — or the Quebec equivalent — will request its money back.

If in 2006 you were required to repay any OAS, CPP, QPP, or EI that was included in your 2005 or prior year's tax returns, you can deduct the repayment on line 232 on your 2006 tax return. EI repayments made in 2006 in respect of EI received in 2005 or prior years are noted in box 30 of your T4E slip.

Repayments of prior-year OAS and EI differ from repayments of OAS and EI, referred to as *social benefit repayments* or *clawbacks* (see "Line 235: Social Benefits Repayment," below). Clawbacks are repayments you may be required to make in connection with OAS or EI received in 2006 — not receipts from prior years. The amount to be repaid is calculated based on your 2006 income, as per line 234 of your return.

Other deductions

Other deductions you may be able to claim include the following:

- **Withdrawals of overcontributed RRSP amounts:** If you remove an RRSP overcontribution (discussed under line 208), you will need to include this in your income as with any RRSP withdrawal. Your RRSP holder will issue you a T4RSP slip. The slip will *not* highlight that the amount you are taking out is an overcontribution. The income inclusion can result in double taxation since you never received a tax deduction for the RRSP contribution (because it was an overcontribution). To prevent double taxation you might be able to claim a deduction on line 232 for the amount of RRSP overcontribution withdrawn. You will need to file form T746, "Calculating Your Deduction for Refund of Unused RRSP Contributions," with your tax return to see if you qualify.

> ✔ **Unclaimed foreign tax credits:** As we detail in Chapter 13, you may not be entitled to claim a full foreign tax credit. When this is the case, the amount of foreign taxes you paid in excess of the foreign tax credit available to you may qualify for a deduction on line 232.

Line 235: Social Benefits Repayment

Canada's social welfare programs — Old Age Security (OAS) for seniors and Employment Insurance (EI) for the unemployed — have limitations. Essentially, if your income is considered too high you are required to repay all or a portion of the benefits received.

OAS clawback

As we explain in Chapter 5, you will be subject to an OAS clawback in 2006 if your line 234 net income exceeds $62,144. For every dollar of income above this, you are required to pay back 15 cents of your OAS income. Your OAS is entirely eliminated once your income reaches $101,031. If you were subject to the clawback rules in 2006, you probably received a reduced amount of OAS from the government. In fact, you might not have received any OAS at all. However, you will still get a T4(OAS) slip indicating that you have received the full OAS. This is guaranteed to confuse you, but the slip is correct; the amount clawed back from you will be indicated as a tax paid.

You can deduct any social benefit repayment (that is, the clawback) in calculating your net income. This makes sense because the full amount of OAS has been included in calculating your total income. Therefore, since you are not allowed to keep all the income, only the portion that you can keep, if any, is taxed. The amount you need to repay, the clawed-back amount, is added to your tax liability on line 422 of your tax return.

 If you have received a T4(OAS) slip, ensure that you complete line 235. The government may owe you OAS! If it does, the amount is paid to you as part of your tax return — it will decrease your tax liability or increase your tax refund.

Since the OAS clawback is based on the line 234 net income, you should plan, where possible, to minimize this net income figure. You can do this by reducing your income subject to tax — perhaps by rearranging your affairs to shift investment income to a spouse or, where it makes sense, to invest to earn capital gains (of which only 50 percent are taxable) versus interest income, which is 100 percent taxable.

EI clawback

Like the OAS clawback, a repayment of EI because your income is considered too high is referred to as a social benefit repayment. If you were required to repay some of the EI you received in 2005 or prior years, the amount repaid can be deducted on line 232 of your 2006 return.

You will usually need to repay all or part of your current year's EI benefits if your line 234 net income is more than $48,750.

A person who received special EI benefits (maternity, parental, and sickness) will not have to repay those benefits.

The repayment of regular EI benefits required is calculated as 30 percent of the lesser of

- ✔ The regular EI benefits you received
- ✔ The amount of your net income in excess of $48,750

Just as with the OAS clawback, any amount of EI to be clawed back is deducted on line 235 ("Social Benefits Repayment") in calculating net income. Since the amount is being repaid, it does not make sense for it to be subject to income tax. Report the amount repaid on line 422 of your tax return. In essence, you are simply adding to your tax liability the EI amount to be repaid.

Part III

Tax Preparation Tips: Claiming Deductions and Credits

The 5th Wave   By Rich Tennant

"That? That's schedule X. We've never had to use it. But, if anyone actually discovers how to grow money on trees, the CRA's got a form to get its fair share of the leaves."

In this part . . .

*N*ow for our favourite part — deductions and credits to lighten your tax burden. After reading through the last couple of chapters and calculating your income, you may feel like there's no hope and be starting to think it would be more efficient next year to simply hand over your paycheques to the CRA. Don't fret — there is a light at the end of the tunnel, and it's shining on the words "deductions and credits."

These next few chapters may be the most important in the entire book, especially given the number of tax changes that have taken place for 2006. So highlight, bookmark, and tag these pages! Do anything you have to do to remind yourself of the deductions you're entitled to: You can be sure that in most cases, the CRA won't remind you to claim them! After all, a dollar deduction not claimed means more money in its coffers. Pay close attention to these chapters — you don't want to miss a single tip!

"Taxes should be proportioned to what may be annually spared by the individual."

—Thomas Jefferson

Chapter 11

Tips for Deductions in Calculating Taxable Income

- -

In This Chapter

▶ Defining taxable income

▶ Taking a look at employee home relocation loans

▶ Dealing with stock options

▶ Making the most of loss carryovers

▶ Using the capital gains exemption

▶ Claiming the northern residents deduction

- -

*N*et income, which we discuss in Chapter 10, is basically a snapshot of your current year's income. You use this snapshot to calculate your entitlement to certain tax credits, such as the GST/HST credit and the Child Tax Benefit, among others. Net income also provides a basis for certain non-refundable tax credits, such as the spousal or common-law partner amount and the medical expense credit. Taxable income, the subject of this chapter, has a different focus altogether. It is the figure you use to calculate how much income tax you owe for the year.

The types of deductions allowed under the taxable income category are not necessarily related to current-year activities. For instance, the calculation of taxable income includes deductions for prior-year losses. In fact, some of the deductions are permissive, meaning they allow for tax deductions based on your personal situation. For example, deductions are available for employee stock options, for residence in northern areas of Canada, and for certain non-taxable payments received in the year.

On many returns, net income and taxable income will be the same; therefore, you won't have to worry about these deductions at all. However, if you do have additional deductions, it's important to keep in mind that there is a difference between net income and taxable income — be sure to use the right figures in the right places!

Tax Planning In Calculating Taxable Income

Sometimes you will have so many deductions to claim, you won't need them all to reduce your taxable income to the point where no taxes are owing.

If you have more deductions than you need in the year, you must claim deductions in this order:

1. Deductions for employee stock options, employee home relocation loans, non-taxable receipts such as social assistance, workers' compensation, Old Age Security (OAS) supplements, treaty-exempt income, and vow of perpetual poverty claims.

2. Loss claims, including non-capital losses, net capital losses, farm losses, and limited-partnership losses.

3. Capital gains exemption.

4. Northern residents deductions.

Some deductions can be carried forward to use in future years, while some can not. So, when given the choice, always try to reduce your "discretionary" deductions to use up all the deductions and credits that can't be carried forward. Discretionary deductions include some items used to calculate your "net income," such as RRSP deductions and moving expenses. Losses from prior years can also be carried forward (although keep in mind the ordering provisions above), so try to use up other deductions before you dip into these!

Use your available tax deductions to reduce your taxable income only to the point that it equals your total tax credits for the year. If you reduce your taxable income to zero, you won't owe any taxes but you might be wasting some deductions. For example, most taxpayers are allowed to claim the basic personal credit amount — this means you would want to report at least $8,839 of taxable income in 2006 since you won't pay tax on that amount of income anyway. To optimize your tax situation, you therefore don't want to waste tax deductions that you can carry forward to future years if it means reducing your taxable income below the amount of your tax credits. Zero taxable income is not the goal.

Where do you find these tax credits? Non-refundable tax credits and other federal tax credits (such as the dividend tax credit, overseas employment tax credit, and alternative minimum tax carryover) are detailed on schedule 1 of your tax return.

Line 248: Employee Home Relocation Loan Deductions

The home relocation deduction is one deduction that you'll know you're entitled to claim. Why? Because it shows up right on the T4 slip you receive from your employer. If an amount is entered in box 37 of your T4 slip, you can claim a deduction for your employee home relocation loan.

So what qualifies as a home relocation loan? Unfortunately, a loan to allow you to move down the street because you want a view of the lake does not. A home relocation loan is a loan your employer gives you, usually at a zero or low interest rate, to help you move for business reasons. Generally, this means you are changing jobs and your new employer is helping you out with a loan, or your current employer is transferring you to a new location.

To qualify for the employee home relocation loan deduction, all of the following must apply:

- ✔ The loan must be received by an employee (or the employee's spouse).
- ✔ You must be moving at least 40 kilometres.
- ✔ You must commence work in a new location in Canada.
- ✔ The loan must be used to acquire a new residence.

When you receive a home relocation loan, the amount received is not included in your T4 slip. However, an amount representing the "interest benefit" you have enjoyed (by not paying the interest!) is included in your T4 slip. Your employer has to report the interest benefit on all loans given to you if the interest rate you are paying (if any) is less than the CRA's prescribed interest rate.

The CRA's prescribed interest rates are posted each quarter of the year. For the first quarter of 2006, this rate was 3 percent. It then rose to 4 percent for the second and third quarter of the year, and finally to 5 percent for the last quarter of the year. Current and historical prescribed interest rates can be found on the CRA's Web site at www.cra-arc.gc.ca/tax/faq/interest_rates/menu-e.html. The rate that should be used to calculate your taxable benefit is the rate in effect when your employee loan was granted. However, if the rate subsequently drops, you can start using this new lower rate. If the rate increases, you can continue to use the rate in effect at the time the loan was received. In other words, you are protected from rate increases after you received the loan, but you benefit from lower rates. This protection lasts for five years, as a new loan is considered to be granted every five years. So, let's say you received a $20,000 loan at the beginning of the year when the CRA prescribed rate was 3 percent. Even though the rate increased to 4 and then 5 percent, provided you are paying 3 percent interest on the loan, you won't have to report any interest benefit in your income. However, if your loan is still outstanding five years from the date the loan was granted and at that time the prescribed interest rate is 6 percent, you'll have to start paying 6 percent in order to avoid any having an interest benefit included in your income.

If you are required to pay at least the CRA's prescribed interest rate on your employee loan, you do not need to calculate a taxable benefit.

Now for the good part: the deduction! When an interest benefit is included in your income for an employee home relocation loan, and you meet the criteria above, you can claim a full or partial deduction from your income.

Your deduction is the lesser of the following:

- ✔ The interest benefit (which is included in your income)
- ✔ The amount of interest benefit that would have been computed if the home relocation loan had been $25,000

In friendlier terms, if you've received a $20,000 interest-free loan from your employer when the prescribed interest rate was 4 percent, and this loan meets the definition of a home relocation loan, your deduction will be the lesser of $800 and $1,000 ($25,000 × 4 percent). In this case, your entire taxable benefit of $800 will be offset by the deduction. Just to keep it interesting, there is another rule that applies to employee home relocation loans. You see, the deduction does not last forever. It is applicable only for a maximum of five years from the day the loan was originally granted, or until the loan is actually paid off, whichever is shorter.

In negotiating your compensation for a new job that will require moving at least 40 kilometres, ask for a $25,000 home relocation loan. Due to the deduction for the interest benefit on the first $25,000 of a home relocation loan, you effectively receive the loan tax-free for five years.

Line 249: Stock Option and Shares Deductions

Stock options are one of the most popular forms of non-monetary compensation offered by employers. But make no mistake about it, they are a taxable benefit. The taxable benefit you receive in the year should be included in your total employment income reported on box 14 of your T4 slip. Here's a brief synopsis of the rules.

The Rules

There are special rules when a corporation agrees to sell or issue shares to an employee as part of a compensation package. Basically the employee is given an option to buy stock (more commonly referred to as shares) of a company for an agreed upon price at a future point in time. When the employee is given this option, there is nothing to report in income. The general rule is that the taxable benefit comes into play when the option is exercised – or when you state that "yes, I would like to purchase the stock now." When the option is exercised, the benefit included in your income is the difference between the fair market value of the shares on the date you exercised your option, and the price you paid for the option and the shares.

Of course, it wouldn't be a tax rule without exceptions. There are exceptions to this general rule when the option is given to buy shares of a publicly traded company or shares of a Canadian-controlled private corporation. We'll take a closer look at these rules below.

Public company shares

Normally in the year you exercise your stock options, you are considered to have received a taxable benefit equal to the difference between the market value of the shares on that day and your actual cost. Thanks to fairly recent legislation in the *Income Tax Act,* this is no longer the case in all instances. In fact, if you have a stock option in a publicly traded company, you may now be able to postpone the taxation of qualifying employee stock options to when the shares are sold, instead of when the option is exercised.

Unfortunately, the rules don't end there. Even if you don't sell your shares in the same year you exercise your option, you may not be allowed to postpone the entire income inclusion. To complicate matters, the maximum benefit that can be deferred is $100,000 per vesting year. This $100,000 is based on the value of the underlying shares when the option was granted to you. The option price doesn't matter — it is the value of the underlying shares that is used to calculate the $100,000 limit.

For example, say you were granted the option to purchase 100,000 shares of your employer corporation, at a price of $2 per share, in 1998. (Assume the shares were trading at $2 at the time the option was granted to you.) At the time you exercise your option, the shares are trading at $5. (If you're quick at math you realize you had a $3 benefit per share, so for 100,000 shares the benefit is $300,000.) If you exercise all your options this year, you will receive only a partial deferral of tax. At the time the options were granted to you, they were worth $200,000 (100,000 × $2). This means that you will manage to defer taxes on only one-half of your options ($200,000 – $100,000 ÷ $2 per share = 50,000 options). Your taxable benefit this year will be $150,000 ($5 – $2 × 50,000 options), and the other $150,000 will be taxed only when you sell the shares ($150,000 taxed now, $150,000 taxed later, $300,000 taxed in total — as expected).

If you wish to take advantage of this deferral for options exercised in 2006 you must make an "election" with your employer before January 15, 2007. The election is simply a letter to your employer that must contain the following:

- ✔ A request for the deferral to apply
- ✔ The amount of the stock option benefit being deferred
- ✔ Confirmation that you were resident in Canada when you purchased the shares
- ✔ Confirmation that you have not exceeded the $100,000 annual limit

You need to inform your employer so that your T4 is prepared correctly. In addition to making this election, you must complete form T1212, "Statement of Deferred Stock Option Benefits," and file it with your return each year you continue to have a deferred stock option benefit.

It usually makes a lot of sense to wait until you want to sell your option shares before you go ahead and exercise your stock options. This will ensure that you have the cash (from the sale of the shares) available to pay your tax bill. We've seen too many situations where Canadians exercised their stock options, accrued a huge tax bill, and then got stung because the shares dropped in value after the exercise date. There is nothing in the Canadian tax laws to remedy this situation, meaning you will still owe tax on the stock option benefit as of the date of exercise, even if the shares are worthless when they are actually sold. What's more, the difference between the sale price and the exercise price is a capital loss (or a capital gain, if it goes up in value). Since capital losses can be used to offset only capital gains, and not any other type of income (such as the employment income a stock option benefit gives rise to), you may be stuck with a useless capital loss. Ouch!

Canadian-controlled private corporations

If your employer is a Canadian-controlled private corporation (CCPC), you're in luck. When you exercise your stock options, you can defer all of your taxable benefit until you actually sell the shares. The taxable benefit for CCPCs is calculated the same way as that for public companies: the market value of the shares on the date you exercise your option less your cost. By the way, your cost includes your exercise price (the amount you must pay for the shares under your option agreement) and amounts you paid (if any) to acquire the option itself.

The rules for CCPC stock options will apply provided your employer was a CCPC at the time the option was granted to you (not when the option is exercised). So, if your company goes public in the future, you can still benefit from the more favourable CCPC stock option rules.

Stock option deductions

Now to the part you really want to know about — the stock option deduction. This deduction is available because the taxable benefit you'll be charged when you exercise your stock options is taxed as employment income (either this year or in a future year when you sell the stock). In other words, 100 percent of the benefit is taxable in your hands. To many people this seems unfair since the benefit is from a stock, which is normally treated as a capital item. As we discuss in Chapter 7, capital gains are only one-half taxable, so you are taxed a full one-half more by exercising an employee stock option rather than purchasing the share yourself on the open market and then selling it for a profit.

But don't fret. Our tax laws understand this difference and allow a deduction, known as the stock option and shares deduction. The deduction is equal to one-half of the taxable benefit you must report. This means that your stock option benefit will effectively be taxed in the same way as a capital gain would be.

Additional deduction for donated shares

An additional stock option deduction of 50 percent is available if you exercise a stock option and then donate the shares to a registered charity on or after May 2, 2006. Yep, that's right. You'll get a tax deduction for *100 percent* of your taxable benefit. For shares donated before May 2, 2006, the additional deduction is 25 percent. So, the total deduction is 75 percent. You'll also get a donation receipt for the full market value of your donation. To take advantage of this incentive, the shares must be donated to the charity within the year and within 30 days of the option being exercised. Note that when you donate such stocks to a registered charity you report the disposition on form T1170, "Capital Gains on Gifts of Certain Capital Property," and not on schedule 3 of your tax return.

Shares qualifying for the deduction

Like most good things, the stock option and share deduction is not available in every case. In order to qualify, some criteria must be met. (You didn't think a tax law would exist without qualifications, did you!)

The stock option deduction is available if *all* of the following conditions are met:

- ✔ Your employer corporation, or a corporation that does not deal at arm's length to the employer (a related company), must be the seller or issuer of the shares.

- ✔ The shares must be common shares of the corporation.

- ✔ The exercise price of the option (that is, the amount you must pay to receive the share of your employer corporation — it's sometimes called the strike price) must be at least equal to the market value of the share at the time the option was granted to you. If you've paid an amount to acquire the option itself, this amount can be added to the exercise price of the option. For example, if you've paid $2 to acquire the option to purchase a share of your employer, and subsequently pay $5 to exercise the option, you will be eligible for the stock option deduction (assuming all other criteria are met) as long as the market value of the employer's shares on the date the option was granted to you was at least $7 ($2 plus $5).

- ✔ You must be dealing at arm's length with your employer. This means that if you control the corporation (that is, you own the majority of the voting shares), or are related to a person who controls the corporation, you will not be eligible for this deduction.

Regulation 6204 of the *Income Tax Act* covers the entire list of criteria (good reading for anyone with insomnia).

If the option was granted to you while the corporation was a CCPC (Canadian-controlled private corporation), you don't necessarily have to worry about the above rules. You see, if you hold the shares you've acquired under your stock option agreement for at least two years, you'll automatically qualify for the stock option deduction. However, if you don't hold the shares for two years, but meet the above criteria, you'll still qualify. (CCPC options are more flexible than public company options in terms of the respective tax rules.)

Although these rules might sound fairly complex, it will not be up to you to determine whether you are eligible for the deduction. Your employer should make this determination, and your T4 slip for the year will indicate that your taxable employment benefit is in fact eligible for the "110(1)(d) or 110(1)(d.1) deduction." (You guessed it — these references are to the *Income Tax Act*.) The amount eligible for the deduction is reported in either box 39 or 41 of your T4 slip. If an amount shows up in these boxes, report it on line 249 of your tax return.

Line 250: Other Payments Deductions

Did you report amounts on line 147 of your tax return? If so, you're likely entitled to a deduction for the full amount reported. You see, the types of payments reported on line 147 are not taxable amounts. And although they must be reported as part of your "net income," they are not intended to be part of your "taxable income." Hence the deduction. (Yes — it's slightly confusing, but these sources of income are received tax-free!)

The types of payments reported on line 147, and then deducted on line 250, are the following:

- ✔ Workers' compensation (form T5007)
- ✔ Social assistance payments (form T5007)
- ✔ Supplements to your Old Age Security pension payments (T4AOAS)

Lines 251 to 253: Loss Carryovers

Filing a tax return is one time that being a loser is to your advantage. If you've incurred losses (including limited partnership losses, non-capital losses, and net capital losses) in prior years, and were unable to use those losses on your prior years' tax returns, you are allowed to carry those losses forward to offset some of your current income.

If you've had losses in the past, you may be able to use those losses on your 2006 tax return to offset your taxable income and reduce your 2006 tax bill! If you're unsure what your unclaimed loss balance is, give the CRA a call. If you forget to claim an amount, the CRA will not apply your unused losses to your current income, because these are optional deductions.

Depending on the type of loss you've incurred, there may be limitations on the amount of loss you can carry forward, and on the number of years it can be carried forward.

It's generally most beneficial to apply a prior year's loss to income that's taxed at a high rate. For example, if your income is low this year but is expected to increase in future years, you may want to forgo claiming the loss carried forward this year. Instead, you can save the loss for a future year when you know you'll be subject to a higher tax rate. Of course, since certain types of losses have a limited carry-forward period (we discuss this in a moment), you'll want to be absolutely certain you'll be able to use the loss in future years. If there's any doubt, claim the loss this year — use it, don't lose it — even if you're in a low tax bracket.

Never claim losses to bring your taxable income to zero. Although you'll have no tax to pay with taxable income of zero, you'd also have no tax to pay if you report income equal to your non-refundable tax credits.

Limited-partnership losses

Limited partnerships are most commonly purchased as tax shelters. A limited partner, as opposed to a general partner, has limited liability with respect to the partnership's liabilities. The main reason (and perhaps not the best reason) for investing in a limited partnership is often the up-front tax losses allocated to partners.

Although some of these partnerships eventually make a profit, there are often huge losses in the first years. These losses are passed on to investors (the partners), to be deducted on their personal tax returns. The tax authorities are not fans of limited partnerships in general, and the tax laws limit the amount of losses that you can claim. Specifically, investors can deduct cumulative losses only up to the investor's "at-risk amount."

Your at-risk amount is the amount you paid to purchase the limited partnership, plus any further capital contributions you made to the partnership (in other words, your *tax cost* of the limited-partnership investment). Put more succinctly, you can deduct losses on your tax return only up to the amount that you paid for your partnership interest.

If you've received form T5013, "Statement of Partnership Income," from your limited partnership in the year, your at-risk amount should be reported in box 45. If not, contact the partnership and ask them for details of this amount — this is something the partnership should track.

If your cumulative limited-partnership losses exceed your at-risk amount, you can carry the remaining losses forward for possible future use. You can deduct the additional losses to offset income produced by the partnership or to offset any additional capital you contributed to the partnership. Limited-partnership losses can be carried forward indefinitely. There is no expiry.

Your limited-partnership losses available for carryover will be reported in box 31 of your T5013 slip. This is the amount that can't be deducted on your current year's tax return, but can be carried forward to offset limited partnership income in the future.

If you have a limited-partnership loss in 2006 (which does not exceed your at-risk amount), this loss can be used to offset income from any source in this year. In fact, the loss must be used this year if it can be. If not, it becomes part of your non–capital loss balance and can be carried back for up to three years to offset a prior year's taxable income or (new for 2006) carried forward for 20 years. But don't forget — if any portion of the loss can't be used because of the at-risk rules, it can only be carried forward to offset against limited-partnership income in the future, unless you increase the at-risk amount of your limited-partnership investment.

Non-capital losses

In general, any business, employment, or property transaction is considered non-capital (see Chapter 7 for details on capital versus non-capital losses). So, if you have your own business and it generates a loss, this is considered to be a non-capital loss. In addition, if you've incurred an allowable business investment loss, otherwise known as an ABIL (see Chapter 10, lines 217 and 226 for more details), this is also considered to be a non-capital loss.

The amount of non-capital loss that is generated in a particular tax year is calculated on form T1A, "Request for Loss Carryback." This is also the form that allows you to carry back any current-year losses to prior tax years, and reports the amount of the loss that can be carried forward to future years.

Form T1A is important because not all items on your tax return are figured into the calculation of your non-capital loss. Therefore, if you have a negative net income or taxable income amount (which is actually reported as a zero balance on lines 236 and 260 of your tax return), you should fill out form T1A so you know how much of the losses can be carried over to other tax years.

Once the CRA receives and processes your form T1A, it will reassess the year to which you carried the loss back . . . *and send you a tax refund cheque!*

Items included in non-capital losses

The items included in the calculation of non-capital losses on your tax return are as follows:

- ✔ **Employment income/loss:** This includes lines 101 and 104, less any amounts reported on lines 207, 212, 229, and 231.

- ✔ **Investment income/loss:** Add together lines 120 and 121 and deduct any amount reported on line 221.

- ✔ **Partnership income/loss:** This includes any amounts reported on line 122. Note that only the allowable loss (not the restricted portion of the limited partnership loss) is included on this line.

- ✔ **Rental income/loss:** This is reported on line 126.

- ✔ **Business, professional, or commission income or losses:** These are reported on lines 135, 137, and 139.

- ✔ **Farming or fishing income or losses:** These are reported on lines 141 and 143. The amount of farming losses you can claim may be restricted if farming is not your chief source of income for the year (see Chapter 9 for more information).

✔ **Taxable capital gains:** This is reported on line 127.

✔ **Non-taxable income:** This is reported on line 147.

✔ **Net capital losses of other years:** This is reported on line 253.

✔ **Certain other deductions:** These include the capital gains deduction, deduction for business investment losses, employee home-relocation loan deduction, stock option and shares deductions, other payments deduction, and income exempt under a tax treaty. Amounts are reported on lines 254, 217, 248, 249, and 250.

Form T1A requires you to separate the income and loss items on your tax return. For example, any deductions claimed would be placed in the "loss" column. You must then total all the income and loss items separately.

If you've claimed any amounts on lines 208, 209, 214, 215, 219, 220, 232, or 235 of your tax return, these amounts are deducted from your total income. It's possible that these deductions will cause you to have negative income; however, these amounts do not result in a non-capital loss. If the deductions claimed on these lines result in negative income (before taking into account allowable deductions in the loss column), your total income is deemed to be nil. You then take your total income, less the total amount reported in the loss column, to calculate the net loss for the year. You must then deduct any farming or fishing losses incurred in the year to come up with your total non-capital loss available for carryover. It is this amount that can be carried back to offset taxable income in any of the previous three taxation years, or carried forward.

Calculation of non-capital losses

Pam had more tax deductions than income in the 2005 tax year. She would like to know if she can take advantage of her losses on her 2006 tax return. Here is a summary of items claimed on her 2005 tax return:

Interest income	1,200
Business income (loss)	($9,000)
RRSP deduction	$2,000

Pam's 2005 non-capital loss is calculated as follows. Note that "personal" streams of income and deductions are handled separately from the business loss.

	Current Year Income ("A")	Current Year Loss ("B")	2005 Non-capital Loss ("A – B")
Interest income	$1,200		
Business loss		$9,000	
Subtotal	$1,200	$9,000	
Subtract: RRSP	($2,000)	n/a	
Subtotal (if negative = 0)	0	$9,000	$9,000

Pam can carry forward the 2005 $9,000 non-capital loss to 2006 to reduce her 2006 taxable income.

Thanks to the 2006 federal budget, non-capital losses can now be carried forward for 20 years (the carry-forward period used to be only 10 years, and prior to 2004, 7 years). However, you should consider carrying your losses back (up to three years back), if possible, to receive a tax benefit from the loss sooner, rather than later.

Like other non-capital losses, an ABIL (allowable business investment loss) can be carried forward 20 years to reduce other types of income. If at the end of the 20 years the ABIL is still unused, it becomes a capital loss and can be carried forward indefinitely to reduce capital gains.

If you are certain you will have taxable income in the future, you may want to forgo a loss carryback and instead carry the losses forward to offset your future income. It is always most beneficial to claim the losses against income taxed at the highest marginal tax rate. So, if you're expecting to generate significant income in the future that will be taxed at a higher marginal tax rate than you're subject to this year, you may want to keep the losses intact until you're in that higher tax bracket.

Net capital losses

Calculate capital losses for the current year on schedule 3 of your tax return. Capital losses will arise whenever you sell capital property (such as shares, mutual fund units, or real estate) for a sales price that is less than the property's adjusted cost base (The adjusted cost base of the property may be the price you originally paid for the property, but not always. See Chapter 7 for more information on calculating your adjusted cost base).

You may have both capital gains and capital losses this year. Your capital losses must first be used to offset any capital gains this year. However, if your losses exceed your total gains, you will have a net capital loss for the year. It is this net loss that can be carried back to offset capital gains taxed in any of the previous three taxation years, or forward to offset any capital gains in the future.

Net capital losses can be used only to offset taxable capital gains of other years. They cannot be used to offset any other types of income. Net capital losses can be carried forward indefinitely to offset future capital gains.

Net capital losses are also known as *allowable capital losses*. Only one-half of capital gains incurred in 2006 are taxable (as discussed in Chapter 7). Likewise, only one-half of any capital losses incurred in 2006 are deductible. It is the taxable, or deductible, portion of the gains and losses that is known as *taxable capital gains,* or net (or allowable) capital losses.

If you've incurred capital losses in prior years, you can deduct these losses on your 2006 tax return against any taxable capital gains reported on line 127 this year. Claim these losses on line 253 of your tax return.

Your Notice of Assessment will normally inform you if you have net capital losses carried forward from prior years. If you haven't kept track of your losses, call your local Tax Services Office and they will give you your net capital loss carry-forward balance.

The allowable portion of capital losses (and the taxable portion of capital gains) has been changing over the years. Therefore, when you're claiming net capital losses of other years on your current year's tax return, it's important to note the year in which the loss arose, and the capital gains inclusion rate in place during that year. The term *inclusion rate* means the portion of the capital gain that was taxable in that year, and the portion of the capital loss that was deductible. Table 11-1 lists the capital gains inclusion rates over the years.

Table 11-1	Capital Gains Inclusion Rates
Year	*Inclusion*
1971 and earlier	0% (Those were the days!)
1972 to 1987	50%
1988 and 1989	66.67%
1989 to February 27, 2000	75%
February 28, 2000 to October 17, 2000	66.67%
October 18, 2000 and later	50%

If you've incurred capital losses in prior years and want to apply them to the current year, you'll have to adjust your net capital loss for that year (that is, the loss after the above inclusion rates have been applied). Basically, the amount of the loss is adjusted to match the inclusion rate in effect for the year in which the loss is being applied. These are the steps to take:

1. Determine the year when your net capital loss occurred.

2. Divide your net capital loss for that year by the inclusion rate in effect during that year. For example, if you have a net capital loss of $50,000 carried forward from the 1988 tax year, you will divide that loss by 66.67 percent. This gives you a total or gross capital loss from 1988 of $75,000.

3. Multiply the total capital loss ($75,000) that you want to apply to your current-year capital gains by the current-year inclusion rate. If you want to apply the loss to gains incurred in 2005, multiply the total loss by 50 percent. Therefore, you can claim up to $37,500 of net capital losses on line 253 of your tax return this year (assuming you have taxable capital gains on line 127 of at least this amount).

You can carry back capital losses for only three taxation years to offset capital gains — so in 2006, 2003 will be the farthest back you can go.

Line 254: Capital Gains Deduction

If you've claimed a taxable capital gain on line 127 of your tax return, it's possible that you are eligible for an additional deduction in computing taxable income. In fact, if you've disposed of qualifying property for a gain, up to $500,000 may be exempt from tax. Of course, not all sales of capital property are eligible for the capital gains deduction. It applies only to disposition of qualified small business corporation shares (QSBC shares), qualified farm property, and thanks to the 2006 federal budget, qualified property used in a family fishing business.

The $500,000 capital gains deduction available is a lifetime limit. You can't double dip — in other words, you can't claim the deduction more than once. Once you've claimed $500,000 in total deductions throughout your lifetime, you're cut off from future deductions.

Between 1985 and 1994, two capital gains exemptions were available. One was the $500,000 capital gains exemption that is still in effect. The other was a $100,000 exemption available on the sale of any capital property. Now that the $100,000 deduction is gone, the only time you can claim a capital gains exemption is when you sell qualifying property — that is, qualified small business corporation shares or qualifying farm or fishing property.

If you've claimed any part of the $100,000 capital gains exemption in the past, the amounts claimed will reduce your $500,000 capital gains exemption available on qualifying property. For example, if you claimed the maximum $100,000 prior to 1994, you'll have only $400,000 of the $500,000 exemption to claim in future years.

Qualified small business corporation (QSBC) shares

If you've disposed of QSBC shares in the year you may qualify for the capital gains exemption, as long as you are a Canadian resident and you haven't used your entire capital gains exemption in the past.

Not just any share of a Canadian corporation will qualify under the QSBC rules. In fact, these rules are quite stringent. To review what criteria must be met for a company to qualify as a "small business corporation," see Chapter 7.

If you hold shares in a Canadian-controlled small business corporation (for example, a family business), visit a tax professional. Steps can be taken to ensure you are eligible for the capital gains exemption (known as "purifying" the corporation), even if your shares do not currently qualify. And even if you're not currently planning on selling your business, remember that should you meet an untimely death, you will be deemed to have disposed of all your assets, including these shares, at their market value at that time (unless you leave them to your spouse). Some current tax planning could save your family from a significant tax bill on your death!

If you own shares in a QSBC that will be going public in the future, ensure you elect to dispose of these shares on your tax return before they become public company shares. You will have to include the taxable portion of any deemed gains on your tax return, but these will be offset by the capital gains deduction. You can then add the deduction claimed to the tax cost of your new shares, effectively sheltering some, or all, of a future tax bill on the sale of the public company shares.

Qualified farm property

To provide an incentive for Canadians to invest in certain types of farm property, the $500,000 capital gains exemption is available to offset gains on the disposition of certain farm properties as well.

A number of criteria must be met to qualify for the exemption. We outline these criteria outlined in Chapter 7.

The definition of qualified farm property is technical and complex. In fact, since there are so many factors to consider, and the potential tax savings are so high, this is one area where a visit to a tax pro is necessary!

Qualified property used in a family fishing business

The 2006 federal budget extended the $500,000 capital gains exemption to include qualified property used in a family fishing business. Qualified property will include such items as fishing vessels and fishing licenses when used principally in a fishing business in Canada. This measure applies to dispositions occurring on or after May 2, 2006.

The CNIL problem

With a name that sounds like a horrid disease, it's no surprise that C-N-I-L spells bad news when you're trying to claim a capital gains exemption. The CNIL's full name is a cumulative net investment loss. It is basically a cumulation of all your investment expenses, less investment income, claimed after 1987. If you've claimed significant investment expenses or losses in the past and little investment income, you may have a problem if you plan to claim a capital gains deduction on your tax return. The problem is that your capital gains deduction will be reduced to the extent of your CNIL. So, if you have a CNIL of, say, $10,000, and your taxable capital gain on the disposition of QSBC shares or qualified farm or fishing property is $200,000, you'll be allowed to claim a capital gains deduction of only $190,000.

If you're planning on claiming a capital gains exemption, you need to know your CNIL balance. Call your local Tax Services Office — they keep track of your CNIL balance and will let you know where you stand.

The CNIL balance is calculated on form T936, "Calculation of Cumulative Net Investment Loss." It's a good idea to fill out this form each year to ensure that you keep an up-to-date running total of your CNIL.

If you expect you will never have a capital gain on QSBC shares or qualifying farm or fishing property, you can forget about the CNIL rules! Sleep easy.

Line 255: Northern Residents Deductions

Rainy Hollow, B.C.; Belcher, Manitoba; Flin Flon, Saskatchewan; Pickle Crow, Ontario. What do these places have in common (other than their intriguing names)? Well, their residents can claim a northern residents deduction. In recognition of additional costs of living incurred by those who live in remote areas of Canada, the CRA allows special tax deductions to help with the extra burden. Living in a remote area does not mean the nearest McDonald's is an hour away. In fact, the CRA has a very detailed (and very long) list of specific areas of Canada where you have to live to claim the deduction.

The actual deductions you can claim depend on where you live. The CRA has set up two different "zones." If you live in a northern zone, you are allowed the full northern residents deduction. If you live in an intermediate zone, you can deduct half the potential amount.

If you think you may live in a northern zone or an intermediate zone, check out the CRA's publication T4039, *Northern Residents Deductions — Places in Prescribed Zones*. (You can find it on the CRA's Web site, www.cra-arc.gc.ca.)

Two types of northern residents deductions are available:

✔ Residency deductions

✔ Travel deductions

If you qualify for the northern residents deduction, you must fill out form T2222, "Northern Residents Deduction," and file it with your personal tax return. Keep any supporting receipts in case the CRA asks to see them.

Residency deduction

To claim the residency deduction you need to live exclusively in one of the prescribed zones. Stopping by for a visit won't do. In fact, to qualify you must have lived, on a permanent basis, in one of the zones for at least six consecutive months beginning or ending in 2005.

You may be able to claim two separate types of residency deductions:

✔ **Basic residency amount.** This is a credit for simply living in a zone. The credit is $7.50 per day for living in a northern zone, and one-half of this, or $3.75, for living in an intermediate zone.

✔ **Additional residency amount.** You can claim an additional credit of $7.50/$3.75 per day if the following situations apply:

  • You maintained and lived in a dwelling during your time up north (generally a house or apartment — sorry, a hotel room or bunkhouse won't qualify).

  • You are the only person claiming the basic residency amount for living in that dwelling for that time.

You are considered to have maintained and lived in a dwelling even if your employer or another person paid for your accommodations and other costs relating to the dwelling.

 If more than one taxpayer lived in the same dwelling at the same time during the year, either each taxpayer can claim the basic residency amount deduction ($7.50 or $3.75 per day), or one taxpayer can claim both the basic residency amount deduction and the additional residency deduction.

 If you are considered to receive a non-taxable benefit for board and lodging at a special work site in a northern or intermediate zone, the non-taxable benefit (as reported on your T4 or T4A slip) is to be deducted in calculating your residency deduction.

 If you received non-taxable board and lodging benefits but the special work site is more than 30 kilometres away from an urban area having a population of at least 40,000, you do not have to reduce your residency deduction.

Travel deductions

The second type of northern residents deduction you may be eligible to claim is the travel deduction. Generally, whenever your employer pays for something on your behalf, you are considered to have received a taxable benefit. This means that some travel benefits that your employer offers to you and your family may be taxable. When you live in a remote northern area, the fact that your employer will pay for some trips for you and your family could be a popular employment perk. Unfortunately, it could also lead to a tax bill. In recognition of the costs involved in travelling in remote areas, there is some relief from the taxable benefit rules. You can claim an additional northern residents tax deduction under these conditions:

✔ You qualify to claim a northern residents deduction (although you don't have to claim it to meet this criterion — *qualify* is the key word).

✔ You were an employee.

✔ You received taxable travel benefits in connection with your employment in a northern and/or intermediate zone.

✔ The travel benefits have been included in your employment income.

Box 32 of your T4 slip, or box 28 of your T4A slip, will report the taxable travel benefits you received in the year. If you received non-taxable benefits, such benefits will not show up on your slips and you are not eligible to claim the travel benefits deduction.

You must claim the travel benefits deduction in the same year that you report the taxable benefit received from your employer.

Types of travel qualifying for deduction

Different rules apply depending on your reasons for travelling. If you are travelling for medical services that are not available where you live, there is no limit on the number of trips you can make in the year. However, if you are travelling for any other reason, you can claim a deduction for only two trips a year for each member of your household.

If you are claiming a travel deduction for trips made for medical reasons, no one can claim the expenditures as medical expenses as well.

If you are travelling for medical reasons, ensure that your employer notes this fact on your T4 or T4A slip.

If you're travelling for medical reasons and cannot travel alone, you can claim a deduction for your travel expenses, as well as those of another member of your household who will act as your attendant (assuming the other conditions for the deduction are met).

Amount of deduction available

Can you take a first-class, whirlwind trip, and hope it qualifies as a travel deduction? Let's not be greedy. As with many of our tax rules, there are maximum amounts that can be claimed. Here are the rules.

The maximum deduction that can be claimed for each eligible trip in the year is the lowest of the following:

✔ The taxable employment benefit considered received for the trip

✔ The total travel expenses for the trip. These travel expenses include such items as:

- Air, train, and bus fares

- Meals. Actual cost (keep your receipts) or claim a flat rate of $15 per meal to a maximum of $45 per day per person

- Motor vehicle expenses. You can claim motor vehicle expenses based on actual costs incurred, or on a fixed per-kilometre amount. The per-kilometre amounts are published in a CRA fact sheet titled *Travel Expenses for Medical Expense, Moving Expense, and Northern Residents Deductions*. It can be found on the CRA Web site at www.cra-arc.gc.ca/tax/individuals/segments/north-res/travel-e.html

- Hotel and motel accommodations

- Other incidental expenses, such as taxis, road tolls, ferry costs

✔ The cost of the lowest return airfare available at the time of the trip between the airport closest to your residence and the nearest designated city, even if you did not travel by air, or to that city.

So, if you are travelling from a northern or intermediate zone to Cape Breton, Nova Scotia, you will have to determine the airfare from the closest airport to your remote location to Halifax, Nova Scotia (which is the closest designated city to Cape Breton). This is the case even if you didn't fly between these two locations, and even though you're not planning on visiting Halifax! A list of designated cities can be found in the CRA guide entitled *General Income Tax and Benefit Guide*.

If you don't know the actual cost of the trip taken (for example, when you're given free airline tickets), include the market value of a similar trip as the actual cost.

Line 256: Additional Deductions

Additional deductions — who doesn't like the sound of that! But don't get too excited. You can't claim any old deduction you think you should be entitled to on your tax return. In fact, the rules for additional deductions are pretty specific. We'll discuss some of them here. And trust us, they're actually not all that common.

Income exempt under a tax treaty

Canada has a number of tax treaties with countries around the globe. These tax treaties outline, among other issues, how each country will treat certain types of income earned within its borders. Sometimes tax treaties state that certain types of income you earn from a foreign country will not be taxable in Canada. It could be that the income is taxed in the foreign country, or is altogether exempt from tax. Whatever the case, when you've received income that is exempt under a tax treaty, it is included in your "net" income but not your "taxable" income. This is why you receive an additional deduction. Income exempt under a tax treaty includes the following items:

- ✔ **United States social security payments:** These payments are only 85-percent taxable in Canada; therefore, you should deduct 15 percent of the total amounts received, on line 256.

- ✔ **Other foreign pensions:** Some pensions received from certain treaty countries, including certain French, German, Italian, and Spanish pensions, are exempt from tax in Canada. If you are unsure whether your pension is exempt from Canadian tax, contact your local Tax Services Office.

- ✔ **Child support payments received from residents of the United States.**

 If you receive income from a foreign source, and you are unsure how it should be taxed in Canada, check with the CRA. Under the terms of a tax treaty Canada has with the foreign country, you may be able to claim tax relief.

Vow of perpetual poverty

Living in a dingy basement apartment in downtown Toronto may make you feel as though you've taken a vow of perpetual poverty, but this tax deduction doesn't apply to you. If you are a member of a religious order, have taken a vow of perpetual poverty, and have turned over your entire earned income and superannuation and pension benefits in the year to your religious order, you're in for some tax relief. In fact, you can deduct the entire amount of this income on line 256 of your personal tax return.

 Earned income includes any salaries, wages, bursaries, scholarships, or research grants. It doesn't include any investment income such as dividends or interest. Even if you give any investment income earned to your order, you are not entitled to a deduction on line 256.

 Want more info? Take a look at the CRA's Interpretation Bulletin #IT86R, *Vow of Perpetual Poverty*.

Employment with a prescribed international organization

If you earn employment income from certain international organizations, you can claim a deduction for your net employment income in the year. The international organizations to which this deduction applies include the United Nations and its specialized agencies. If this deduction applies to you, you must include your employment income and any related employment expenses in your net income, then deduct the income, net of related employment expenses, on line 256.

Tuition assistance payments

You may have received and included in your income certain tuition assistance payments received from the Employment Insurance Commission (EIC) or Human Resources and Skills Development Canada (HRSDC). If so, you can claim a deduction on line 246 for the amount of qualifying assistance shown in box 21 of your T4E slip.

Chapter 12

Tips for Non-Refundable Tax Credits

● ●

In This Chapter

▶ Understanding credit amounts and non-refundable tax credits

▶ Claiming the basic personal amount

▶ Knowing when to claim the spouse or common-law partner amount

▶ Considering the new adoption expense amount

▶ Maximizing special credits for disabled persons

▶ Making the most of student loan interest, tuition, and education amounts

▶ Claiming medical expenses

● ●

*N*on-refundable tax credits directly reduce the amount of income tax you owe — they do not reduce your taxable income. In this way they differ from tax deductions, which are subtracted in computing your taxable income. These credits are referred to as "non-refundable," because if they exceed your tax you do not get a refund of the excess. (Some tax credits are *refundable*: refer to Chapter 13 for comments on federal refundable tax credits, and to Chapter 14 for more on provincial/territorial credits.)

For all but one of the non-refundable tax credits, the reduction in federal taxes is 15.25 percent. Charitable donations over $200 get a 29 percent credit.

Report federal non-refundable tax credits in schedule 1 of your tax return. Each province/territory also calculates its own non-refundable tax credits to help offset provincial/territorial taxes. These credits are reported on your provincial/territorial tax calculation forms.

Line 300: Your Basic Personal Amount

For 2006, you are eligible to claim $8,839 as a personal amount on line 300 of schedule 1. In other words, the first $8,839 you earn this year is not subject to tax! Let's see how this actually works.

Assume your taxable income is $8,839. You calculate your federal tax at the top of schedule 1. The tax rate at this income level is 15.25 percent, so your tax equals $1,348. Next on schedule 1 you calculate the non-refundable tax credits available to you. The basic personal amount is $8,839 — the 15.25 percent tax credit on this equals $1,348. See a pattern? The tax credit completely offsets the tax, so your final tax liability is nil.

If you are entitled to more non-refundable tax credits, such as the credits detailed below, you would not get a refund since these credits are . . . well . . . non-refundable.

Line 301: Age Amount

You qualify for a maximum age amount of $4,066 if you were 65 years of age or older on December 31, 2006. You can claim the maximum amount of $4,066, reduced by 15 percent of your net income (from line 236 of your tax return) in excess of $30,270. The age amount you are able to claim is reduced as your income exceeds this level. If your income is $30,270 or less, you will be able to claim the maximum age amount.

For example, suppose Alice turned 65 in 2006, and she is wondering if she is entitled to claim the age credit. Her income for the year as reported on line 236 is $35,000. Her age credit is reduced by $709: ($35,000 – $30,270 × 15%). This means she can claim $3,357 ($4,066 – $709) on line 301 of her tax return.

You won't be entitled to any age amount if your net income exceeds $57,377. The credit amount will work out to zero.

Line 303: Spouse or Common-law Partner Amount

You may claim a maximum credit amount of $7,505 if at any time during the year you were legally married or had a common-law partner and supported that spouse or common-law partner.

Who is your spouse? For income tax purposes, "spouse" includes the person you are legally married to or a person who is your common-law partner. (Of course, if you happen to have both, you can make a claim for only one these "spouses"!) Common-law partners are defined as two persons, regardless of sex, who cohabit in a conjugal relationship that has been continuous for at least 12 months or, if fewer than 12 months, have a child, natural or adopted, together.

If your spouse had net income for the year, the $7,505 credit amount is reduced by the amount of your spouse's income over $768. Therefore, if your spouse's income was greater than $8,273, the credit amount available to you is reduced to zero. Your spouse's net income is the amount reported on line 236 of his or her tax return.

If you separated during the year and were not back together by December 31, reduce your claim by your spouse's net income before the separation only.

If you cannot claim the spousal amount (say, because the credit amount calculation works out to zero), or you have to reduce the credit claimed because of your spouse's net income, you still may be able to claim the credit, or an increased credit amount, if your spouse's income for the year includes dividend income from Canadian corporations. You do this by claiming your spouse's dividend income on your return so that his or her income is lowered to permit the credit amount you claim — or, perhaps, a greater credit amount than originally calculated. See Chapter 6 for a full explanation.

Make this spousal "dividend transfer" only if the increased spousal credit amount results in tax savings that, when combined with your spouse's tax savings from not reporting the dividend income, exceeds the increase in tax that you will pay on the dividend income transferred from your spouse. Don't forget that the effective tax rate for dividends is lower because of the dividend tax credit. Table 1-2 in Chapter 1 details the difference in tax rates for dividends, capital gains, and interest.

 If you were paying spousal support (not child support) for part of 2006 after a breakdown of your marriage or common-law partnership, you can choose between claiming the spousal or common-law partner amount and deducting the spousal support payments on line 220 of your return.

Line 305: Amount for an Eligible Dependant

This credit amount (often referred to by its previous moniker, the "equivalent-to-spouse" amount) of $7,705 is available to you if you have a dependant and you were single, divorced, separated, or widowed at any time during the year. In other words, you did not have a spouse or a common-law partner, or if you did you were not living together. Not just any dependant will qualify for this credit, so unfortunately you can't claim a credit for your 28-year-old son who still lives in your basement, even if he does eat all your food. Your dependant must be the following:

- ✔ Your parent or grandparent
- ✔ Your child, grandchild, brother, or sister who was under 18, or if not under 18, was physically or mentally infirm
- ✔ Living with you in a home you maintain

This claim is usually made by a single parent for a child, although claims by children for a parent and by one sibling for another are fairly common as well. Give details of the claim for an eligible dependant (name, age, income) on schedule 5 of your tax return.

 Like the spousal or common-law partner amount, the amount for an eligible dependant of $7,505 is reduced by the dependant's income over $768. If the dependant's net income is $8,273 or greater, the amount for an eligible dependant will be zero.

 You cannot claim this amount if someone else in your household is claiming it for the same dependant.

 You can claim this credit for a dependant who lives away from home while attending school, if that dependant ordinarily lives with you when not in school.

Line 306: Amount for Infirm Dependants Age 18 or Older

You may be able to claim a credit amount of up to a maximum of $3,933 for each relative who is 18 or older and is dependent on you, or you and others, by reason of physical or mental infirmity. The credit is reduced by the dependant's net income in excess of $5,580. The credit is completely eliminated once the dependant's income reaches $9,513. Give details of the claim for an infirm dependant (name, age, income, nature of infirmity) on schedule 5 of your tax return.

If more than one person is supporting the dependant person, the available credit must be allocated between those supporting people. That is, the total credit claimed for one dependant, cannot exceed $3,933.

A dependent relative may include your or your spouse's child, grandchild, parent, grandparent, brother, sister, uncle, aunt, niece, or nephew. To claim this amount the dependant must be:

- ✔ Age 18 or older at the end of the year
- ✔ A resident of Canada at some time during the year, if a credit amount is being claimed for a dependant other than a child or grandchild
- ✔ Dependent on you by reason of mental or physical infirmity
- ✔ Dependent on you, or you and others, for support

You may be able to claim an "amount for infirm dependants" in respect of children or grandchildren even if they live outside Canada, provided they depended on you for support. The CRA can ask you to provide proof of support paid. Dependants other than your children or grandchildren must have been resident in Canada at some time during the year.

Note that unlike the "line 315: caregiver amount" (see below), the dependant is not required to live with you to be considered an infirm dependant for this claim.

You cannot claim this credit if someone other than you is claiming the eligible dependant amount (line 305) for the same dependant. However, if you are claiming the eligible dependant amount, you may also claim the amount for infirm dependants age 18 or older on line 306. You cannot claim the amount for infirm dependants age 18 or over, if you, or anyone else, have claimed the caregiver amount (line 315) for the same dependant.

Generally, an individual is dependent on you for support if he or she does not have income in excess of the basic personal credit amount — $8,839 in 2006 — and you have contributed to the maintenance of that person (food, clothing, and other bills).

Lines 308 and 310: Canada Pension Plan (CPP)/Quebec Pension Plan (QPP) Contributions

The total, or a portion, of the CPP or QPP you paid in the year will qualify for the 15.25 percent federal non-refundable tax credit. Enter the total of the amounts shown in boxes 16 (CPP) and 17 (QPP) of your T4 slips (or see the next section if you're self-employed). Do not enter more than $1,910.70.

If you contributed more than $1,910.70, enter the excess amount on line 448 of your return. This situation often occurs when you've worked for more than one employer in the year. If you've paid more than you should, don't worry. The CRA will refund this over-payment to you, or use it to reduce your tax balance owing. If you lived in Quebec on December 31, 2006, and contributed more than the max of $1,910.70, claim the overpayment on your Quebec provincial return.

If you would like to calculate your CPP overpayment yourself, use form T2204, "Employee Overpayment of 2006 Canada Pension Plan Contributions and 2006 Employment Insurance Premiums." Other-wise, the CRA will calculate the overpayment for you and will adjust your tax return for the difference.

CPP or QPP contributions payable on self-employment and other earnings

If you are self-employed, you are required to pay *both* the employer and employee portion of CPP/QPP contributions to a maximum of $3,821.40 ($1,910.70 × 2). If you have employment and self-employment earnings, the amount of CPP or QPP contributions that you have to make on your self-employment earnings will depend on how much you have already contributed to the CPP or QPP as an employee. Schedule 8 will help you with these calculations.

Self-employed individuals can claim a deduction on line 222 for the portion of CPP or QPP contributions that represents the employer's share (that is, one-half of the premiums paid). Only the portion of the CPP or QPP contributions that represent the employee's portion qualify for the 15.25 percent federal non-refundable tax credit.

Line 312: Employment Insurance (EI) Premiums

As with CPP and QPP contributions, all or a portion of the EI premiums you've paid will qualify for the 15.25 percent federal non-refundable tax credit. Enter the total of the amounts shown in box 18 of all your T4 and T4F slips at line 312 of schedule 1. Do not enter more than $729.30.

If you contributed more than $729.30, enter the excess amount on line 450 of your return. The CRA will refund this overpayment to you, or, if applicable, will use it to reduce your tax balance owing.

In some cases, you may have an overpayment even if you contributed less than $729.30. If so, the CRA will calculate your overpayment and show it on your Notice of Assessment.

If you would like to calculate your EI overpayment yourself, use form T2204, "Employee Overpayment of 2006 Canada Pension Plan Contributions and 2006 Employment Insurance Premiums."

If the total of the Employment Insurance (EI) insurable earnings shown in box 24 of all your T4 slips (or box 14, if box 24 is blank) and box 16 of your T4F slips is $2,000 or less, the taxman will refund your total EI premiums to you or will use the amount to reduce your tax balance owing. In this situation, do not enter your total EI premiums on line 312. Instead, enter the amount on line 450.

Line 313: Amount for Adoption Expenses

The 2005 federal budget included proposals to permit a non-refundable tax credit for adoption expenses. Eligible adoption expenses include fees paid to an adoption agency; travel costs for the parents and child; and court, legal, and administration fees. The expenses must be claimed in the year the adoption is finalized, and they can be shared by the parents. For 2006, the total amounts claimed cannot exceed the lesser of the actual adoption expenses or $10,220 per child.

Line 314: Pension Income Amount

Thanks to the 2006 federal budget you can claim up to a $2,000 credit amount (formally $1,000) if you reported pension and/or annuity income on line 115 or line 129 of your return. But watch out! Only pension or annuity income you report on line 115 or 129 qualifies for the pension income amount.

Amounts such as Old Age Security benefits, Canada Pension Plan benefits, Quebec Pension Plan benefits, Saskatchewan Pension Plan payments, death benefits, and retiring allowances do not qualify for the pension income amount. Non-annuity income you withdraw from your RRSP similarly does not qualify for the pension amount.

If you are age 65 or over but do not have sufficient pension income to qualify for the full credit (that is, your pension income is less than $2,000), you can create pension income by converting all or part of your RRSP to an RRIF or a life annuity. Or, you can purchase a life annuity with other available funds. The income from these investment vehicles is eligible for the pension income amount.

If your spouse does not need all or a portion of the non-refundable tax credit that arises from the pension amount to reduce his or her federal tax to zero, it may be transferable to you. See the comments below under "Line 326: Amounts transferred from your spouse."

If you are under 65, the pension amount is available only if you have received payments from a pension plan and/or received annuity payments due to the death of your spouse.

Line 315: Caregiver Amount

If at any time in 2006 you maintained a dwelling, alone or with another person, where you and a dependant lived, you may be able to claim this $3,933 credit amount. Your dependant must be one of the following:

- ✔ Your child or grandchild
- ✔ Your or your spouse or common-law partner's brother, sister, niece, nephew, aunt, uncle, parent, or grandparent

In addition, the dependant must be

- ✔ Age 18 or over at the time he or she lived with you
- ✔ Dependent on you due to mental or physical infirmity, or, if he or she is your or your spouse or common-law partner's parent or grandparent, at least 65 years of age

Note the details of the claim for a caregiver amount on schedule 5 of your tax return. The maximum credit amount of $3,933 is reduced dollar for dollar by the dependant's income in excess of $13,430. Once your dependant's income reaches $17,363, the credit is completely eliminated.

The claim for the caregiver amount is different from the credit amount for infirm dependants age 18 or older claimed on line 306 (see above). For you to be able to claim the caregiver amount, the dependant must have lived with you at some time during the year. This is not a requirement in claiming the credit amount for infirm dependants age 18 and older. Since the caregiver credit amount will always be greater than or equal to the credit amount for infirm dependants aged 18 or older, you should claim the caregiver amount if the dependant lived with you. You cannot claim both credit amounts. However, you can claim both the amount for an eligible dependent (line 305) plus the caregiver amount for the same dependant in the same year.

If you and another person support the same dependant, you can split the claim. However, the total of your claim and the other person's claim cannot be more than the maximum amount allowed for that dependant.

You cannot claim this amount for a dependant if anyone claims an amount on line 306 (amount for infirm dependants age 18 or older) for that dependant, or if anyone other than you claims an amount on line 305 (amount for eligible dependant) for that dependant.

You may have noticed by now that if you have a dependant who is infirm or disabled there are many potential credits you can claim. Correspondingly, the rules surrounding infirm and disabled persons are some of the most confusing in our tax laws. At times, the permutations and combinations of credits you can claim seem impossible to figure out. We recommend you read the CRA guide RC4064, "Information Concerning People with Disabilities," which discusses all the potential credits and who can claim them. It's a good start to help ensure you don't miss out on any potential tax savings!

Line 316: Disability Amount for Yourself

You may be able to claim a disability amount of $6,741 if a qualified person certifies both of the following:

> ✔ You had a severe mental or physical impairment in 2006, which caused you to be markedly restricted all or almost all of the time in any of the basic activities of daily living.

> ✔ Your impairment was prolonged — meaning it lasted, or is expected to last, for a continuous period of at least 12 months.

The only people who are qualified to certify that your impairment was severe and prolonged are medical doctors, optometrists, psychologists, occupational therapists, audiologists, speech-language pathologists, and physiotherapists.

 You may be markedly restricted in the basic activities of daily living if you are blind or are unable to feed or dress yourself, control bowel and bladder functions, walk, speak, hear, or lack the mental functions for everyday life (perceive, think, or remember). Individuals who undergo therapy to sustain their vital functions, such as dialysis, and cystic fibrosis patients also qualify.

You may also be markedly restricted if it takes you an extremely long time to perform any of these basic activities of daily living, even with therapy and the use of appropriate aids and medication.

 Eligibility for the disability tax credit was extended in 2005 to include those individuals who have more than one impairment and, although each individual impairment does not markedly restrict basic activities of daily living (which in the past would have disqualified the individual from claiming the credit), the cumulative impact of those impairments is equivalent to having a single marked restriction.

 If you are under 18 you may qualify for the "disability supplement for persons under 18." If so, your disability amount can increase to $10,674 — the regular credit amount of $6,741 plus the supplement amount of $3,933. The supplement amount is decreased by the amount of any childcare expenses (line 214) claimed for you and the disability supports deduction (line 215) claimed by you (see Chapter 10).

If you are applying for the disability amount for the first time, you have to submit with your return a completed and certified form T2201, "Disability Tax Credit Certificate." The CRA will review your claim to determine if you qualify before it assesses your return. Once your application is approved, you will be able to claim this amount for future years as long as your circumstances do not change.

Line 318: Disability Amount Transferred from a Dependant Other Than Your Spouse

You may be able to claim all or part of a dependant's disability amount that is not needed to reduce the dependant's taxes — because, say, the dependant's federal taxes are already zero. You can claim the unused portion if he or she lived in Canada at any time in 2006 and was dependent on you because of mental or physical infirmity. The disability supplement can also be transferred. In addition, one of the following must apply:

- You claimed an "amount for eligible dependant" on line 305 for that dependant, or you could have if you did not have a spouse and if the dependant did not have any income.

- The dependant was your or your spouse's child, grandchild, parent, grandparent, brother, sister, aunt, uncle, niece, or nephew and you made a claim on line 306 (amount for infirm dependant age 18 or older) or line 315 (caregiver amount) for that dependant, or you could have made a claim if he or she had no income and was 18 years of age or older in 2006.

If you are required to make child-support payments for your child, you cannot claim a disability amount for that child.

In the first year you claim this amount, you must attach to your return a properly completed and certified form T2201, "Disability Tax Credit Certificate," for each dependant.

If you are splitting this claim for a disability amount transferred from a dependant with another supporting person, attach a note to your return including the name and social insurance number of the other person making this claim. The total claimed for one dependant cannot be more than $6,741, or $10,674 if the disability supplement can be transferred as well.

You can claim this credit only if (1) the spouse of the person with a disability is not already claiming the disability amount or any other non-refundable tax credit (other than medical expenses) for the person with a disability, and (2) you supported that person.

If you can claim this amount, you also may be able to claim an amount on line 315, the caregiver amount, for the same dependant.

If you have a child with a severe and prolonged impairment, you may qualify for the Child Disability Benefit (CDB). The CDB is a tax-free supplement to the Canada Child Tax Benefit and Children's Special Allowance. For the period July 2006 to June 2007, the CDB provides up to $2,300 per year (191.66 per month) for each child who qualifies for the disability amount. Ensure the CRA has a form T2201 on file for your child and that you file your tax return so the government can assess your eligibility for this credit.

Eligibility for the CDB is determined based on your family net income and the number of children in the family eligible for the disability tax credit. Enhancements introduced in the 2006 federal budget extend the eligibility for the CDB to nearly all families caring for children eligible for the disability tax credit.

Line 319: Interest Paid on Your Student Loans

In calculating your federal non-refundable tax credits, you can claim the amount of the interest you, or a person related to you, paid on loans made to you for post-secondary education under the *Canada Student Loans Act,* the *Canada Student Financial Assistance Act,* or similar provincial or territorial government laws.

Interest on personal or family loans will not qualify for this credit. Likewise, loans obtained through a bank that are not official government student loans do not qualify.

If you do not wish to claim these amounts on the return for the year they are paid — say, because you do not need the credit as your federal tax bill is already zero — you can carry the amounts forward and apply them on any one of the next five years' returns.

Be careful about consolidating government student loans with other debts you might have. Even though your borrowing was initially under one of the government acts noted above, once you've extinguished that debt the interest paid is no longer tax deductible. You might find a lower interest rate at a commercial bank, but since that interest will not be tax deductible you might find you're better off, after tax, paying the higher interest rate under the government programs. Plus, the government has interest forgiveness measures that you might qualify for — you can be sure that a bank won't be so forgiving! More information on Canada Student Loans can be found on the Human Resources and Social Development Canada website at: `http://www.hrsdc.gc.ca/en/gateways/topics/cxp-gxr.shtml`. In addition, the website for the province under which your loan is administered should have additional information on interest relief provisions.

As a result of the 2006 federal budget, you'll see a few new tax credits on your return this year — the public transit tax credit and the Canada employment tax credit. Let's take a look at them, and, hopefully, you can take advantage of one or two to reduce your tax bill this year!

Public Transit Tax Credit

If you use public transportation, you may be able to offset the cost of your transit pass by a new non-refundable credit. Starting July 1, 2006, individuals can claim a non-refundable tax credit for the cost of public transit passes (monthly or longer).

Public transit includes transit by local bus, streetcar, subway, commuter train, commuter bus, and local ferry. The credit can be claimed by you or your spouse for eligible transit costs incurred by you, your spouse, or dependent children under the age of 19. If this credit applies to you, be sure to keep your receipts and passes in case the CRA asks for proof.

Canada Employment Tax Credit

Commencing July 1, 2006, employees can claim a new non-refundable credit to help offset some of the work-related expenses incurred by employees. For 2006, the credit is calculated as the lesser of $250 (rising to $1,000 in 2007) and the individual's employment income for the year.

Line 323: Tuition, Education, and Textbook Tax Credit Amounts for Yourself

A 15.25 percent non-refundable federal tax credit is available for eligible tuition and education amounts incurred in 2006 and any unused amounts carried forward from previous years. Amounts carried forward are shown on your 2005 Notice of Assessment. Enter the details of your tuition and education amounts on schedule 11 of your return.

Beginning in 2006, students can also receive a 15.25 percent non-refundable federal tax credit for the cost of their textbooks.

Tuition tax credit

You can claim only the tuition paid for courses you took in 2006. Qualifying courses include most at the post-secondary level or those that develop or improve skills in an occupation.

You must have paid more than $100 during the year to each educational institution whose fees you claim. You cannot claim other expenses related to pursuing your education, such as board and lodging. These costs are the reason that an education amount is available to students (see below).

To claim tuition fees paid to an educational institution in Canada you must obtain from your educational institution an official tax receipt or a completed form T2202A ("Tuition and Education Amounts Certificate"). To claim tuition fees paid to an educational institution *outside* Canada, you must receive from your institution a completed form TL11A, "Tuition Fees Certificate — University Outside Canada," which you can obtain from any Tax Services Office.

Education tax credit

You can claim the education tax credit for each whole or part month in 2006 in which you were enrolled in a qualifying educational program. Your educational institution has to complete and give you form T2202, "Education Amount Certificate," or form T2202A, "Tuition and Education Amounts Certificate," to confirm the period in which you were enrolled in a qualifying program.

The following amounts apply:

- You can claim $400 for each month in which you were enrolled as a full-time student.

- You can claim $120 for each month in which you were enrolled in a qualifying part-time program.

You cannot claim more than one education amount for a particular month.

A full-time program is a program at the post-secondary level that lasts at least three weeks and requires at least ten hours per week on courses or work in the program. A part-time program must also last at least three weeks, but it does not have a ten-hour per week course or workload requirement.

You can claim $400 a month if you attended your educational institution only part-time because of a mental or physical impairment. In this case, you have to complete form T2202, "Education Amount Certificate," to make your claim.

Textbook tax credit

In the past, the only credit available to offset some of the additional costs of going to school, including books, board, and lodging, was the education amount. Now, thanks to the 2006 federal budget, students can claim a non-refundable credit for the cost of their textbooks.

The credit is calculated as follows:

- $65 for each month for which you qualify for the full-time education tax credit amount; and

- $20 for each month for which you qualify for the part-time education tax credit amount.

Transferring and carrying forward tuition, education, and textbook tax credit amounts

In many cases, students simply do not have the cash flow to pay for their own education. However, for tax purposes, the student — not the person who paid the fees — gets first crack at the tuition, education, and textbook tax credit amounts. It is only when you do not need the full tax credit from these amounts to reduce your tax bill to zero that you can transfer the tuition, education, and textbook tax credits to another person.

Again, you must use all the tuition, education, and textbook tax credit amounts necessary to reduce your taxes to zero before you can transfer the amounts to another person. If you do not transfer your unused amount to your spouse, you can transfer it to your or your spouse's parent or grandparent, who would claim it on line 324 of his or her return. Complete the back of form T2202 or form T2202A, as well as schedule 11 on your tax return, to calculate and designate this transfer.

The maximum amount you may transfer to a spouse, parent, or grandparent is $5,000 (for federal tax purposes) less whatever amount you needed to reduce your taxes payable to zero. You can carry forward and claim in a future year the part of your tuition, education, and textbook tax credit amounts that you did not need to use and did not transfer for the year in which they were incurred. However, if you carry forward an amount, you will not be able to transfer it to anyone else in the future. You must claim your carry-forward amount in the earliest year possible — that is, when you have a federal tax liability that needs to be sheltered with a federal tax credit. In other words, you can't pick and choose the tax years in which to claim the credits. The federal carry-forward amount and the amount used in the year, if any, to reduce a tax bill are to be detailed on schedule 11 of your tax return.

If you are transferring a tuition, education, or textbook tax credit amount to another person, do not transfer more than the person needs to reduce his or her federal income tax to zero. That way, you maximize the benefit of the credit and can carry forward the unused amount to a future year to offset your future tax bill.

Line 324: Tuition, Education, and Textbook Tax Credit Amounts Transferred from a Child

A student who does not need all of his or her 2006 tuition, education, and textbook tax credit amounts to reduce federal income tax to zero may be able to transfer the unused portion to you if you are a parent or grandparent of the student or of the student's spouse. The maximum amount that each student can transfer is $5,000 (federally) minus the amount the student needs, even if there is still an unused amount greater than this.

To calculate the transfer amount and to highlight who the amount is being transferred to, the student has to complete the reverse side of form T2202, "Education Amount Certificate," or form T2202A, "Tuition and Education Amounts Certificate."

If a student's spouse claims amounts on line 303 (spousal or common-law partner amount) or 326 (amounts transferred for spouse) for the student, a parent or grandparent cannot claim the tuition and education amounts transfer.

Line 326: Amounts Transferred from Your Spouse

Your spouse can transfer to you any part of certain tax credit amounts that he or she qualifies for but does not need to reduce his or her federal income tax to zero.

The credits that may be transferred from one spouse to another are the age credit, the disability credit, the pension credit, and tuition, education, and textbook tax credits. For additional details and to calculate the amounts that can be transferred, refer to schedule 2 of your tax return. In the identification area on page 1 of your return, be sure to report your marital status and your spouse's name and social insurance number so your claim is not rejected.

Lines 330 and 331: Medical Expenses

You can claim medical expenses paid by you or your spouse for any of the following persons:

- ✔ You or your spouse;
- ✔ Your or your spouse's child born in 1989 or later and who depended on you for support;

You can claim medical expenses paid in any 12-month period ending in 2006 and not claimed in 2005. Generally, you can claim all amounts, even if they were not paid in Canada. Your total expenses have to be more than either $1,884 or 3 percent of your net income (line 236), whichever is less. This limit makes it more beneficial, in most cases, to claim the medical expenses on the tax return of the spouse with the lowest net income.

You can also claim medical expenses for other dependants including:

- ✔ Your or your spouse's child or grandchild born in 1988 or earlier who depended on your for support; and

- ✔ Your or your spouse's parent, grandparent, brother, sister, uncle, aunt, niece, or nephew who lived in Canada at any time in the year and depended on you for support.

- ✔ If you are claiming medical expenses paid on behalf of a relative who depended on you for support (i.e., those expenses incurred for someone other than you, your spouse and any minor dependant children) the maximum amount that you can claim for each dependant is the lesser of $1,884 and 3 percent of the dependant's net income, up to a maximum of $10,000.

Checklist of allowable medical expenses

- ✔ **Fees for professional medical services:** These include the services of doctors, dentists, surgeons, chiropractors, acupuncturists, registered or practical nurses, physiotherapists, speech therapists, naturopaths, professional tutors that a medical practitioner certifies as necessary because of a person's learning disability or mental impairment, and so on.

- ✔ **Payments for apparatus and materials, and repairs thereto:** Eligible apparatus and materials might include artificial limbs, wheelchairs, crutches, hearing aids, prescription eyeglasses or contact lenses, dentures, pacemakers, iron lungs, orthopedic shoes, reasonable expenses relating to renovations or alterations to a dwelling of an impaired person, reasonable moving expenses if incurred by an impaired person moving to a more accessible dwelling, and so on.

- ✔ **Medicines:** These might include costs of prescriptions, insulin or substitutes, oxygen, and so on.

- ✔ **Fees for medical treatments:** These treatments might include blood transfusions, injections, pre- and postnatal treatments, psychotherapy, speech pathology or audiology, and so on.

- ✔ **Fees for laboratory examinations and tests:** These include blood tests, cardiographs, X-ray examinations, urine and stool analyses, and so on.

- ✔ **Fees for hospital services:** These include hospital bills, use of the operating room, anesthetist, X-ray technician, and so on.

✓ **Amounts paid for attendant care, or care in an establishment:** Seniors who are eligible to claim the disability amount and who live in a retirement home can claim full or part-time attendant care expenses as medical expenses. The claim is the portion of salaries and wages of attendants that can reasonably apply to the senior, limited to $10,000 per year or $20,000 in the year of death. If more than these amounts are claimed, then the disability amount cannot be claimed in regard to that person.

✓ **Ambulance charges**

✓ **Expenses for guide and hearing-ear animals**

✓ **Premiums paid to private health services plans** (other than those paid by an employer) and premiums paid under the Quebec Medical Insurance Plan, including travel medical insurance.

✓ **Group home:** If you paid fees to a group home in Canada for individuals who qualify for the disability amount (line 316), the portion of those fees paid to someone to care for or supervise such an individual — if nobody has claimed it as an attendant or institutional care medical expense on line 330, a childcare expense on line 214, or a disability supports amount on line 215 for that person.

✓ **Travel expenses, if medical treatment is not available locally.**

Recent additions to the list of eligible medical expenses include:

✓ **Real-time captioning** for individuals with a speech or hearing impairment

✓ **Note-taking services** for individuals with mental or physical impairments

✓ **Voice recognition software** for individuals with a physical impairment

✓ **Incremental costs associated with the purchase of gluten-free food** for those with celiac disease

✓ **Phototherapy equipment** for skin disorders

✓ **Oxygen concentrators**

✓ **Deaf/blind intervening services**

✓ **Reading services for the blind**

✓ **Marijuana,** under restricted circumstances.

Individuals who have a severe or prolonged mobility impairment may be eligible to claim as medical expenses the renovation costs incurred to make their homes more accessible. The list of eligible medical expenses includes expenses relating to the construction of a principal residence if the expenses enable the individual to gain access to or to be mobile or functional within the home.

Items you cannot claim as medical expenses

Things you cannot claim as medical expenses include the following: toothpaste; maternity clothes; athletic club memberships; funeral, cremation, or burial expenses; illegal operations; illegal treatments; illegally procured drugs; and so on. Similarly, you are not allowed to claim any vitamins, herbs, bottled water, or organic or natural foods, even if prescribed by a licensed medical practitioner, if those items are not "recorded by a pharmacist." In other words, only prescription drugs that you need to buy from a pharmacist will qualify.

Attach your receipts and other documents (other than your health services plan premium receipts) to your tax return. Receipts for attendant care or therapy paid to an individual should show the individual's name and social insurance number.

Line 349: Donations and Gifts

You can claim federal non-refundable tax credits in respect of charitable donations and government gifts made by either you or your spouse. Enter your claim from the calculation on schedule 9 and attach it to your return.

These donations and gifts do not include contributions to political parties. If you contributed to a federal or provincial political party, see Chapter 19 to find out about claiming a credit.

Allowable charitable donations and government gifts

Add up all of the donations made in 2006, plus any donations made in any of the previous five years that you have not claimed before. Don't forget any donations you made through payroll deductions — these donations will be shown on your T4 slip. Generally, you can claim all or part of your total donations, up to the limit of 75 percent of your net income reported on line 236. For the year a person dies and the year before that, this limit is 100 percent of the person's net income.

 It is generally most beneficial to claim donations made by both spouses together on one tax return. This is because the first $200 of donations is eligible for only a 15.25 percent tax credit, while any additional donations attract a 29 percent tax credit. That's quite a difference! Combining your donations will ensure you are subject to the 15.25 percent limit on the first $200 only once — not twice.

 You do not have to claim on your 2006 return the donations you made in 2006. It may be more beneficial for you not to claim them for 2006 but rather to carry them forward to claim on your return for one of the next five years. This may be to your benefit, for example, if you already have sufficient non-refundable tax credits to completely eliminate your taxes payable.

 You can claim only amounts you gave to Canadian registered charities and other qualified donees. A registered charity will show its charity registration number on the receipt. The slip must also indicate the Web address of the CRA. In fact, the CRA Web site has a full list of registered charities in Canada, in case you want to check if a particular charity is legitimate (see www.cra-arc.gc.ca/tax/charities/). These receipts must be attached to paper-filed tax returns. The CRA will not accept cancelled cheques, pledge forms, or the like as proof of payment.

Donating assets

Rather than donating cash to a charity, some individuals choose to give other types of assets. When you "gift" an asset, in most cases you are considered to have sold the asset for a price equal to the market value at the time. This is referred to as a *deemed disposition* and can trigger a capital gain on the asset, which in turn triggers a tax liability despite the fact that you did not receive any cash to fund the tax. However, there likely will not be any tax to pay, as you will receive an official receipt to claim a charitable donation equal to the market value of the property.

Donations of publicly traded securities

Beginning on May 2, 2006, taxes triggered on the direct donation of publicly traded shares or mutual funds to a registered charity will be eliminated. Any capital gains triggered on donations made prior to this date will be included in income at 50 percent of the normal one-half inclusion rate for capital gains — that is, only 25 percent of the capital gain will be subject to tax. Whether the donation is made before or after May 2, 2006, you still get a charitable receipt for 100 percent of the market value of the securities at the time of donation.

Rather than selling securities and donating the cash, you should donate the securities. The charity is free to sell the securities, and charities do not pay tax! This way, you'll pay no tax and still get the same donation credit.

Donations of RRSPs, RRIFs, and life insurance

You can name a charity as the beneficiary of an RRSP, RRIF, or insurance policy and obtain a tax credit for the donation in the year of death. When gifts of a life insurance policy are made, it may also be possible to claim the insurance premiums as charitable donations as they are paid.

Cultural and ecological gifts

Unlike other donations, the donation claim for cultural and ecological gifts is not limited to a percentage of net income. You can choose the portion you want to claim in 2006, and carry forward any unused portion for up to five years.

Donations of cultural property and ecologically sensitive land also enjoy an exemption from capital gains tax. That's an added tax advantage!

Donations to charities in the United States

Generally, donations to foreign charities are not eligible for a credit on your Canadian tax return. However, you can claim donations to U.S. charities, subject to a limitation of 75 percent of your U.S. source income, as long as the charitable organization is recognized as such by U.S. law and would have qualified in Canada if it had been a Canadian organization.

If you make a donation to a qualifying foreign university, the donation can be treated as if it were a Canadian donation; that is, you do not have to have U.S. source income in order to benefit from the donation. A qualified university is one where the student body normally includes students from Canada. A listing of these universities can be found in schedule VIII of the Income Tax Regulations. Most large U.S. universities are included on the list.

Chapter 13

Figuring Out Your Federal Tax

- -

In This Chapter

▶ Calculating federal tax credits

▶ Calculating social benefits repayment

▶ Qualifying for the GST/HST rebate

- -

*T*o help you calculate the total federal tax you have to pay, we provide tips for tax credits in this chapter. We hope they help!

Most of the line references in this chapter refer to schedule 1 of the tax return. This is where you calculate federal tax and federal tax credits. Some of the references are to lines on page 4 of the tax return.

Line 425: Federal Dividend Tax Credit

In Chapter 6 we talk about the special tax treatment available when your receive dividends from Canadian corporations. Although all Canadian dividends receive special tax treatment, the type of "special treatment" differs depending on the type of corporation paying the dividends. Starting in 2006, Canadian dividends are classified as either "eligible" or "non-eligible." Eligible dividends generally include dividends paid by public corporations, and non-eligible dividends are generally those paid by private corporations. If you don't own shares of your own incorporated business, but rather invest in publicly traded stocks, your dividends will be eligible dividends. What's the difference? If you receive eligible dividends, you will pay less tax on the dividends than you have in the past! Good news!

The special tax treatment for Canadian dividends involves including the entire dividend in income and then "grossing up" or adding an additional amount of the dividend into your income (see Chapter 6 for a full explanation). Tax-techies call this the dividend gross-up (perhaps gross *out* would be a better term.) For now, you need to believe us that there is logic in including "more income" than you actually received in your tax return. There is method to the madness . . . we promise.

For eligible dividends, the gross-up is 45 percent. For non-eligible dividends the gross-up is 25 percent. If you receive $10,000 in eligible dividends this year, you'll include $14,500 in your calculation of total income, while if the dividend was non-eligible, $12,500 will be included in your income. Enter the grossed-up amount on line 120 of your tax return.

With a 45 percent gross-up compared to 25 percent, it seems like you are being penalized for investing in public companies in Canada with a higher income inclusion! However, the calculations don't stop there. You are also entitled to a dividend tax credit, which works to reduce your tax bill. In fact, although it seems like you are exposing yourself to more tax if you earn eligible dividends, the tax credit on these dividends works in such as way that you will pay less tax on eligible dividends versus non-eligible dividends.

In other words, the interrelated workings of the dividend gross-up and dividend tax credit in respect of eligible dividends is significantly better in terms of tax minimization than the same with non-eligible dividends.

We agree this is all quite confusing! We suggest you take a look at our comments in Chapter 6 to put your mind at ease.

Federal dividend tax credit on eligible dividends

The federal dividend tax credit on eligible dividends (dividends from public Canadian corporations) is 19 percent of the grossed-up amount. Looking again at the $10,000 example above, the 45 percent grossed-up amount included in income was $14,500 ($10,000 × 145%). The federal dividend tax credit is 19 percent of $14,500, or $2,755.

Federal dividend tax credit on non-eligible dividends

A federal dividend tax credit of 13⅓ percent applies to the grossed-up amount of non-eligible dividends (dividends from private corporations). If the $10,000 was a non-eligible dividend, the grossed up amount would be $12,500 ($10,000 × 125%). The federal dividend tax credit would be 13⅓ percent of $12,500, or $1,667.

Provincial and territorial dividend tax credits

Don't forget your calculation of provincial and territorial taxes will also include another dividend tax calculation!

Chapter 14 deals with provincial and territorial taxes and tax credits.

No dividend tax credit on foreign dividends

Foreign dividends do not qualify for the dividend tax credit — only dividends from Canadian corporation qualify. So, do not gross up foreign dividends on your tax return or report them on line 120. Foreign dividends are included on line 121 of your return as part of "interest and other investment income."

Line 426: Overseas Employment Tax Credit

The overseas employment tax credit may be available to you if you are a Canadian resident but worked abroad for six months or longer in connection with a resource, construction, installation, agricultural, or engineering project. Your employer must complete and sign form T626, "Overseas Employment Tax Credit." If you qualify, you'll find that some (and maybe most!) of your overseas income is exempt from tax in Canada.

Calculate the credit amount on form T626 and then carry it to line 426 of schedule 1.

If you have severed your ties with Canada and become a non-resident, you will not be eligible for the credit because your income as a non-resident will generally not be taxable in Canada.

Line 427: Minimum Tax Carryover

What is minimum tax, you might be wondering? It is a special tax that is charged if someone has a high amount of gross income but many favourable tax deductions or "tax preferences" (in the eyes of the government, that is), resulting in a significantly reduced (again, in the eyes of the government) tax liability for the year.

The types of deductions that may lead you to pay minimum tax include limited-partnership losses (see Chapter 11), resource expenses (see Chapter 10), and stock option deductions (see Chapter 11). If you have these types of deductions on your tax return, you should fill out form T691, "Alternative Minimum Tax," to see if the minimum tax will apply to you. If so, don't fret. You can use that minimum tax to offset regular taxes payable in any of the next seven years. Assuming you will pay regular tax during those years, you will get your money back. Consider it a prepayment of your future tax bill. Minimum tax is often more of a cash-flow issue than a true income tax.

Lines 431 and 433: Federal Foreign Tax Credit

If you've received income from foreign sources this year, you may have already paid tax to foreign tax authorities. But as we learn throughout this book, Canadians are taxed on their worldwide income, which means that this same income is being taxed in Canada. Does this mean you're being double taxed? Probably not. Luckily for you, Canada lets you claim a tax credit for the foreign taxes you've paid.

Claiming the foreign tax credit can take a bit of work. First, there are two types of foreign tax credits, one for foreign tax paid on *non–business* income, perhaps better known as "investment income," and foreign tax paid on *business* income. Second, you need to do a separate calculation for each country you paid to the foreign tax to.

If you paid a total of $200 or less in foreign non-business taxes you do not need to do a separate calculation for each country.

Generally, the foreign tax credit you can claim for each foreign country is the lowest of the following:

- ✔ The foreign income tax you actually paid to the foreign country
- ✔ The Canadian federal tax due on your income from that foreign country

Use form T2209, "Federal Foreign Tax Credits," to calculate the amount of your foreign tax credit. Once you've calculated the amount of foreign tax credits you're entitled to, enter the total in box 14 of schedule 1.

If you paid tax on income from foreign investments (that is, foreign non-business income), your foreign tax credit cannot be more than 15 percent of your income from that investment. However, you may be able to deduct the excess amount on your return at line 232.

If you can't use all of your foreign business income taxes in 2006, you can carry unclaimed foreign business income taxes back three years and forward ten years.

If your federal foreign tax credit on non-business income is less than the tax you paid to a foreign country, you may be able to claim a provincial or territorial foreign tax credit. Complete form T2036, "Provincial Foreign Tax Credit," to determine the amount, if any, of the credit available.

Here's how to claim the federal foreign tax credit. First, ensure you complete the federal foreign tax credit area on schedule 1 and attach form T2209 to your return. Also attach the following:

- ✔ A note showing your calculations. (Remember: show all amounts in *Canadian* dollars.)
- ✔ Proof, such as an official receipt, showing the foreign taxes you paid. For example, if you paid taxes in the U.S., attach your W-2 information slip, U.S. 1040 tax return, and any other supporting documents. Foreign taxes paid may also be noted on your T3 and T5 slips.

Lines 409 and 410: Federal Political Tax Credit

If you contributed to a federal political party or a candidate in a federal election, enter the total amount of your contribution directly on line 409 on schedule 1 of your tax return.

You may deduct from your federal tax payable a *portion* of the political contributions you made. The amount of the credit deductible depends on the amount contributed.

The credit is calculated as the total of the following:

75% for the first $400 contributed ($0 to $400)

50% on the next $350 contributed ($401 to $750)

33 1/3% on the next $525 contributed ($751 to $1,275)

0% on additional contributions above $1,275.

If you work through the math, the *maximum* credit you will be able to claim in a year is $650, and that's when you have contributed $1,275. More credit is not available for contributed amounts over $1,275.

Enter the amount of the credit calculated on line 410.

 The federal political contributions tax credit applies only to — you guessed it — federal political contributions. If you've made provincial political contributions, you're likely eligible for credit against your provincial taxes owing (take a look at Chapter 14). Contributions to candidates in municipal elections do not qualify for a credit on your tax return.

Line 412: Investment Tax Credit

You may be eligible for an investment tax credit (ITC) if you have made an investment where certain tax incentives apply such as investments in scientific research and development (SRED) projects. You are eligible for an ITC if you receive any of the following tax reporting information:

- ✔ There's an amount shown in box 13 of your T101 or T102 slip

- ✔ There's an amount shown in box 41 of your T3 slip

- ✔ There's an amount shown in box 38 of your T5013 slip

To claim an ITC, complete form T2038, "Investment Tax Credit (Individuals)" and send it as part of your tax return.

If you have not used ITCs generated in earlier years (perhaps because the ITCs exceeded your tax liability), you can carry over these amounts to offset 2006 or future-year taxes.

The 2006 federalbudget extended the carryover period for unused ITCs from 10 years to 20 years!

Lines 413 and 414: Labour-Sponsored Funds Tax Credit

A *labour-sponsored venture capital corporation* (LSVCC), otherwise known as a labour-sponsored fund, is a venture capital mutual fund established under specific federal or provincial legislation and managed by labour unions or employee groups. You can claim the labour-sponsored fund tax credit if you purchased an approved share of the capital stock of an LSVCC between January 1, 2006 and February 28, 2007. If you bought a share between January 1, 2007 and February 28, 2007, you can claim a credit for that share either on your 2006 return or on your 2007 return, but not both.

Enter the cost of purchasing your labour-sponsored fund on line 413 of schedule 1 of your tax return. Enter the amount of the credit on line 414. The allowable federal credit is 15 percent of the cost, to a maximum of $750.

You can contribute labour-sponsored funds to your RRSP (Chapter 10, line 208). If you choose to do so, don't forget to claim an RRSP deduction as well as the federal (and perhaps provincial) tax credit for your investment!

If the first registered holder of the labour-sponsored fund units is a spousal RRSP, either the RRSP contributor or the RRSP annuitant (the spouse) may claim the credit for the investment.

Attach to your return either a T5006 slip, "Statement of Registered Labour-Sponsored Venture Capital Corporation Class A Shares," or an official provincial or territorial slip documenting your investment. If the labour-sponsored funds went into your RRSP, you must attach an official RRSP receipt to your return as well.

Line 418: Additional Tax on RESP Accumulated Income Payments

Many Canadians are purchasing Registered Education Savings Plans (RESPs) to help fund their children's education. (We give lots of information about RESPs in Chapter 6.) But when the moment of truth arrives, and your child decides to forgo post-secondary school, who do you think may be stuck paying the tax on the RESP growth? You guessed it — you!

You are liable for additional tax when you have contributed to an RESP that has been running for at least ten years and the beneficiary of the plan does not pursue a post-secondary education by age 21. You are then entitled to the accumulated investment income in the plan.

Don't get us wrong, we think RESPs are a great tax-deferral and income-splitting tool. We're just warning you of one of the repercussions. You see, if you received an accumulated income payment from an RESP in 2006, you may have to pay regular tax plus an additional tax of 20 percent on all or part of the amount received. It is reported in box 40 of your T4A slip. You need to complete form T1172, "Additional Tax on Accumulated Income Payments from RESPs."

You can use this accumulated income to avoid the additional tax. For example, you are able to transfer the income to your RRSP or that of your spouse, subject to available RRSP contribution room and an overall total of $50,000. However, any surplus amount will be subject to the additional 20 percent tax.

You can withdraw the capital you contributed to the RESP at any time without paying additional tax because you have already paid tax on these funds.

Line 421: Canada Pension Plan Contributions on Self-Employment Earnings

 If you are self-employed, you must fill out schedule 8, "CPP on Self-Employment and Other Earnings," to calculate the Canada Pension Plan (CPP) contribution you owe on your self-employment earnings. (See Chapter 12 for more on CPP/QPP contributions for the self-employed.)

Enter the CPP contributions you have to pay on your self-employment earnings on line 421 on page 4 of your tax return. If you are a resident of Quebec, this line does not apply to you; enter on your Quebec tax return the Quebec Pension Plan (QPP) contributions you have to pay.

 If you pay CPP or QPP contributions on your self-employment income, you can claim a deduction for half of your contributions on line 222 on page 3 of your tax return. You can also claim the other half as a non-refundable tax credit on line 308 on schedule 1.

Line 422: Social Benefits Repayment

Did you receive social benefits this year, such as employment insurance (EI) benefits or the Old Age Security (OAS) pension? Well, you could be in for a surprise. You see, you can't always have your cake and eat it too. Some taxpayers will actually have to repay the benefits they received in the year. If this applies to you, you must enter the amount of social benefits you have to repay, from line 235 of your return, on line 422. You can find more details at the end of Chapter 10.

Employment Insurance (EI) clawback

Your EI payments may be subject to a "clawback" (that is, repayment) to the extent that your net income is greater than 125 percent of 2006 maximum insurable earnings of $39,000, or $48,750. The government claws back EI payments at a rate of 30 percent on every dollar of income in excess of $48,750.

If you received maternity, parental, or sickness EI benefits, you do not have to repay any of those benefits even if your income exceeded $48,750. If you received regular EI benefits, in addition to the above EI benefits, you may need to repay some or all of the regular EI benefit.

Old Age Security (OAS) clawback

Your Old Age Security benefits will be taxed back ("clawed back" or returned to the government) at a rate of 15 percent of every dollar your income exceeds $62,144 in 2006. If your maximum OAS benefit for 2006 ends up being $6,000 then you would need to pay back your entire OAS if your income exceeded $102,144.

Line 448: CPP Overpayment

Finally, a breath of fresh air! After pages of pay this, pay that, here's one area where you can recoup some of the money you've paid in the year. As you probably know, your employer has to take CPP premiums off your pay. However, it's possible that you paid too much! This most commonly happens when you held more than one job in the year. Since each employer is obligated to withhold CPP without regard to your other employers, you may have maxed out your payments for the year.

If you were not a resident of Quebec and you contributed more than you were required to, as we explain in Chapter 12, enter the difference on line 448. The CRA will refund the excess contributions to you, or will apply them to reduce your balance owing. If you were a resident of Quebec, this line does not apply to you; claim the excess amount on your Quebec provincial tax return.

Don't worry if you do not realize that you made a CPP overpayment. The CRA will catch it when assessing your return.

Line 450: EI Overpayment

As with the CPP overpayment, you may have had too much EI deducted from your pay in the year. If you contributed more than you had to, enter the difference on line 450. Refer to Chapter 12 if you need help calculating the correct amount. The CRA will refund the excess amount to you or use it to reduce your balance owing.

If you repaid some of the EI benefits you received, do not claim the repayment on this line. If you were required to repay any of your 2005 or previous-year EI received, enter the repayment on line 232. If the repayment was in connection with EI received in 2006, you need to include the amount on line 235. Refer to Chapter 10 for a discussion on lines 232 and 235.

Again, if you fail to calculate that you have overpaid EI premiums, the CRA will catch it on assessing your return.

Line 452: Refundable Medical Expense Supplement

The refundable medial expense supplement provides monetary assistance to low-income taxpayers who incur significant medical- and disability-related expenses. This supplement may be available to you if you have claimed medical expenses (line 332 of schedule 1) and/or disability supports expenses (line 215 of your tax return). See Chapter 12 for more details on these deductions.

To claim this credit, complete the calculations on the federal worksheet included with the guide to completing your tax return.

The 2006 federal budget increased the maximum amount of the supplement from $767 to $1,000.

The supplement is calculated as the lower of $1,000 and 25 percent of the aggregate of medical expenses claimed and the disability supports deduction.

The available supplement is reduced where family income (i.e., both spouses' incomes together) exceeds $22,150. The reduction is 5 percent of every dollar of family income over $22,150. At a family income of $42,150 or above the supplement would be zero.

Line 457: Goods and Services Tax (GST)/Harmonized Sales Tax (HST) Rebate

If you were able to deduct expenses from your income as an employee or as a partner, you may be eligible for a rebate of the GST/HST you paid on those expenses. If your employer (or partnership) paid for these expenses directly, the employer would have been able to claim an input tax credit for the GST/HST paid. Since you paid for the expense yourself, the GST/HST rebate works as though you are getting the input tax credit instead. In Chapter 10 we detail the calculations of the GST/HST rebate.

Generally, you can claim this rebate if either of the following applies:

- ✔ Your employer has a GST/HST registration number.

- ✔ You are a member of a GST/HST–registered partnership, and you have reported on your return your share of the income from that partnership.

If your employer is not registered for GST purposes (perhaps because your employer is a financial institution, health-care provider, or non-profit organization that provides "GST exempt" services), you won't be able to take advantage of this rebate.

You can claim a GST/HST rebate only if you paid GST/HST on your expenditures. If you've paid for expenses that do not require GST, such as insurance or interest, you're out of luck. To claim the GST/HST rebate, complete form GST 370, "Employee and Partner GST/HST Rebate Application." Attach a completed copy of this form to your return, and enter on line 457 the rebate you are claiming.

The GST/HST rebate is taxable in the year following the year you claim it. For example, if you claim a rebate on your 2006 return, you have to report the rebate as income on your 2007 return. (It would be included on line 104 of your 2007 return.)

Chapter 14

Provincial and Territorial Taxes and Credits

*I*n Canada, we pay taxes to both the federal government and a provincial or territorial government — although it may not seem this way because, with the exception of Quebec, the Canada Revenue Agency (CRA) administers income taxes on the provinces' behalf.

In this chapter we discuss the tax rates that apply in your province or territory of residence, the respective tax rates, and the tax credits that may apply to you.

Provincial and Territorial Tax Rates

As we explain in Chapter 1, our federal government levies taxes based on the taxable income you earn in a year. The federal tax rates that apply in 2006 are as follows:

Taxable Income	Federal Marginal Tax Rate
$0–$36,378	15.25%
$36,379–$72,756	22%
$72,757–$118,285	26%
$118,286 and over	29%

Calculate your federal tax using the above rates, then deduct any federal tax credits such as non-refundable tax credits (Chapter 12), dividend tax credits (Chapter 6) foreign tax credits (Chapter 6), and others. Use schedule 1 of your personal tax return to do this federal tax calculation. Then take your taxable income figure and multiply it by the appropriate provincial/territorial tax rate. You may then deduct tax credits available in that province/territory to come up with your provincial tax payable. Provincial or territorial surtaxes are added if they apply. Table 14-1 shows the provincial tax rates as a percentage of taxable income.

Table 14-1	Provincial Tax Rates for 2006
Taxable Income	*Tax Rate as a Percentage of Taxable Income*
Alberta	
All levels of taxable income	10.00
British Columbia	
$0–$33,755	6.05
$33,756–$67,511	9.15
$67,512–$77,511	11.70
$77,512–$94,12	13.70
Over $94,121	14.70
Manitoba	
$0–$30,544	10.90
$30,545–$65,000	13.50
Over $65,000	17.40
New Brunswick	
$0–$33,450	9.68
$33,451–$66,902	14.82
$66,903–$108,768	16.52
Over $108,768	17.84

Newfoundland and Labrador

$0–$29,590	10.57
$29,591–$59,180	16.16

Taxable Income	Tax Rate as a Percentage of Taxable Income
Over $59,180	18.02
Top rate, with surtax	19.64

(Surtax is 9% of Newfoundland and Labrador tax over $7,032)

Northwest Territories

$0–$34,555	5.9
$34,556–$69,110	8.6
$69,111–$112,358	12.2
Over $112,358	14.05

Nova Scotia

$0–$29,590	8.79
$29,591–$59,180	14.95
$59,181–$93,000	16.67
Over $93,000	17.50
Top rate, with surtax	19.25

(Surtax is 10% of Nova Scotia tax over $10,000)

Nunavut

$0–$36,378	4.00
$36,379–$72,756	7.00
$72,757–$118,285	9.00
Over $118,285	11.50

Ontario

$0–$34,758	6.05
$34,759–$69,517	9.15

(continued)

Table 14-1 *(continued)*

Taxable Income	Tax Rate as a Percentage of Taxable Income
Over $69,517	11.16
Rate, with first surtax	13.39
Top rate, with first and second surtaxes	17.41
(First surtax is 20% of Ontario tax in excess of $4,016)	
(Second surtax is 36% of Ontario tax above $5,065)	
Prince Edward Island	
$0–$30,754	9.80
$30,755–$61,509	13.80
Over $61,509	16.70
Top rate, with surtax	18.37
(Surtax is 10% of Prince Edward Island tax over $5,200)	
Quebec	
$0–$28,710	16.00
$28,711–$57,430	20.00
Over $57,430	24.00
Saskatchewan	
$0–$37,579	11.00
$37,580–$107,367	13.00
Over $107,367	15.00
Yukon	
$0–$36,378	7.04
$36,379–$72,756	9.68
$72,757–$118,285	11.44
Over $118,285	12.76
Top rate, with surtax	13.40
(Surtax is 5% of Yukon tax over $6,000)	

If you lived in more than one place in 2006, you may be wondering which province or territory you should pay tax to. In the past, wherever you lived on December 31 was considered your province or territory of residence for the entire year. However, now the answer may not be as simple. According to the CRA's interpretation bulletin IT-221R3, *Determination of an Individual's Residence Status,* an individual is considered to be resident in the province where he or she has significant residential ties. So even if you reside in one province on December 31, you will be considered resident in the province where you have the most ties. Most often this will be the province where your house, spouse, or dependants are located. (And no, your Friday night poker buddies are not considered your residential ties. So even if you leave them behind, you're still considered to have closer ties to your family.)

If you are planning to move this year, time your move carefully to save taxes. As we highlight above, each province and territory has different tax rates. So, if you're moving from a higher-taxed place to a lower-taxed place, you're better off moving as soon as possible in order to take advantage of the lower tax rates. By doing so, all your income from the entire year, even when you lived in the higher-taxed jurisdiction, will be subject to the lower tax rates in your new province or territory of residence. On the other hand, if you're moving to a higher-taxed jurisdiction, consider postponing your move until next year. So, given the choice between moving in December and January, if you're moving to a province with a lower tax rate, you'd prefer to move in December. However, if you're moving to a highly taxed province, you're better off postponing the move until January.

Provincial and Territorial Tax Credits

Once you have calculated your provincial or territorial tax liability, you may reduce this liability using the tax credits available to you. Below we take a look at the common credits available in each province and territory.

Alberta

If you don't like paying high income taxes, Alberta is the place to be. Moreover, if you want your tax calculation to be simple (yes, we said simple), consider making a move to Alberta. You see, Alberta made the headlines a few years back when it became the first province to implement a flat tax: a single rate of provincial tax

(10 percent) of taxable income, regardless of the amount of income you earn — and to top it off, there are no surtaxes. (We told you it was easy!) Alberta's tax calculations are easy . . . and so are the calculations for Alberta's tax credits. Table 14-2 provides the details of the tax savings for some of the common non-refundable credits available in Alberta.

Table 14-2   Alberta Non-Refundable Tax Credits

	Amount	Percentage	Tax Savings
Basic personal amount	$14,899	10.00	$1,490
Spouse or common-law partner amount	$14,899	10.00	$1,490
Amount for an eligible dependant	$14,899	10.00	$1,490
Age amount	$4,152	10.00	$415
Infirm dependant credit (over age 18)	$4,015	10.00	$402
Caregiver amount	$4,015	10.00	$402
Disability amount	$6,883	10.00	$688
Education amount (per month) full time	$459	10.00	$46
Education amount (per month) part time	$138	10.00	$14

If you made charitable donations in 2006, you'll receive a credit equal to 10 percent on the first $200, and 12.75 percent on the excess over $200.

The non-eligible dividend tax credit for Alberta is 6.4 percent of the grossed-up amount of non-eligible Canadian dividends. In September of 2006, the provincial government announced that the eligible dividend tax credit would be staged in over five years as follows:

Year	Dividend Tax Credit on Eligible Dividends
2005	6.4%
2006	7.5%
2007	8.0%
2008	9.0%
2009	10.0%

For 2006, the combined top marginal tax rate in Alberta on eligible dividends is 18.12 percent.

Other tax credits can be found on form AB428.

British Columbia

Table 14-3 provides the details of the tax savings for some of the common non-refundable credits available in B.C.

Table 14-3	B.C. Non-Refundable Tax Credits		
	Amount	Percentage	Tax Savings
Basic personal amount	$8,858	6.05%	$536
Spouse or common-law partner amount	$7,585	6.05%	$459
Amount for an eligible dependant	$7,585	6.05%	$459
Age amount	$3,972	6.05%	$240
Infirm dependant credit (over age 18)	$3,877	6.05%	$235
Caregiver amount	$3,877	6.05%	$235
Disability amount	$6,644	6.05%	$402
Additional credit for mental or physical impairment for child under age 18	$3,877	6.05%	$235
Education amount (per month) full time	$200	6.05%	$12
Education amount (per month) part time	$60	6.05%	$4

British Columbia has introduced a low-income tax credit that will reduce or eliminate provincial tax for individuals whose net income in 2006 is under $26,558.

If you are a British Columbia resident and made charitable donations in 2006, you are entitled to a non-refundable tax credit of 6.05 percent on the first $200 you donated. Any donations in excess of $200 will give rise to a 14.7-percent non-refundable tax credit.

The non-eligible dividend tax credit is 5.1 percent of the grossed-up amount of non-eligible Canadian dividends. The government announced in its budget that it plans to make changes to the dividend gross-up and credit amount for eligible dividends to parallel the federal changes. No specific details have been released at the time of writing.

Other tax credits can be found on forms BC428 and BC479.

Manitoba

Manitoba taxpayers are entitled to claim non-refundable tax credits as detailed in Table 14-4. These amounts are unchanged from 2004.

Table 14-4	Manitoba Non-Refundable Tax Credits		
	Amount	Percentage	Tax Savings
Basic personal amount	$7,734	10.90	$843
Spouse or common-law partner amount	$6,482	10.90	$707
Amount for an eligible dependant	$6,482	10.90	$707
Age amount	$3,728	10.90	$406
Infirm dependant credit (over age 18)	$3,605	10.90	$393
Caregiver amount	$3,605	10.90	$393
Disability amount	$6,180	10.90	$674
Education amount (per month) full time	$400	10.90	$44
Education amount (per month) part time	$120	10.90	$13

The first $200 of charitable donations will receive a 10.9-percent non-refundable tax credit in Manitoba, while any further donations will receive a 17.4-percent credit.

The non-eligible dividend tax credit for Manitoba is 5 percent of the grossed-up amount of non-eligible Canadian dividends. For eligible dividends, a dividend tax credit of 11 percent of the grossed-up amount of eligible dividends is available.

Other credits can be found on forms MB428 and MB479.

New Brunswick

For residents of New Brunswick, there are no new taxes and no tax increases to be concerned with in 2006. After calculating your New Brunswick tax payable, claim the non-refundable tax credits you are entitled to. Table 14-5 shows some of the more common tax credits available.

Table 14-5	New Brunswick Non-Refundable Tax Credits		
	Amount	*Percentage*	*Tax Savings*
Basic personal amount	$8,061	9.68	$780
Spouse or common-law partner amount	$6,845	9.68	$663
Amount for an eligible dependant	$6,845	9.68	$663
Age amount	$3,936	9.68	$381
Infirm dependant credit (over age 18)	$3,807	9.68	$369
Caregiver amount	$3,807	9.68	$369
Disability amount	$6,386	9.68	$369
Education amount (per month) full time	$400	9.68	$39
Education amount (per month) part time	$120	9.68	$12

If you are a resident of New Brunswick and make a charitable donation in 2006, the first $200 will entitle you to a non-refundable credit of 9.86 percent, while any further donations will receive a 17.84-percent credit.

The non-eligible dividend tax credit for New Brunswick is 3.7 percent of the grossed-up amount of non-eligible Canadian dividends.

Additional credits can be found on form NB428.

Newfoundland and Labrador

After calculating Newfoundland and Labrador tax payable (see Table 14-1), you calculate the non-refundable tax credits you are entitled to claim. The common credits are detailed in Table 14-6. The base amount for the credits is still set at 1999 levels (don't ask us why!).

Table 14-6	Newfoundland and Labrador Non-Refundable Tax Credits		
	Amount	Percentage	Tax Savings
Basic personal amount	$7,410	10.57	$783
Spouse or common-law partner amount	$6,055	10.57	$640
Amount for an eligible dependant	$6,055	10.57	$640
Age amount	$3,482	10.57	$368
Infirm dependant credit (over age 18)	$2,353	10.57	$249
Caregiver amount	$2,353	10.57	$249
Disability amount	$5,000	10.57	$529
Disability amount supplement under age 18 $249		$2,353	10.57
Education amount (per month) full time	$200	10.57	$21
Education amount (per month) part time	$60	10.57	$6

If you make a charitable donation, the first $200 will entitle you to a non-refundable credit of 10.57 percent (equal to the lowest tax rate in the province), while any further donations will receive an 18.02-percent credit.

The non-eligible dividend tax credit for Newfoundland and Labrador is 5 percent of the grossed-up amount of non-eligible Canadian dividends. In its budget, the provincial government announced that it will consider mirroring the federal changes to the dividend tax credit for eligible dividends. No announcements have been made to date.

Additional credits can be found on form NL428.

Northwest Territories

The Northwest Territories didn't introduce any new tax changes this year. So once you've calculated your Northwest Territories tax liability using the new rates found in Table 14-1, you can reduce this tax payable by claiming tax credits you are entitled to. Table 14-7 illustrates some of the common credits available.

Table 14-7 Northwest Territories Non- Refundable Tax Credits

	Amount	Percentage	Tax Savings
Basic personal amount	$11,864	5.9	$700
Spouse or common-law partner amount	$11,864	5.9	$700
Amount for an eligible dependant	$11,864	5.9	$700
Age amount	$5,803	5.9	$342
Infirm dependant credit (over age 18)	$3,933	5.9	$232
Caregiver amount	$3,933	5.9	$232
Disability amount	$9,621	5.9	$568
Education amount (per month) full time	$400	5.9	$24
Education amount (per month) part time	$120	5.9	$7

If you make a charitable donation in the Northwest Territories, the first $200 will entitle you to a non-refundable credit of 5.9 percent, while any further donations will receive a 14.05-percent credit.

The non-eligible dividend tax credit for the Northwest Territories is 6 percent of the grossed-up amount of non-eligible Canadian dividends.

Additional credits can be found on forms NT428 and NT479.

Nova Scotia

No new tax changes were announced this year in Canada's Ocean Playground, so preparing your tax return shouldn't bring on any unwanted surprises. Table 14-8 details the tax savings provided by the commonly used credits to help reduce your provincial taxes.

Table 14-8 Nova Scotia Non-Refundable Tax Credits

	Amount	Percentage	Tax Savings
Basic personal amount	$7,231	8.79	$636
Spouse or common-law partner amount	$6,140	8.79	$540

(continued)

Table 14-8 *(continued)*

	Amount	Percentage	Tax Savings
Amount for an eligible dependant	$6,140	8.79	$540
Age amount	$3,531	8.79	$310
Infirm dependant credit (over age 18)	$2,386	8.79	$210
Caregiver amount	$4,176	8.79	$367
Disability amount	$4,293	8.79	$377
Education amount (per month) full time	$200	8.79	$18
Education amount (per month) part time	$60	8.79	$5

If you make a charitable donation in Nova Scotia, the first $200 will entitle you to a non-refundable credit of 8.79 percent, while any further donations will receive a 17.50-percent credit.

The non-eligible dividend tax credit for Nova Scotia is 7.7 percent of the grossed-up amount of non-eligible Canadian dividends. With respect to eligible dividends, Nova Scotia has announced that it will introduce legislation matching that of the federal government, although nothing formal has been brought forward at the time of writing.

Additional credits can be found on forms NS428 and NS479.

Nunavut

Nunavut announced no new tax changes for 2006 (which is good if you hate change, we guess). To calculate your Nunavut tax liability, start with the rates found in Table 14-1. Then you may be eligible for some deductions. The common non-refundable credits are illustrated in Table 14-9.

Table 14-9   Nunavut Non-Refundable Tax Credits

	Amount	Percentage	Tax Savings
Basic personal amount	$10,909	4.0	$436
Spouse or common-law partner amount	$10,909	4.0	$436
Amount for an eligible dependant	$10,909	4.0	$436

	Amount	Percentage	Tax Savings
Age amount	$8,181	4.0	$327
Infirm dependant credit (over age 18)	$3,933	4.0	$157
Caregiver amount	$3,933	4.0	$157
Disability amount	$10,909	4.0	$436
Education amount (per month) full time	$400	4.0	$16
Education amount (per month) part time	$120	4.0	$5

If you are a Nunavut resident and make a charitable donation, the first $200 will entitle you to a non-refundable credit of 4 percent, while any further donations will receive an 11.5-percent credit.

The non-eligible dividend tax credit for Nunavut is 4 percent of the grossed-up amount of non-eligible Canadian dividends.

Other credits can be found on forms NU428 and NU479.

Ontario

Table 14-10 details the common non-refundable tax credits and the respective tax savings available to Ontario residents.

Table 14-10   Ontario Non-Refundable Tax Credits

	Amount	Percentage	Tax Savings
Basic personal amount	$8,377	6.05	$507
Spouse or common-law partner amount	$7,113	6.05	$430
Amount for an eligible dependant	$7,113	6.05	$430
Age amount	$4,090	6.05	$247
Infirm dependant credit (over age 18)	$3,948	6.05	$239
Caregiver amount	$3,948	6.05	$239
Disability amount	$6,768	6.05	$409
Education amount (per month) full time	$451	6.05	$27
Education amount (per month) part time	$135	6.05	$8

If you made a charitable donation during the year, in addition to the federal credit you'll also be entitled to an Ontario donation tax credit. For the first $200 you will receive a credit calculated at the lowest Ontario tax rate of 6.05 percent, and any donations above this level will receive a credit at Ontario's highest tax rate of 11.16 percent.

The non-eligible dividend tax credit for Ontario is 5.13 percent of the grossed-up amount of non-eligible Canadian dividends. The dividend tax credit on eligible dividends is 6.5 percent of the grossed-up amount of eligible dividends.

Additional credits can be found on forms ONT428 and ONT479.

Prince Edward Island

The home of Anne of Green Gables didn't announce any major tax changes in 2006. So, to calculate your 2006 PEI tax liability, apply the rates found in Table 14-1 to your taxable income this year. After that, you'll be able to deduct the provincial non-refundable tax credits, shown in Table 14-11. These credit amounts have remained unchanged since 2004.

Table 14-11   Prince Edward Island Non-Refundable Tax Credits

	Amount	Percentage	Tax Savings
Basic personal amount	$7,412	9.8	$726
Spouse or common-law partner amount	$6,294	9.8	$617
Amount for an eligible dependant	$6,294	9.8	$617
Age amount	$3,619	9.8	$355
Infirm dependant credit (over age 18)	$2,446	9.8	$240
Caregiver amount	$2,446	9.8	$240
Disability amount	$5,400	9.8	$529
Education amount (per month) full time	$200	9.8	$20
Education amount (per month) part time	$60	9.8	$6

Charitable donations by a resident of Prince Edward Island will earn a 9.8-percent tax credit on the first $200, and further donations will result in a 16.7-percent credit.

The non-eligible dividend tax credit for Price Edward Island is 7.7 percent of the grossed-up amount of non-eligible Canadian dividends. The PEI government announced that the provincial dividend tax credit would be adjusted to reflect the changes made by the federal government. That being said, at the time of writing, no specific details have been released.

Additional credits can be found on form PE428.

Quebec

If you are a resident of Quebec, you must file two tax returns this year. Your federal return will be sent to the Canada Revenue Agency (CRA), while your Quebec return must be sent to the Ministère du Revenu du Québec. Your Quebec return is due the same day as your federal return — April 30, 2007 (or June 15, 2007 if you or your spouse is self-employed).

Preparing your Quebec tax return is, for the most part, the same as preparing your federal tax return. The types of income you must report and many of the deductions are identical, although they may be reported on different slips. For example, for Quebec taxation purposes a T4 slip is called the RL-1. In addition, many of the forms that apply to your federal return also apply to your provincial return — the only difference is the names. For example, if you've moved in the year, you should fill out form T1M, "Moving Expenses," with your federal return, and form TP-347-V, "Moving Expenses," with your Quebec return. You can use the tips in the rest of this book to calculate your Quebec income.

If you are a resident in Quebec, you must report your income from all sources on your Quebec tax return. Even if you worked outside Quebec during the year, you must still report this income on your return.

You may be entitled to provincial credits and deductions. Table 14-12 details some of the more common ones.

Table 14-12   Quebec Non-Refundable Tax Credits

	Amount	Percentage	Tax Savings
Basic personal amount	$6,520	20%	$1,304
Amount with respect to age	$2,200	20%	$440
Amount for a person living alone	$1,130	20%	$231

(continued)

Table 11 12 (continued)

	Amount	Percentage	Tax Savings
Amount respecting dependent children:			
Child over 17 who is a full-time student:			
—For first child[1]	$2,875	20%	$575
—Additional children[2]	$2,650	20%	$530
Child in full-time professional training or post-secondary studies	$1,825	20%	$365
Amount if you are head of a single-parent family	$1,435	20%	$287
Other dependants 18 or over	$2,650	20%	$530
Amount respecting a severe and prolonged mental or physical impairment	$2,250	20%	$450

1. A person who has a child under age 18 will receive child assistance payments quarterly. These payments will replace credits for those families with dependants under the age of 18. However, this credit remains in place for dependents 18 years of age and over who are full-time students.

2. An additional amount can be claimed for the child designated as the first dependant if that child is 18 years of age and over and if the individual claiming this amount does not have any children under the age of 18.

3. Credit is reduced if net family income exceeds $28,710.

The credit amount for a dependant with a physical or mental infirmity has been removed and has been replaced by a new refundable tax credit for caregivers of adults. The maximum credit of $1,000 is reduced if the eligible relative's income exceeds $20,000.

The disability (under-18 supplement) credit is replaced with a $37.50 per month increase in the handicapped children supplement included in child assistance payments.

If you are a Quebec resident and make a charitable donation, the first $200 entitles you to a non-refundable credit of 20 percent, while further donations receive a 24 percent credit. Prior to 2006, you had to make total donations of $2,000 before you were eligible for the 24 percent credit rate.

The dividend tax credit for Quebec for non-eligible dividends paid before March 24, 2006 is 10.83 percent of the grossed-up amount of

Canadian dividends. (For non-eligible dividends paid after March 23, 2006, the dividend tax credit is 8.00 percent.) On eligible dividends paid after March 23, 2006, Quebec will offer a 45 percent gross-up and an 11.9 percent dividend tax credit on the grossed-up amount.

You may be entitled to other deductions and credits. Be sure to refer to your Quebec tax return guide (TP-1.G-V) for more information.

Don't forget that a Quebec resident can claim a special credit on his or her federal return. This credit is referred to as the "refundable Quebec abatement" and is found on line 440 on page 4 of the federal personal tax return. This credit is provided as part of the federal–provincial fiscal arrangement, in place of direct cost-sharing by the federal government. The credit reduces your federal balance owing — and can even result in a federal refund to you. The credit is calculated as 16.5 percent of your basic federal tax (line 13 on federal schedule 1).

Saskatchewan

Table 14-13 provides the details for the various non-refundable credits available to residents of Saskatchewan.

Table 14-13 Saskatchewan Non-Refundable Tax Credits

	Amount	Percentage	Tax Savings
Basic personal amount	$8,589	11.00	$945
Spouse or common-law partner amount	$8,589	11.00	$945
Amount for an eligible dependant	$8,589	11.00	$945
Dependant child amount	$2,684	11.00	$295
Senior supplement	$1,074	11.00	$118
Age amount	$4,066	11.00	$447
Infirm dependant credit (over age 18)	$3,933	11.00	$433
Caregiver amount	$3,933	11.00	$433
Disability amount	$6,741	11.00	$742
Education amount (per month) full time	$400	11.00	$44
Education amount (per month) part time	$120	11.00	$13

The tax credit for the first $200 of charitable donations made by Saskatchewan-resident taxpayers is calculated at 11.0 percent, and the tax credit for donations in excess of $200 is determined at 15 percent.

The non-eligible dividend tax credit in Saskatchewan is 8 percent of the grossed-up amount of non-eligible Canadian dividends.

Other tax credits can be found on form SK428.

Yukon

Yukon made no new tax changes this year, so after calculating your taxes using Table 14-1, take a look at Table 14-14, which illustrates some of the common credits you may be entitled to.

Table 14-14   Yukon Non-Refundable Tax Credits

	Amount	Percentage	Tax Savings
Basic personal amount	$8,328	7.04	$586
Spouse or common-law partner amount	$7,071	7.04	$498
Amount for an eligible dependant	$7,071	7.04	$497
Age amount	$4,066	7.04	$286
Infirm dependant credit (over age 18)	$3,933	7.04	$277
Caregiver amount	$3,933	7.04	$277
Disability amount	$6,741	7.04	$475
Education amount (per month) full time	$400	7.04	$28
Education amount (per month) part time	$120	7.04	$8

If you make a charitable donation in Yukon, the first $200 will entitle you to a non-refundable credit of 7.04 percent, while any further donations will receive a 12.76-percent credit.

The non-eligible dividend tax credit for Yukon is 5.87 percent of the grossed-up amount of non-eligible Canadian dividends.

Additional credits can be found on forms YT428 and YT479.

Part IV
After You've Filed Your Tax Return

The 5th Wave
By Rich Tennant

"Death and taxes are for certain, Mr. Dooley, however, they're not mutually exclusive."

In this part . . .

So you've filed your return; now what? Well, you sit and wait for a thank-you card in the mail from the CRA called a Notice of Assessment. Does getting this hot little item in your hands mean you're free and clear? Unfortunately, not always. You see, the CRA likes to perform random checks on people — think of it as a lottery you don't want to win. Sometimes they request little pieces of information, while sometimes they make larger requests for *all* your information. (Did you guess that "larger requests" is simply a nicer term for "audit"?)

So, even the good, law-abiding folks out there will sometimes find themselves hassled by the tax police. For those of you in that boat, all we can say is . . . we're sorry, and you'll live. But don't panic. This part will tell you everything you need to know about dealing with the CRA.

> *"The best measure of a man's honesty isn't his income tax return. It's the zero adjust on his bathroom scale"*
>
> —Arthur C. Clarke

Chapter 15

CRA Administration

• •

• •

*C*ongratulations! You've completed your tax return and sent it in. One of these days (in two to three weeks if you NETFILED or EFILED your return, or four to six weeks if you mailed it), you will receive a Notice of Assessment. What does this mean? Has the CRA audited your return and given it final approval? Unfortunately, the answer is no.

What you have in the Notice of Assessment is an acknowledgment that your return has been received, and usually a confirmation that a basic review of your return has produced no *obvious* errors or omissions. "Obvious" means things like your math adds up, you have not claimed a northern residents deduction (see Chapter 11) from your home in Windsor (which is in southern Ontario!), and you have filed your return in the correct province of residence. You can interpret your receipt of the notice to mean that the CRA accepts your return as filed and does not require more information at this time. In the majority of cases, you will never need to concern yourself with this return again.

Understanding Your Notice of Assessment

The typical Notice of Assessment (form T451) contains a date — the day the notice was mailed to you, your social insurance number, the tax year being assessed, the Tax Centre where the return was assessed, a summary of your return by line number, the amount you owe or are owed, plus an explanation of any changes.

The "explanation of changes" area typically states that the return was assessed as filed, or that some changes were made due to calculation errors or omissions. The notice will go on to say that no additional interest will be charged on amounts owed if the debt is paid within 20 days, and it gives you a telephone number to call if you have any questions. At the bottom of the notice is your RRSP deduction limit statement, which tells you how your RRSP limit was calculated and how much RRSP deduction room you have for next year. This figure includes all your unused RRSP deduction room from 1991 on.

If you have made RRSP contributions but did not deduct them in your return, the amount of your "unused RRSP contributions available" for deduction in future years is noted. (This amount is not considered in calculating your RRSP deduction limit. Therefore, be careful to "net" the two figures to ensure you do not overcontribute to your RRSP.)

Your Notice of Assessment also contains some useful information for future years, including loss carry-forward and alternative minimum tax carry-forward amounts (see Chapter 7). Keep this notice to help you in preparing your tax return for next year.

If you don't agree with any change made by the CRA on your Notice of Assessment, don't wait too long to follow up! The date on your Notice of Assessment — referred to as the "assessment date" — is of particular importance because if you don't agree with changes made by the CRA, you have until the later of 90 days from the assessment date or one year from the original due date of your tax return (usually April 30, or June 15 if you or your spouse are self-employed) to object to the changes. If you miss this deadline you may be out of luck. (The CRA does have the power to grant time extensions, but it's not something you should rely on getting.)

We tell you how to go about objecting to your Notice of Assessment in Chapter 16.

If your Notice of Assessment contains incorrect information, it is your responsibility to contact the CRA and correct the error. Errors most commonly found include incorrect carry-forward amounts and incorrect RRSP deduction limits. If you know that these amounts are wrong and you still use them to your advantage, the CRA will view this as an intentional misstatement and penalize you accordingly. Examples of misused information include individuals who overcontribute to their RRSP because the contribution limit is incorrect or individuals who stop paying tax because the notice has incorrectly declared them dead. (Hmmm. . . .)

Requests for More Information

During the initial tax assessment, or as a result of a re-review of your return, the CRA may have additional questions. To obtain information to answer these questions, the CRA will send you a letter called a "Request for Additional Information." This letter will usually ask for specific information and will include an address where this information is to be sent, a CRA reference number, the name and phone number of the person requesting the information, and a date the information must be received by (usually 30 days from the date of the request).

Is this letter the beginning of a full audit of your return? Should you seek professional advice? Should you run screaming into the hills? The answer is no.

The first thing to remember is that a request for information is not an unusual thing. It is a normal part of the CRA's verification process. Second, a request for information does not automatically mean you will owe more tax.

In fact, the CRA may be sending a request to you for many reasons. One of the most common is that a particular receipt or slip of paper — such as a charitable donation or RRSP receipt — was not included in your paper-filed return. Perhaps the information you supplied was unclear or incomplete, or the CRA is doing random compliance checks to test the accuracy of returns. For example, if you are claiming carrying charges or child-care expenses, the CRA may ask to see proof of these deductions, since you were not required to submit these receipts with your return.

This later request is usually the result of a "desk audit." Such audits are done at the Tax Services Office and are primarily done to test a large number of returns and identify potential problems that will be forwarded for a full audit. As long as the information you've reported on your tax return is truthful, supportable, and within the tax laws, you should have nothing to worry about.

If you did not send receipts to the CRA because you NETFILED or EFILED (electronically filed) your return, a request for information is very common. You see, when you NETFILE or EFILE, you do not send receipts to the CRA. By asking you to send in receipts, the CRA is trying to maintain the integrity of the system by testing the accuracy of your return. With this in mind, it's best to read the letter carefully and respond with the correct information within the time limit set out.

If you cannot get the information within the time limit, call the number on the request and ask for an extension. In most cases, a further 30-day extension will be granted. This extension is usually a one-shot deal, however, and will not be granted a second time.

Record the name and phone number of the person on the letter. Most Tax Services Offices have hundreds of people with hundreds of phone numbers, and it's unlikely that you'll be able to locate this person if you lose the name and contact number.

If you ever have contact with someone at the CRA and find them to be helpful, keep a record of their name and number and call them if you have a question in the future. A knowledgeable person inside a huge bureaucracy can be worth his or her weight in gold.

The worst thing to do if you receive a request for additional information is to ignore it. Ignoring the CRA will not make your problems magically disappear. If you don't provide the information in the time allowed, or if you do not make suitable arrangements for an extension, the auditor will simply conclude that the information does not exist and reassess you accordingly. This type of reassessment usually includes penalties and interest. As well, once this reassessment is complete, the CRA is under no compulsion to accept the supporting information at a later date, and can legally even refuse to accept it.

For more serious situations, where a substantial amount of money is involved or potential criminal activities are suspected, the CRA can invoke a requirement or a judicial authorization forcing you to provide information. The *Income Tax Act* gives it authority to do so.

Fixing Your Mistakes on a Return You've Already Filed

If you think you have forgotten or omitted information on your already filed return, or if you discover new information that pertains to a previously filed and assessed return, will the CRA allow you to submit this information late? The answer is yes!

As you can imagine, this is a common problem. But don't worry — you can change or add information to both assessed and soon-to-be-assessed returns. The process is as follows:

✔ The CRA asks that if you need to make a change to a return already sent in, you *do not file another return for the year*.

✔ Either complete form T1-ADJ, "T1 Adjustment Request," available at all Tax Services Offices (and on the CRA Web site, www.cra-arc.gc.ca), or write a letter detailing the changes (including the years involved, the specific details, your address and social insurance number, and your home and daytime phone numbers). This letter must be dated and signed by you.

✔ Provide *all* supporting documents for the requested changes.

✔ Send this adjustment request to the Tax Centre where you filed your return.

If you follow this process, you will greatly assist the CRA in making the correct changes in a timely manner. Upon review of the information, the CRA will take one of three steps:

✔ Accept your changes and send you a Notice of Reassessment (or Notice of Assessment, if the return had not yet been assessed).

✔ Deny your request. A letter will explain the reasons.

✔ Request additional information.

The CRA accepts online requests for changes to your return. Go to "My Account" on the CRA's Web site (www.cra-arc.gc.ca). You can make online changes to this year's tax return or the prior two years. Beyond that, you will have to file a T1ADJ. Once you have made the desired changes online, the CRA will issue you a confirmation number. Be sure to keep this number for your records.

Before you can access the services under My Account for the first time, you have to register for a Government of Canada "epass." You can apply for an epass online at www.cra-arc.gc.ca/eservices/tax/individuals/myaccount/register-e.html.

What if I discover an error several years back that would have resulted in a refund had I filed correctly?

The CRA will allow you to ask for a refund for up to ten preceding calendar years (prior to 2005 you could request adjustments all the way back to 1985) if it is satisfied that the request would have been accepted had it been made in the normal reassessment period and if all the relevant information is provided. For example, changes requested in 2007 must relate to the 1997 or a subsequent tax year to be considered. The policy of allowing late refund requests is covered in the CRA's Information Circular 92-3 *Guidelines for Refunds beyond the Normal Three-Year Period,* available at Tax Services Offices or on the CRA's Web site (www.cra-arc.gc.ca).

If the filing deadline is approaching — that is, April 30 or June 15 if you're self-employed — and you are missing slips or information, it is best to file your return on time to avoid the late filing penalties. Do your best to calculate your income and deductions, and then follow the above adjustment process when the information is available. The CRA suggests that you include any partial information you have, a description of the missing information, and an explanation of what you are doing to obtain it.

Voluntary Disclosures

If you have never filed a return, you sent a return that was incomplete or incorrect, or you stopped filing returns for two or more years, a voluntary disclosure could help you out. Late returns and false or incomplete information can attract heavy penalties. To avoid these penalties, you can voluntarily come forward and provide all the missing information. Under these circumstances the CRA will waive penalties if you tell it before it catches you, and you will be responsible only for paying the tax you owe plus interest. Here are the CRA's stipulations:

- ✔ **You must provide full and complete information.** If you intentionally provide incomplete information, the CRA will not consider this a voluntary disclosure and will assess penalties.

- ✔ **The CRA must not have requested the information or started an action against you prior to the voluntary disclosure.** If the CRA has already requested the information, or if an audit has been initiated, yours is not considered a voluntary disclosure.

Refunds: Show Me the Money!

The rule is simple: To get a refund, you need to file a tax return. However, if you failed to file a return in the past, and you would have received a refund had you filed, you should still file a return for the missing years. The CRA does not have to send you your refund if your return is more than three years late. However the CRA is prepared to accept returns requesting refunds back ten years if you provide *all* the pertinent information and the CRA is satisfied that the refund would have been issued had the information been supplied on time.

The CRA doesn't have to accept your return if you file late. By filing outside the three-year limit, you are putting yourself at the mercy of the CRA's discretion as to whether it will accept or reject your request. Information Circular 92-3, *Guidelines for Refunds beyond the Normal Three-Year Period,* available at Tax Services Offices or on CRA's Web site (www.cra-arc.gc.ca), provides details of this policy.

The real scoop on refunds

An important point to mention at this juncture is that refunds come from taxes you've already paid. Creating a big loss on a tax return will not get you a refund unless you have already paid tax (sorry to burst your bubble). The *Income Tax Act* requires the Minister of National Revenue (through the CRA) to determine if an overpayment of tax has occurred and to pay a refund. Usually the refund arrives with your Notice of Assessment. If a refund is owed and you have not received it with your assessment, the CRA is required to issue a refund upon receipt of your written application.

If you have any other tax liabilities outstanding (or even federal student loans in arrears!), the CRA will apply your refund against these taxes or loans instead of sending you the money.

Interest on refunds

The CRA pays interest on refunds based on a "prescribed" interest rate that is set quarterly. The amount it pays on refunds is set at 2 percent below the interest it charges on balances owing. The rates can be found on the CRA Website at www.cra-arc.gc.ca/tax/faq/interest_rates/menu-e.html.

Interest on refunds is compounded daily starting on the latest of the following three dates:

✔ 30 days after you filed your return

✔ 30 days after the balance due date for the year (May 30 if your return was due April 30, July 15 if your return was due June 15)

✔ The day after you overpaid your taxes

If a tax refund arose as a result of a loss carry back, interest is calculated on the refund beginning 30 days after your request for the loss carry back was received.

Direct deposit

Your refund can be automatically deposited into your bank account. If you paper file, complete form T1-DD, "Direct Deposit Request," and send it with your tax return. For EFILING, complete part C on form T183, "Information Return for Electronic Filing of an Individual's Income Tax and Benefit Return." (The T183 form will be provided to you by the person or firm responsible for EFILING your return.)

Once you have asked for direct deposit you do not need to request it again. It stays on the CRA's computer records *forever!* If you close a bank account it is imperative you provide the CRA with your new bank account information. Trust us, it takes weeks or months to trace a tax refund sent to a bank account that no longer exists. Avoid the hassle — and avoid the delay in getting your refund!

Refund interest as income

Refund interest is income and must be included in your return in the year you receive it. If you were reassessed and required to repay some of the refund interest, you may deduct repayments made in the current year to the extent of the interest income you have previously included in income.

Balances Owing

The *Income Tax Act* requires that all tax for a year be paid by the balance due date. This date is April 30 of the year following the taxation year in question.

Even if your tax return is not due until a later date (for example, if you or your spouse is self-employed, your tax return is not due until June 15), you must estimate your taxes payable and remit the amount to the CRA by April 30.

Your tax bill is considered to be paid on the day that it was mailed to the CRA, if it is sent by first-class mail or courier. If you're filing your tax return at the last minute, don't just drop it in any old mailbox. Ensure that your return is postmarked April 30 so it will not be considered late-filed. If the mail doesn't get picked up until the next day, you'll be stuck with a late-filed tax return! (Yes, there are penalties for late-filing — these are discussed below.)

If you are filing a tax return for a person who has died during the year, any balance owing on his or her final personal tax return (sometimes referred to as a terminal return) is payable on April 30 following the year of death, except if death occurred in November or December. In this case, the final tax liability is not due until six months after death. If death occurs in January to April, payment for the prior year's return is due six months following death. For example, if George died on February 1, 2006, his 2005 tax bill is not due until August 1, 2006. Any tax liability for 2006 would be payable by April 30, 2007.

Interest on balances due

If you owe taxes for the current year, the CRA charges compound daily interest starting April 30 on any unpaid taxes. This also applies to taxes owing that are included in Notices of Reassessment. If you are reassessed for 2006, the interest calculation starts May 1, 2007 — one day after the tax should have been paid.

If you incur any penalties, interest is also charged on the penalty starting the day after your return is due. The interest charged by CRA is based on the prescribed interest rate. Prescribed interest rates are discussed earlier in the chapter. The rates can be found on the CRA Web site at www.cra-arc.gc.ca/tax/faq/interest_rates/menu-e.html.

Pay your tax by April 30 to avoid significant interest charges. Pay them by that date even if you are filing your return late. Estimate your tax payable and send it in.

Instalments

Taxpayers who earn income that is not subject to withholding tax, and who earn sufficient amounts of this income to regularly create a tax liability, will be asked by the CRA to pay their tax liabilities throughout the tax year, instead of just at tax filing time. Generally you will have to pay installments for the following tax year if your tax owing for the current year is more than $2,000, and you expect that your tax liability for the following year will be more than $2,000. This prepayment of your tax liability is called an instalment. If you are subject to instalments, the CRA will send you a reminder, and you should pay the required amount unless you are certain that you will not have a tax liability this year.

Instalments are payable quarterly, on March 15, June 15, September 15, and December 15. If you are required to pay instalments during the year, be aware that late or deficient instalment payments also attract interest at the high prescribed interest rate.

If you are deficient or do not make an instalment payment, you can avoid interest by paying your next instalment early. The CRA will give you credit for the overpayment interest (at the same rate as the late payment) and net the interest owed against the interest earned.

Non-deductible interest

Interest paid to the CRA is generally non-deductible for tax purposes. As we note above under "Refund interest as income," if you were reassessed and required to repay all or some of the refund interest you had received previously and included it in your income, the repayment of the interest can be deducted.

Penalties and Interest

Penalties are in addition to the interest payments made on late or deficient taxes. Penalties also attract the same interest as do unpaid balances. (So, you can have interest charged on outstanding taxes, interest charged on outstanding interest, and interest charged on outstanding penalties!)

Late-filing penalty

If you file your return late — after April 30 or perhaps June 15 — a penalty of 5 percent of the tax owing will immediately be applied. A further penalty of 1 percent of the unpaid tax will also be added for each full month the return is late, up to a maximum of 12 months (so, there's an additional 12 percent maximum penalty).

If you are late a second time within three years of the first late filing, the penalty is bumped up to 10 percent of the unpaid tax plus 2 percent per month, to a maximum of 20 months (so, there's an additional 40 percent maximum penalty!).

Even if you cannot pay your tax, make sure you file your return on time to avoid the late-filing penalties.

Repeated failure to report income

If you have failed to report income, and this has been reassessed by the CRA, any subsequent failure to report income within the next three years will earn you a penalty of 10 percent of the unreported income.

Failure to provide complete information

If you fail to provide complete information, you'll face a fine of $100 per occurrence. Some examples include not providing a SIN on your return or omitting information that the CRA requires to correctly assess your return. Don't be sloppy — complete *all* the information asked for on your tax return.

If the information you need had to be obtained from a third party, and this person (or company) would not cooperate, the CRA can waive your penalty. Attach a note to your tax return, outlining the steps you took to try to obtain the information.

Tax evasion, gross negligence, false statements, or false credit returns

For serious situations where taxpayers intentionally try to misstate or misrepresent their returns, a penalty of 50 percent of the tax avoided will be added to their tax liability. Cheating does not pay!

Criminal prosecutions

Tax evasion usually involves a criminal prosecution in addition to the above penalties. The courts can impose fines of up to 200 percent of the tax evaded and sentence you to five years in prison.

In one case, an individual was fined $36,000 after pleading guilty to two counts of tax evasion. The fine represented 120 percent of the amount of federal tax the individual was trying to evade. In addition to the fines, the individual was required to pay (obviously) the full amount of taxes owing, plus interest and penalties, for a total of $214,000! We can't say it enough — cheating does not pay!

Waiving of interest and penalties

As we discuss in Chapter 16, the CRA, through its Fairness Committees, can waive penalties and interest in certain circumstances, such as illness or natural disaster.

Chapter 16

Disagreeing with the Taxman

● ●

In This Chapter

▶ Filing a notice of objection to your Notice of Assessment

▶ Proceeding to tax court

▶ Making an application for fairness

● ●

A reality of our tax system is that occasionally the CRA will dis-agree with the way you prepared your tax return. If the CRA disagrees with you the first time it assesses your return you will receive a *Notice of Assessment* detailing the changes. (For more on the Notice of Assessment, see Chapter 15.) Any adjustments after the original Notice of Assessment will be communicated to you by means of a *Notice of Reassessment.*

This chapter details how to go about disagreeing with the CRA if you think an error has been made in assessing your return.

Objecting to Your Notice of Assessment

If you disagree with (or perhaps simply don't understand) how you've been assessed by the CRA, your first step is to call the CRA at 1-800-959-8281 and discuss the problem.

If you're still not satisfied, you have the right to a formal review of your return through the CRA's Appeals Branch at no charge. The Appeals Branch is completely independent of other CRA branches, so you can be assured that the person who originally assessed your return will not be the same person assigned to review your appeal!

A Notice of Objection is the document you use to notify the CRA's Appeals Branch that you disagree with an assessment or reassessment and that you would like the return to be re-reviewed. File a Notice of Objection by completing form T400A, "Objection — Income Tax Act," or by writing a detailed letter outlining the reasons for your objection. Send the form or letter to the Chief of Appeals at the Tax Services Office or the Tax Centre where you filed your return. (This office or centre is noted on your notice of assessment.) An example of an objection letter is provided on page 19 of CRA's publication P148, "Resolving Your Dispute: Objection and Appeal Rights Under the *Income Tax Act.*" This publication is available on the CRA Web site (www.cra-arc.gc.ca).

Use form T400A if you file an objection. Though not mandatory, it will act as a precise guide to the information that the Appeals Branch will need in order to deal quickly with your situation. To speed up the process a little at CRA's end, attach a copy of your Notice of Assessment to the Notice of Objection.

When can I file a Notice of Objection?

A Notice of Objection must be filed before the *later* of the following:

✔ One year from the due date of the return; or

✔ 90 days from the mailing date (referred to as the "assessment date" or "reassessment date") of the Notice of Assessment or Notice of Reassessment.

Let's say that the due date of your 2006 tax return is April 30, 2007. Assume your return's assessment date is July 2, 2007. You will have until the later of 90 days after the date of mailing of the Notice of Assessment (assessment date), September 30, 2007, or one year after the return was due, April 30, 2008, to object to the assessment. In this case, you will have until April 30, 2008, to object to the assessment.

In the case of a Notice of Reassessment, the rules are slightly different. Since a reassessment usually happens well after the original Notice of Assessment, one year after the return was due has usually passed. As a result, you must file your Notice of Objection within 90 days of the mailing date of the Notice of Reassessment (reassessment date).

Can I file a Notice of Objection late?

Yes, you can file a Notice of Objection late — if circumstances beyond your control prevented you from filing the Notice of Objection on time.

You need to write to the Chief of Appeals at the Tax Services Office or the Tax Centre where you filed your return (again, it will be noted on your Notice of Assessment) to request an extension. The letter must detail why you did not file the objection on time. File the Notice of Objection along with the letter. The letter must be sent within one year from the date the Notice of Objection should have been filed.

Should I pay the disputed amount?

The answer is yes, you should pay the disputed amount, even though your objection has not beenresolved. This may seem strange, since the core of your argument is that you do *not* owe this money. The truth is that the CRA will begin charging interest on the disputed amount if it is not paid within 20 days of your assessment or reassessment date. If you win the appeal, you will get your money back plus interest. If there's a chance you'll lose, why pay the extra interest?

Will collection actions start while my case is under appeal?

The CRA will stop collection actions against you while your case is under appeal. Unfortunately, you will still continue to receive notices of outstanding amounts from the CRA Collections Division throughout the period, but no action will be taken against you — yet. If you lose your appeal, however, watch out. The collections people at the CRA mean business, and you should make every effort to cooperate with them — either pay them or work out a payment schedule. If you work out a payment schedule, interest continues to be charged on unpaid taxes.

Collections staff are specially selected for their easygoing approach to recovering money owed to the CRA — NOT! Remember, they are "bill collectors" with significant powers!

How long will the appeal take? What if I lose but still think I'm right?

Generally speaking, appeals take many months to be resolved. It can take from six months to a year for a decision to be rendered.

If your appeal has been rejected by the CRA, the Tax Court of Canada is your next stop. We look more closely at the court system in the next section, but for now you need to know that to be able to advance to Tax Court you must have filed a Notice of Objection within the time limits set out above. If you didn't follow the rules, the Tax Court will not hear your case.

As you can see, the Notice of Objection, filed correctly and within the required time limit, is a powerful tool for protecting your right to appeal. If in doubt, file a Notice of Objection to protect your rights to appeal.

How long after I file my return can I be reassessed?

The general rule is that a return can be reassessed any time within three years of the mailing date of the original Notice of Assessment (the assessment date). After the three years have passed, the return becomes "closed," or what tax-techies call *statute-barred*. When a return is statute-barred, neither you nor the CRA can go back and reopen the year for reassessment.

Let's say you mailed your 2006 return on April 30, 2007. A month later you receive your Notice of Assessment. The date on the notice is May 30, 2007. If the CRA wants to reassess the 2006 tax return, it must do so before May 30, 2010. Even if your return is reassessed, the original Notice of Assessment date is the key date used to determine when the return goes statute-barred. Subsequent Notices of Reassessment do not affect this original date.

Reassessment outside the three-year limit

The *Income Tax Act* does allow the CRA the discretion under specific circumstances to reassess beyond the normal reassessment period of three years. Reasons for reassessment outside the three-year limit include the following:

- ✔ **The taxpayer has made misrepresentations in his or her tax return due to fraud, neglect, carelessness, or willful default.** If the CRA can prove that you intentionally or unintentionally misrepresented information on your return because of fraud or carelessness, you can be reassessed at any time with no limitations.

- ✔ **The taxpayer signs a waiver of the three-year limit.** If it's to your benefit to extend the limit, you can sign a waiver to do so. (We discuss waivers in the next section.)

- ✔ **The special "six-year rule" applies, which includes the carry back of losses.** Since the law allows you to carry losses back three years, any prior return within that carry-back period stays open for six years from the original assessment date rather than the usual three. For example, say you had a $5,000 non-capital loss in 2003 that you requested be carried back to 2000. Later, say the CRA decides to reassess your 2003 tax year, and adjusts the loss previously claimed to only $4,000 and let's say this reassessment takes place in 2006. If the CRA was bound by a three-year reassessment period for this loss adjustment, it would not be possible to reduce the losses applied to the 2000 tax year. The "six-year rule" ensures that the 2000 year is not statute-barred by the time the 2006 reassessment takes place, and allows the loss to be adjusted to $4,000.

- ✔ **Transactions with related non-residents.**

- ✔ **Transactions involving the payment of tax to a foreign government.**

- ✔ **Consequential changes.** Consequential changes are changes that occur in a year as a result of a court decision or a settlement with the CRA that affect other taxation years. In these cases, the CRA can reassess returns for otherwise statute-barred years.

In addition to the above rules, the CRA has the power to reassess beyond the normal statute-barred period for certain taxpayer-requested adjustments.

Individuals are able to late-file tax returns or request adjustments to old returns for ten preceding tax years if it would be to their advantage tax-wise. This may occur if they had been entitled to a refund or if they had been entitled to certain credits but did not file for these items when they filed their tax returns.

It is a good idea to do a thorough review of your past tax returns (with the help of this book) from time to time to ensure you claimed all the credits (and tax deductions!) you were entitled to. Credits we often see missed and that you might want to pay close attention to include provincial tax credits, the disability tax credit, and age credits.

Waivers

Sometimes you won't want the regular three-year assessing period to apply to you because it is to your benefit to have the tax year remain open. In these cases, you should file a waiver with the CRA. A waiver is a document that specifies the items reported on your personal income tax return that you don't want the regular three-year assessing period to apply to. You must file a waiver on form T2029, "Waiver in Respect of the Normal Reassessment Period," and it must be received by the CRA within three years of the assessment date in question.

When signing a waiver, be very specific about which items you want to remain open. If you are too general, you are leaving the door open for the CRA to reassess items you had not intended it to consider. The CRA is limited to looking at only the items mentioned in the waiver. Since the CRA is allowed to assess more tax, include only items that you expect will reduce your tax liability.

Why and when to sign a waiver

There are basically two situations in which waivers come into play:

- ✔ The CRA asks you to sign a waiver on a particular issue because the three-year limit is approaching and the issue may not be resolved before the return goes statute-barred. If you do not sign the waiver, the CRA will assess the issue and force you to file a Notice of Objection and appeal its decision. This can be a long process, so you'll save a lot of time, effort, and money if you simply sign the waiver and hope the issue is resolved without additional tax being levied.

- ✔ You are asking the CRA to reduce the tax you owe, and the three-year limit is approaching. By signing the waiver you can ensure that the issue will still be open for discussion, and you can avoid taking the entire return to appeal.

As mentioned earlier, the CRA is given the discretion to reassess returns beyond the three-year limit if the effect is to reduce the tax originally assessed and the CRA is satisfied that the adjustment would have been accepted if filed on time. By filing a waiver, you can avoid being victim to the CRA's discretion and protect your right to appeal.

Can I revoke a signed waiver?

Yes, a waiver can be revoked on six months' notice by filing form T652, "Notice of Revocation of Waiver." After revocation, the waiver is permanently revoked and no reassessment can be made after this date.

 In some cases, it's a good idea to sign a waiver and file the revocation at the same time. For example, if the CRA requests the waiver, your filing both forms at once gives them only six months to resolve the issue and does not leave your return open for years to come.

Here Comes the Judge

As we discussed in the previous section, the Appeals Branch is the last level of recourse within the CRA. If you continue to disagree with the decision, your next step is the *Tax Court of Canada*. To proceed to Tax Court, you must have filed a Notice of Objection to your original assessment. If so, then a letter stating you are appealing a CRA decision must be sent to the Tax Court – together with the $100 filing fee:

- ✔ Within 90 days of the date of mailing of the confirmation of your assessment (or reassessment) to the Notice of Objection (translated — correspondence from the CRA denying your objection); or

- ✔ After 90 days have passed since you filed the Notice of Objection if you have not received a decision from the CRA Appeals Branch

The Tax Court has two procedures, informal and general. If the amount of federal tax in dispute is not more than $12,000, you can have your case heard under the informal procedure. If the amount of federal tax is more than $12,000, you must follow the court's general procedure.

Informal procedure

Under the informal procedure, you do not need a lawyer to represent you. You may appear on your own or be assisted by a lawyer, accountant, or adviser. This court does not necessarily follow the "normal" rules of evidence and procedure, nor are decisions precedent-setting. The decisions of this court are quick and are usually delivered within a year of your appeal. (Yes, a year can be considered "quick" in court decisions!) If you want to appeal a decision, you are limited to issues of law or gross error, and must apply for a "judicial review" before the Federal Court of Appeal.

If you go to Tax Court using the informal procedures, it is advisable to seek the advice of an experienced tax professional (although you are not required to do so). The expert's advice can better prepare you for the proceedings and help you avoid costly errors that may jeopardize your case.

General procedure

The general procedure operates in a formal court atmosphere — and lawyers are required. These cases will involve all the usual aspects of a trial. As is the case in most formal court proceedings, the time involved can be several years from the initiation of the process until a decision is made. The amount of money involved is also substantial, with the added downside that you could end up paying the court costs if the decision goes against you. Beyond Tax Court, cases heard under the general procedure can be appealed to the Federal Court of Appeal and eventually to the Supreme Court of Canada — but only if the Supreme Court lets you appeal! If you are not given permission to appeal — tough; it dies.

Making an Application for Fairness

Within each Tax Services Office there exists a committee responsible for reviewing a taxpayer's request to do the following:

- ✔ Waive penalties and interest on an assessment
- ✔ Accept late, amended, or revoked income tax elections
- ✔ Allow refunds beyond the normal three-year period

Adjustments to returns are made for compelling reasons on compassionate or equitable grounds, or for circumstances beyond the taxpayer's control. Examples include serious illness or accident; incorrect information supplied by the CRA, including errors in CRA publications; a natural disaster, postal strike, or civil disobedience; or legitimate delays in receiving information. In the case of late-filed elections, the CRA is also willing to accept honest mistakes as a legitimate reason for filing incorrectly.

Visit the CRA's Web site at www.cra-arc.gc.ca to get a copy of CRA Information Circulars IC 92-1 (Guidelines for Accepting Late, Amended or Revoked Elections), IC 92-2 (Guidelines for Cancellation and Waiver of Interest and Penalties), and IC 92-3 (Guidelines for Refunds beyond the Normal Three-Year Period). These guidelines will help you to better understand the situations where you can request a "fairness" review. In addition to the above factors, the CRA wants to see that the taxpayer has made every effort to minimize or correct the errors where possible.

To request that the CRA conduct a "fairness" review, you must write a letter to the director of your Tax Services Office requesting a review. The letter needs to detail all the facts and the reasons the fairness provisions should be applied to your situation, so it is in your best interest to review the information circulars noted in this section before writing the letter!

Part V
The Part of Tens

The 5th Wave

By Rich Tennant

In this part . . .

Well, you've made it to the end. These final few chapters provide short tidbits of useful information you can read any time and any place. To be honest, these chapters are filled with information we thought you should know but couldn't place anywhere else in the book. So here they are — on their own.

Read these chapters over to find out the ten major tax changes that have taken place in the last year that will have an impact on your return this year, the top ten ways to reduce your risk of an audit, and the top ten planning tips for families and investors. Lots of great tips are packed into these last few pages, so be sure not to miss them!

"The nation ought to have a tax system which looks like someone designed it on purpose."

—William E. Simon

Chapter 17

Top Ten Tax Changes for 2006

In This Chapter

▶ Checking out new tax cuts

▶ Looking at new credits

▶ Good news for students, seniors, and parents

*J*ust when you thought you understood all there was to know about tax!

This chapter highlights the top ten tax changes for 2006.

Goods and Services Tax (GST) Rate Decreased to 6%

As of July 1, 2006, the GST rate dropped from 7% to 6%. (Okay, it is not an income tax change but any change that puts money in your pocket has to be mentioned!)

Universal Child Care Benefit

The federal government began sending out payments in July! Each family is entitled to $100 per month for each child under the age of six — no matter what the family income is. Payments were automatic if a child tax benefit was already being sent out. If not you must apply for the benefit. Go to www.universalchildcare.ca or call 1-800-959-2221 or stop by a Service Canada Centre to apply. Although getting money from the government is great, the bad news is that these payments are taxable in the hands of the lower income spouse. So, you may want to tuck a portion of it away, to avoid a nasty surprise in April.

Income Tax Lowered on Dividends Received from Canadian Public Corporations

Beginning in 2006 you pay less tax on dividends received from Canadian public corporations. Changes were made to the way public company dividends are taxed in order to get the after-tax returns of public company dividends on similar footing to the after-tax returns of income trust distributions. You can find more information on these new rules in Chapter 6.

Scholarships Now Tax-Free, and a Tax Credit for Textbooks

Previously, a student was taxed on the amount of a scholarship over $3,000. Now the entire scholarship is tax-free.

Students can also begin to claim a tax credit amount to assist with textbook purchases. The tax credit amount is $65 a month for a full-time student and $20 a month for a part-time student.

Tax Assistance for Employees

To assist in the costs of doing your job, the Canada Employment Credit was introduced in 2006. A credit amount of $250 can be claimed by employees this year ($1,000 in 2007) to offset the costs of work-related expenses like uniforms, home computers, Internet fees, and supplies.

Do you take public transit to work? Beginning on July 1 the cost of monthly (or longer) public transit passes qualify for a tax credit. You need to save your passes (and receipts showing the cost) to support your claim. You can also claim a credit for your spouse's transit passes and for any children you have under the age of 19. (Well, assuming they don't make the claim themselves!)

Tradespeople are now entitled to a tax deduction when they acquire tools required to perform their job. The deduction is calculated as the total cost of tools in excess of $1,000 to a maximum deduction of $500.

Increased Pension Credit

The maximum amount of the pension credit amount has doubled from $1,000 to $2,000. This may mean seniors can receive an extra $1,000 of pension income (excluding OAS and CPP/QPP) tax-free! (See Chapter 5 for more info.)

Donating Securities to Charities

Starting May 2, 2006, you can donate publicly traded securities, *with accrued capital gains*, to a charity and pay no capital gains tax! (Previously, you paid tax on 25 percent of the accrued capital gain.) Don't forget you receive a charity receipt for the full market value of the securities which qualifies for the charitable donation tax credit. We tell you more in Chapter 11.

Tax Breaks for Fishers

Fishers have now been put on equal footing with farmers in that they can make use of the $500,000 capital gains exemption. They can now also transfer their fishing business to their children without triggering a tax liability at the time of transfer. See Chapter 7.

Improvements to Disability and Medical Tax Assistance

The child disability tax benefit amount has increased to $2,300 (from $2,044) and the family income threshold has increased to permit more families to claim.

The maximum refundable medical expense supplement has increased to $1,000 from $750. The family income threshold at which a full supplement can still be claimed has also increased slightly. For more details, see Chapter 10.

Children's Fitness Tax Credit

This credit begins in 2007. Parents will be eligible to claim a maximum credit amount of $500 per child under 16 who participates in an eligible physical activity program. The federal government is to release information on what is considered an eligible program

Chapter 18

Ten Ways to Reduce the Risk of an Audit

In This Chapter

▶ Becoming your own tax auditor

▶ Being consistent

▶ Learning from your mistakes

*W*hat are the two most dreaded words in the English language? For some, they're "tax audit." Chances are, if you are reading this chapter you're just putting the finishing touches on your tax return and are looking for ways to reduce your risk of getting anything other than a thank-you note — called a Notice of Assessment — from the CRA.

Here are our pointers to help you avoid becoming the CRA's target for an audit or review.

Audit Your Own Tax Return

Make sure you double-check your return before you send it in. Check first for mathematical accuracy. Make your life easy and use tax software or an online service to ensure your numbers add up properly. Also check that you've included all relevant information, including your name, address, and social insurance number. Avoiding these simple mistakes is the first step in keeping the CRA from reviewing your return more closely.

Report All Your Income

Make sure that you've reported *all* income, including interest and dividends from all accounts. If you forget something, you can be sure the taxman will eventually find it. You see, the CRA gets a copy of the same income slips you receive, and they cross check them by computer to make sure everything is reported. One handy tip is to compare this year's return to last year's to ensure that you haven't missed anything.

Avoid Claiming Ongoing Losses

Be careful if you run your own business and are reporting a loss on this year's return. In order to claim these losses, you must be able to prove that your business is not a "personal" endeavour and is in fact a true commercial enterprise. If there are personal or hobby aspects to your business, your losses can be denied if your business does not have a reasonable expectation of profit. The tax collector generally only flags your return the first year you report business losses, but if you continue to report losses in the next two or three years, you could be a prime candidate for an audit.

Tax Planning 101: File a Return and File on Time!

Some people argue that the only way to ensure your return doesn't get audited is simply not to file a return at all. After all, the CRA can't audit what isn't there. To these people we say . . . try again. In fact, every year the CRA sends out countless letters to individuals requesting them to file a tax return — proof that the taxman knows who these people are. Non-filers risk not only getting caught and getting hit with interest and penalties, but also going to jail. In addition, if the CRA has to ask you to file a return, you can bet the chances are greater that they'll take a closer look. So make sure you file every year. And if you've been a non-filer in the past, remember — it's never too late to make things right.

Be Consistent with Your Expenses

Claims for expense deductions must be reasonable, and the expenses must be incurred to earn income. This means that claiming personal expenses is not only a bad idea, it's also not allowed under our tax law. And if you own your own business, make sure your expenses are consistent from year to year. Of course, you still must be able to support all expenses claimed, but a significant jump in travel or entertainment costs may catch the taxman's eye.

If you are self-employed, make sure salaries paid to family members continue to be "reasonable" in view of the services provided.

Don't Cheat

Sounds simple enough, right? Well, those of you who are tempted to cheat should be aware that the taxman has ways to track you down. The CRA has identified the industries that have in the past had a higher incidence of cheaters, including construction, subcontracting, carpet installation, unregistered vehicle sales, auto repair, independent courier businesses, and direct sales. If you're in one of these industries, don't be offended by our comments. You are probably aboveboard with your tax filings. But not everyone is, and so the list of industries the CRA keeps its eye on grows longer each year.

Think Twice about Taking Cash Under the Table

Many people think that taking cash payments for services will get them out of paying tax. What the taxman doesn't know won't hurt him, right? Don't be so sure. There is no shortage of Canadians who are willing to quietly report you for offering services on a cash basis. In one instance we're aware of, a business owner offered a customer services at a discount if the customer was willing to pay cash. Turned out that the customer worked for the CRA. *Oops!* The business owner's tax affairs were examined, and he was eventually reassessed for underreporting revenues.

Learn from Your Mistakes

If you're caught cheating, it's almost guaranteed that the CRA will look at that particular item again the next year. Suppose, for example, that you receive a request to substantiate your child-care expenses and find that, whether by accident or design, you've overstated the amount claimed. You can be sure that the CRA will ask you to submit your receipts next time around — perhaps for the next couple of years. The moral of the story? There's absolutely no excuse for getting caught making the same mistake twice.

Don't Give the Taxman Something to Audit

Some tax returns have very little worth auditing. An employee with one T4 slip has less chance of being audited than a self-employed person with significant expenses. The CRA likes to flag the more risky items to get more bang, so to speak, for its time spent assessing. Items such as losses from tax shelters, significant interest deductions, rental or business losses, moving expense deductions, and clergy residence deductions (believe it or not) have an increased likelihood of being flagged for an audit. These deductions may be legitimate, but if you choose to complicate your tax affairs by reporting deductions that can be higher risk, be sure you have the information necessary to back up your claim — just in case the taxman comes knocking.

Keep Your Fingers Crossed

Even if you do everything right on your return, you may be selected for an audit or receive a request for information because of plain old bad luck. Every year, the CRA selects taxpayers at random, and uses the results of these audits or requests to determine where people make the most mistakes and in which areas people most often cheat. So even if you've crossed all your t's and dotted your i's, you may still receive an unwelcome letter in the mail on CRA stationery. Don't assume you've done anything wrong — just be sure you can prove that you did it right!

Chapter 19

Top Ten Tax Planning Tips for Families

- -

In This Chapter

▶ Extending loans to family members

▶ Using "second-generation" income

▶ Splitting tax by pension sharing

▶ Keeping it in the family

▶ Contributing to a spousal RRSP

▶ Contributing to an RESP

- -

*O*ne of the most effective ways for a family to save tax is to split income. So what is income splitting? Income splitting involves shifting income from the hands of one individual who pays tax at a high tax rate to another who will pay tax at a lower tax rate. For example, if a husband gives money to his wife for investment purposes, and the wife is taxed at a lower rate than the husband (because she is in a lower tax bracket), income splitting can be achieved provided the tax rules let the investment income be taxed in the wife's hands. The after-tax income retained by the couple is greater than if it was taxed in the husband's hands.

The key to income splitting is to ensure that the income will be taxed in the hands of the lower-income family member — that's the hard part. To make income splitting difficult, the *Income Tax Act* includes a bunch of rules, called the "attribution rules," which state that if you try to split or shift investment income (i.e., interest, dividends, and rents) to your spouse (or common-law partner), or to a minor child, grandchild, niece, or nephew, *you* — not they — will be taxed on the income earned on the invested funds . In addition, if you wish to split or shift capital gains with a spouse or common-law partner, you may find that the attribution rules will also work against you! Oddly, perhaps, the attribution rules will not negatively impact your plans to shift capital gains to your minor child. Hey, here is a tax planning opportunity! More on this below!

The good news is that there are ways (legal ways — of course!) around the attribution rules so that you can make income splitting work for you and your family. Here are the top ten income splitting strategies.

Lend Money to a Family Member to Use for Investing

If you give your spouse or minor child funds to invest the interest and dividends (i.e., investment income) earned on the invested funds will be subject to tax in your hands — not the in the hands of your spouse or minor child. The investment income earned will be "attributed" to you and your tax return where it will be subject to tax at your tax rate. In other words, you are in the same position as if you had invested directly yourself — you have not income split!

If you loan, instead of gifting, money to a spouse or minor child to be used for investment purposes you can avoid the investment income earned on the loaned funds being taxed in your hands. However, as with everything, there's a catch. Interest-free loans or even low-interest loans won't cut it! To avoid the attribution rules, you must charge interest on the loan at an interest rate at least equal to the CRA's prescribed interest rate at the time of the loan. Your spouse or minor child must pay the interest owing to you by no later than January 30 (not 31!) of the year following the year in which the interest was incurred — and must be included in your income. Your spouse or minor child can deduct this interest from the income earned on the investment. (See Chapter 10, line 221 for more on deducting interest expense.)

The CRA announces its prescribed interest rates every quarter. The rates can be found on the CRA's Web site at www.cra-arc.gc.ca/tax/faq/interest_rates. (At the time of writing, the CRA prescribed interest rate was 5 percent!)

Consider Julie, who wants to transfer some investment income to her husband, Jim, because he is in a lower tax bracket. She knows that she can't simply give him the money to invest, as the attribution rules will thwart her income-splitting plans. So, on January 1, 2006, she decides to lend him $100,000 at 5 percent interest, resulting in an interest cost to Jim of $5,000 per year.

Jim takes the $100,000, invests it, and in the first year earns $7,000. If Jim pays Julie the $5,000 in interest by January 30, 2007, he can report the $7,000 of investment income on his 2006 tax return — saving Julie from reporting it on hers. As well, Jim can deduct the $5,000 in interest paid to Julie, so the "net" addition to his total taxable income is just $2,000 ($7,000 of investment income less the $5,000 interest expense). Julie reports the $5,000 interest received from Jim in her income.

If your head is spinning, here's the end result: Julie has managed to transfer $2,000 of her investment income to Jim, who will pay tax at a lower rate. The overall tax for Julie and Jim combined is less than if Julie had simply invested herself — and the happy ending is that there is more after-tax money available for Julie and Jim to use as they wish!

You'll manage to split income, and save tax, only if the investments earn a rate of return higher than the CRA prescribed interest rate at the time the loan is made.

You can lock in the prescribed interest rate that was in effect at the time the loan was made for the entire term of the loan, so you're not at risk should the CRA's prescribed interest rates go up in the future. If the rates drop, consider repaying your loan and taking out a new loan to lock in at the low rate.

When a lower-income family member borrows money to invest — from, say, a bank — make sure that a higher-income family member doesn't guarantee the loan or give the borrower funds to make the repayment. The attribution rules will apply, causing any income earned on these borrowed funds to be taxed in the hands of the person guaranteeing the loan or providing the funds to make repayments. In other words, you will not have avoided the attribution rules.

As noted above, if you give money to a minor child to invest, the investment income (i.e., interest and dividends) will be taxed in your hands. However, if the funds were invested and capital gains were incurred (due to a sale of an investment, where proceeds are greater than the cost of the investment, or a capital gain allocated from a mutual fund), the capital gain will not be taxed in your hands — it will be taxed in the hands of the child. Because individuals can have a taxable income of $8,839 and pay no tax, a minor child can actually report capital gains of $17,768 and pay no tax since only 50 percent of capital gains are subject to tax.

If you're giving a minor child funds to invest, make sure that the investments selected focus on generating capital gains (stocks and equity-based mutual funds) as opposed to interest and dividends.

Use "Second-Generation" Income

You now know that if you give or lend money to a spouse or minor child to invest (with no interest or at an interest rate below the CRA prescribed interest rate at the time of the loan), any income earned on the investments will be attributed back to you and taxed in your hands. The good news? Second-generation income — that is, "income on income" — is not attributed back. It works like this: lend or give money to your spouse or minor child, then transfer any income earned each year to a separate investment account in the spouse's or minor child's name. Future earnings in that second account are not subject to the attribution rules. Income splitting has been achieved!

Split Tax on CPP Payments by "Pension Sharing"

You know how it works in a marriage: "What's mine is yours, and what's yours is mine." Well, the same holds true for Canada Pension Plan (CPP) retirement payments. You see, married or common-law partners that are at least 60 and live together can elect to share CPP payments on the portion of CPP earned during their time together. A portion of CPP payments of a high-tax-bracket individual can be *shifted* — or *shared* — with a lower-tax-bracket individual. This will result in tax savings! The high-tax-bracket individual reports less income and pays less tax. The lower-tax-bracket individual will have a greater tax burden on the shifted CPP but this tax will be less than the tax that would have been paid by the person in the higher tax bracket. Voila — there is an overall tax savings for the two individuals combined!

If only one individual was a CPP contributor, the two individuals can share one pension.

For further information on pension sharing, take a look at Chapter 5. You can also contact Human Resources and Social Development Canada (HRSDC) at 1-800-277-9914 (TTY 1-800-255-4786), or visit its Web site at www.hrsdc.gc.ca. Remember, you must apply to share your CPP pension!

Pay Salary or Wages to Family Members

If you have your own business, consider paying a salary or wage to members of your family. Of course, they must actually work in the business (and no, you won't get away with paying your four-year-old son to colour pictures you use for advertising). In addition, the salary you pay them must be reasonable for the work they do.

 The advantage to paying wages to family members is that you can claim the amount paid as a deduction on your business statement, so your taxable income, and your taxes, is reduced. On the flip side, the family member includes this amount in his or her income. You can pay a child who has no other source of income up to $8,839 in 2006 without generating a tax bill for that child. Assuming your marginal tax rate is 45 percent, that's a savings of almost $4,000 in tax!

By paying your spouse or child a salary, you'll generate "earned income" in their hands. This gives rise to valuable RRSP contribution room, so even though there may be no tax owing, your spouse or child should still file a tax return each year. (More on RRSPs in Chapter 10, line 208.)

Transfer Money for Business Purposes

If you give or lend money to family members to be used in a business as opposed to be used for investing, you can avoid the dreaded attribution rules. Even if it's a loan, there's no need to charge interest. Since the funds will earn business income and not investment income or capital gains, you don't have to worry about having the business income or gains taxed in your hands.

 If the business goes sour, there are favourable tax rules that you may be able to take advantage of. The company you invest in must be a Canadian-controlled private corporation, and while in operation must have had at least 90 percent of its assets used in a non-investment business operated primarily in Canada. If you won't recover your loan, you may be eligible to claim an allowable business investment loss (ABIL) on your tax return. See Chapter 10 (line 217) for more details on ABILs.

Pay an Allowance to a Working Child

If you're paying your child an allowance for work around the house, don't stop paying once your child starts working. We know — you're probably thinking, "Why should I pay them, if they have their own spending money?" Here's why: Paying your child an allowance will free up his or her earnings for investment. When they invest their own income, the attribution rules won't apply and you effectively will have split income — and reduced the family's tax burden.

Get the Higher-Income Spouse to Pay the Household Expenses

Another way to get more funds into the hands of the lower-income spouse is to have the higher-income spouse pay all the daily living expenses. This includes groceries, mortgage or rent payments, credit card bills, gas for the car, and so on. This frees up more cash in the hands of the lower-income spouse to earn investment income that is taxed at a lower tax rate.

Similarly, another way to transfer funds is for the higher-income spouse to pay the income tax liability and instalments of the lower-income spouse. Since the amount is paid directly to the CRA and is not invested by the spouse, the attribution rules won't apply. Any funds the lower-income spouse would have used to pay the tax liabilities are now free to be used for investment purposes.

Invest Child Tax Benefit Payments in the Child's Name

The federal government pays the Child Tax Benefit monthly to qualifying families until their children reach 18 years of age. The CRA takes the position that these benefit payments can be invested in your child's name and earn any type of income without the attribution rules kicking in. Make sure these funds are deposited directly into an investment account for your child. Keep them separate from other funds that you may have given your child previously, because the attribution rules still apply to these gifted funds.

At press time, the CRA had not agreed to treat the new Universal Child Care Benefit (UCCB) in the same manner, so the attribution rules would apply to investment income (but not capital gains) earned on UCCB payments invested in the child's name.

Contribute to a Spousal RRSP

The optimum goal is for spouses (including common-law spouses) to have equal incomes during retirement. This will accomplish perfect income splitting and keep the total family tax bill to a minimum. Spousal RRSP contributions work like this: You contribute to an RRSP under which your spouse is the annuitant. You claim the tax deduction for the amounts put into the plan, and when money is withdrawn for retirement your spouse is taxed on the withdrawal. Talk about shifting retirement income from one spouse to the other!

If your spouse makes a withdrawal from a spousal plan in the year or within two calendar years of when you last made a spousal RRSP contribution, you, not your spouse, will be subject to paying tax on the withdrawn amount. Have your spouse wait until the third calendar year after your last spousal RRSP contribution to withdraw the funds.

Make a spousal contribution on December 31 — say, December 31, 2006. Your spouse then has to wait only two years plus one day — until January 1, 2009 — to begin making withdrawals that will *not* be taxed in your hands as no withdrawal was made in the calendar year in which the RRSP contribution was made, 2006, or the next two calendar years — 2007 and 2008.

The amount you can contribute to a spousal RRSP is not affected by your spouse's RRSP contribution limit — it is based on *your* RRSP contribution limit. If your 2006 RRSP contribution limit is $18,000, you have the option of contributing $18,000 to a spousal RRSP, contributing $18,000 to your own RRSP, or contributing to both RRSPs provided the aggregate contribution doesn't exceed $18,000. You'll find more on RRSPs in Chapter 10 (line 208).

Contribute to an RESP

Registered Education Savings Plans (RESPs) are used to help build an education fund for your child or grandchild. But did you realize that RESPs are a great way to income-split with your family? Although contributions made to an RESP are not tax deductible like contributions to an RRSP, they do grow tax free. When the funds are taken out for educational purposes, you won't be the one to foot the tax bill. The income earned in the plan is taxed in the child's hands, not yours. As a student, that child will probably have minimal income and will be eligible for tuition, textbook, and education tax credits, and therefore likely won't pay tax. Read more about RESPs in Chapter 6.

Chapter 20

Top Ten Tax Planning Tips for Investors

. . . .

In This Chapter

▶ Investing tax efficiently

▶ Using losses to reduce your taxes

▶ Minimizing taxes on capital gains

▶ Borrowing to invest

▶ Making interest tax deductible

▶ Using investments for charitable giving

▶ Considering specialty investments

. . . .

*A*t least once a week we hear people say, "My taxes are too high. What can I do to reduce them?" Although we don't have the magical solution that will make your tax bill disappear, there are some things you can do to reduce the amount you pay, particularly if you are an investor. Keep in mind, however, that you should always weigh your investment *and* tax objectives before making any investment decision. Even though a particular investment suits you tax-wise, it may not fit your investment risk profile.

Choosing Tax-Efficient Investments

Investment returns are not created equal in the eyes of the taxman. In fact, the amount of tax you pay depends on the type of income your investment is earning. You'll find interest income is always the least tax efficient (i.e., taxed the most!) because it is fully taxed at your marginal tax rate. Investments that earn interest income include term deposits, guaranteed investment certificates (GICs), Canada Savings Bonds, corporate and government bonds, and money market mutual funds.

Canadian dividends generally sit in the middle of the tax efficiency scale, since they qualify for the dividend tax credit and effectively are taxed at a lower rate than interest. In fact, starting in 2006, if you earn eligible dividends (which are generally those paid from Canadian public companies) you'll find you receive even more of a tax credit, and pay less tax, than you had in the past. If you're looking to generate dividend income, you may want to invest in Canadian equities that pay dividends annually.

Capital gains are often the most tax efficient, since they are taxable only when realized (that is, when your shares are sold, or, if you invest in mutual funds, when the securities in the mutual fund are sold). Further, capital gains are just one-half taxable. (For more on capital gains, see Chapter 7.) If you're looking for potential capital gains outside of your registered account, equities are your best bet.

Capital gains are not always taxed more efficiently than dividends — it depends on your tax bracket, province/territory of residence, other sources of income, and the type of dividend. However, you are generally better off earning capital gains versus non-eligible dividends (those paid from private companies) if your income is greater than about:

- ✔ $72,800 in Alberta, Saskatchewan, and Yukon
- ✔ $69,000 in the Northwest Territories
- ✔ $33,450 in New Brunswick
- ✔ $29,600 in Newfoundland and Labrador, and
- ✔ $36,400 in the other provinces and Nunavut

Assuming you have no other sources of income, you can earn approximately $30,000 in non-eligible dividends and pay no tax in most of the provinces and all of the territories!

Use Capital Losses to Your Advantage

We all hate to lose money on an investment. However, you can use losses to reduce your current-year taxes and even to get some of the tax you paid in prior years back! Keep in mind that these strategies require the losses to be in a non-registered, or open, investment account. Losses in your RRSP or RRIF account won't work.

Sell your losing investments only if you no longer like them and do not wish to repurchase that same investment for at least 30 days after the sale. If you repurchase that same investment within 30 days, your loss will be denied. (For the techies out there, these are known as the "superficial loss rules.") If you want to purchase the investment back, wait for 31 days.

Consider selling your loss investment and then contributing the proceeds to your RRSP up to your contribution room limit. This will trigger the loss for tax purposes while also providing you with cash to put into your RRSP — for even more tax relief! Do not directly transfer the investment into your RRSP: A capital loss in this case is considered to be nil by the *Income Tax Act.* You also cannot repurchase that same investment you sold for a loss within your RRSP for at least 30 days. This is also a superficial loss, which means that your loss will be . . . well . . . lost. Instead, choose a different investment altogether inside your registered account or wait until your 30-day period is up.

If you have capital losses in 2006 but do not have capital gains to use the loss against on this year's tax return, consider carrying the loss back to your 2003, 2004, or 2005 return to apply against capital gains you previously reported and paid tax on. This will result in a tax refund! If you cannot use a capital loss to reduce your taxes for 2006 or get a refund of some of your prior years' taxes, the loss can be carried forward to 2007 and future years. The loss does not expire — make sure you keep track of it!

Minimize Taxes on Capital Gains

Consider triggering capital gains periodically in your open investment accounts, especially in years when your income is particularly low. In 2006, taxpayers with no other sources of income (such as minors, for whom you may have set up "in trust for" investment accounts) can trigger up to $17,678 in capital gains (only $8,839, or 50 percent, is taxable) and not attract any tax. This is because each taxpayer has a basic personal tax credit ($8,839 in 2006 for federal taxes) to reduce taxes payable. The advantage to this strategy is seen in the future when you actually sell the investment for good.

By triggering gains in years you have low income, you manage to increase the tax cost of the investment. For example, say you have an investment with a current value of $10,000 and a purchase price, or tax cost, of $4,000. If you choose to trigger the capital gain on the investment this year, you will have a $3,000 taxable gain ($10,000 less $4,000 × 50 percent) to report on your tax return. Assuming you have no other sources of income, you'll face no tax on that gain. However, you've managed to increase the tax cost of the investment to $10,000. If you sell the investment for $12,000 next year, you'll only be subject to tax on 50 percent of that increase in value, or $1,000.

Borrow to Invest for Tax Savings

Leveraged investing — that is, taking out a loan and using the proceeds to invest — is popular because you use other people's money (usually the bank's) to make money for yourself! The idea is that over the long term you can achieve higher effective rates of return on your investments and may even reach your financial goals faster than if you simply used your free cash flow to invest.

From a tax point of view, leveraged investing can help reduce the taxes you pay on any source of income you have. As long as your purpose in borrowing is to earn income from interest, dividends, or rent, the interest on your loan is tax deductible. Even if your interest cost exceeds your investment income, you are still entitled to deduct the excess against other sources of income if you are expecting income in the future. (Well, this last statement is not completely true. The excess of interest expense over investment income can be deducted for federal tax purposes, and in all provinces and territories except Quebec.)

Just because the initial purpose of your borrowing is to invest, this does not mean that you are guaranteed a tax deduction for the interest paid in the future. To ensure your interest remains tax deductible, avoid withdrawing any capital from your investment account (which includes both the growth and any reinvested distributions) for personal purposes. Doing so will result in losing a portion of your interest deduction, unless you are withdrawing the funds to put into another investment.

If you borrow to invest in an RRSP, your interest is not tax deductible. Consider using your tax refund to pay off at least part of your loan in order to keep your non-tax-deductible debt to a minimum.

Make Interest Tax Deductible

Many of us pay interest on personal borrowing, such as mortgage interest, car loans, lines of credit, and credit cards, but few of us can deduct that interest on our tax returns. There is a way, however, that some of us can convert that non-deductible interest into a tax deduction. This strategy is commonly known as debt-swapping.

Debt-swapping is possible if you have both non-deductible interest and non-RRSP investments such as shares, bonds, or mutual funds. The first step is to sell your investments, ideally choosing those that have not greatly appreciated in value since you purchased them (since you will be responsible for paying tax on any capital gains you trigger on the sale). You then use the proceeds from the sale to pay down your non-deductible debt. Finally, you will take out a new loan with the bank and use it to repurchase the investments you sold. At the end of the day you will have the same amount of debt and the same amount of investments as before the sale (assuming you didn't have tax to pay on any capital gains), but because there is a direct trace between the borrowing and the investments the interest you pay each year can be deducted on your tax return!

Consider Labour-Sponsored Funds

The federal and most provincial governments offer fairly generous tax credits to investors who invest in labour-sponsored venture capital corporations (LSVCCs, or labour-sponsored funds, for short). You'll be entitled to a federal credit equal to 15 percent of your investment and a provincial credit equal to, in most provinces, another 15 percent. (Bad news for readers in Alberta, New Brunswick, Newfoundland, and Labrador: You won't receive any provincial credits. In addition, if you purchase a fund that does not entitle you to provincial or territorial credits, you can't claim federal credits either!) There is a cap of $1,500 on the total credits you'll be eligible for in a year, so you may not want to contribute more than $5,000 to a labour-sponsored fund in any one year.

If you made an investment in a labour-sponsored fund after March 6, 1999, you are encouraged (by the tax rules!) to keep these units invested, without redeeming them, for eight years. If you redeem them before the eight years are up, you'll have to repay the tax credits you received in the year of purchase!

Use Insurance for Investment Purposes

Life insurance is commonly used to cover tax liabilities on death and to help provide a source of income for heirs. However, if you purchase a "permanent" life insurance policy, such as a *universal life* policy, you can combine your insurance policy with a side investment fund. From a tax standpoint this side fund works very much like an RRSP in that the investments inside grow tax-free and you won't face a tax bill until the funds are withdrawn or the policy is surrendered (you don't get a tax deduction for amounts put into the fund, though). Most universal life policies have a decent selection of investments to choose from, which means that the investment component of the policy has the potential to grow at a respectable rate of return.

Before you go and put all your excess cash into a universal life policy so that the investment can grow tax-free, be aware of the limits. Unlimited tax-sheltered growth sounds too good to be true — and it is. Our tax law places a ceiling on the amount that can be in the investment account, and penalties are charged if too much investment is built up in your side fund. Your insurance company will work with you to ensure you keep onside.

This type of strategy isn't for everyone. Since you will have to pay premiums for insurance, you must weigh these costs against the benefits of tax-free growth. Generally, it makes sense for individuals holding investments in excess of $500,000 who have already maxed out their RRSP contributions.

Life insurance proceeds received on the death of the insured are received tax-free.

Donate Investments to Charity

Normally when you sell or otherwise dispose of an investment, any increase in value is taxed as a capital gain. As we learned in Chapter 7, 50 percent of that gain is taxable and must be reported on your personal tax return. However, thanks to the 2006 federal budget, if a publicly listed investment, such as a stock or mutual fund, is directly donated to a registered charity or public foundation in Canada, the entire capital gain can be sheltered from tax. Therefore, if you are charitably inclined, you are better off to directly donate your appreciated investments, rather than first selling those investments and then donating the residual cash.

This incentive also applies to donations of stock options.

In addition to avoiding capital gains tax, when you donate investments you will receive a donation tax credit for the full fair market value of the investment donated.

Hugh, a supporter of numerous charities, owns a stock that he paid $1,000 for, and that is now worth $10,000. He is considering making a donation to a public foundation. In Table 20-1 we compare the donation under two scenarios: (1) Hugh sells the stock and then donates the after-tax cash to the foundation, and (2) he directly donates the stock to the foundation. Assume Hugh is taxed at the highest marginal rate.

Table 20-1	Donating Cash or Stock	
	Sell Stock	*Donate Stock*
Current Value of Stock	$10,000	$10,000
Adjusted Cost Base	$1,000	$1,000
Capital Gain	$9,000	$9,000
Taxable Gain (at 50 percent)	$4,500	$0
Tax (at 46 percent)	$2,070	$0
Donation Value	$7,930	$10,000
Donation Tax Credit	$3,648	$4,600
Net Tax Savings	$1,578	$4,600

Do you see what happened here? Not only does the charity benefit from a higher donation, Hugh is also better off because he pays less tax! Talk about a win-win situation!

Most of the large charities and public foundations in Canada have the processes in place to accept your donation of publicly listed securities. Give your favourite charity a call, or check its Web site to see what steps to take.

This tax incentive has not been extended to donations made to private foundations.

Consider Specialty Investments

If it's tax savings you're looking for, you may want to consider some specialty investments, including:

- ✔ **Flow-through shares:** These shares can benefit you in a year when you are expecting higher than normal income that you do not want to see eroded by tax. How? They offer large tax deductions in the year the investment is made (probably about 90 percent of the investment) with the remainder of the deductions available in the next year or the year after. The adjusted cost base ("tax cost") of flow-through shares is considered nil, so whenever you decide to sell them you will have a guaranteed capital gain. Flow-through shares, therefore, manage to reduce current taxes and to defer taxes until the future when the shares are sold.

- ✔ **Real estate investment trusts (REITs):** REITs, and their cousins, royalty trusts, may interest you if you require an income from your investments. These trusts will pay you an income, but due to some unique features not all of this income will be taxable — a portion is considered a "return of capital," not income. The adjusted cost base of your investment is reduced by the return of capital payments, so you will generally have a capital gain to claim when you eventually sell your trust units.

Flow-through shares, REITs, and royalty trusts may benefit you if you have unused capital losses, because you will have a high chance of generating a capital gain on these investments in the future.

Watch Out for Tax Shelters

In the past, some taxpayers bought into tax shelters where quantities of certain property (i.e., art, comic books, etc.) were purchased at a discount. The taxpayers then donated the property to charity and received a donation tax credit equal to the market value of the property donated. The net result was that the value of the donation tax credit exceeded the net cost of the property to the purchaser. The government was not impressed by these tax shelters and began to track them more closely. Since 2003, tax shelters can no longer be sold without an identification number from the CRA. If there is no number, there is no tax credit. And even then, if the CRA is offended by any of the activities of the tax shelter tax benefits will be disallowed. Buyer beware!

Index

• P •

parking spaces, as non-taxable benefit, 39
partial dispositions, and capital gains, 84
partnership income, and business income, 142
past-service contributions, defined, 167–168
payroll costs, deductibility of, 143
penalties, for late or deficient taxes, 300–302
pension adjustment (PA), 166–167
pension adjustment reversal (PAR), 167
pension assets, transferring, 59–60
pension income
  the allowance, 48–49
  Canada/Quebec pension plan (CPP/QPP), 49–56
  credit, 59, 317
  Guaranteed Income Supplement (GIS), 48
  and non-refundable tax credit, 244
  non-taxable, 58–59
  Old-Age Security (OAS), 43–47
  other pensions, 56–58
pension sharing, 326
personal amount, basic, 238
personal counselling, as non-taxable benefit, 38
personal-use property, and capital gains, 93–94
political tax credit, federal, 264
prepaid expenses, deductibility of, 143–144
preparation of tax return
  filing options, 30–32
  Internet resources, 26–28
  software for, 24–25
  tax professionals, 29–30
prescribed prizes, as income, 131
Prince Edward Island tax credits, 284–285
Prince Edward Island tax rates, 274
principal residence, sale of, 95–99

prize in your field of endeavour, as income, 131
proceeds of disposition, 83
professional dues, deductibility of, 177–178
professional income, reporting, 155–158
promissory notes, and capital gains, 91–92
provincial and territorial tax credits
  Alberta, 275–277
  British Columbia, 277–278
  Manitoba, 278
  New Brunswick, 279
  Newfoundland and Labrador, 279–280
  Northwest Territories, 280–281
  Nova Scotia, 281–282
  Nunavut, 282–283
  Ontario, 283–284
  Prince Edward Island, 284–285
  Quebec, 285–287
  Saskatchewan, 287–288
  Yukon, 288
provincial and territorial tax rates, 271–275
provincial and territorial tax systems, 9
public company shares, 217–219
public transit tax credit, 249, 316
publicly traded securities, donation of, 257–258, 317, 336–337

• Q •

qualified farm property, 101–102, 230
qualified fishing property, 102, 230
qualified small business corporation (QSBC) shares, 99–101, 229
Quebec Pension Plan (QPP), 49–51. *See also* Canada Pension Plan (CPP)
Quebec tax credits, 285–287
Quebec tax rates, 274
Quebec tax system, 10, 285–287